You are a cool guy! Just try and not be too girl crazy! —Brittany

SO-CNG-005

CES YOUTH AND FAMILY PROGRAMS 2001

Remember
THE PROMISE

Favorite Talks from
Especially for Youth

You are the best. Thanx for dancing w/ me!

Tiffany Davis
4497 Waterfront Farms Dr.
Draper, UA 24334

EAGLE
GATE

Special appreciation is expressed to the contributors to this work for their willingness to share their thoughts and testimonies with youth. Each author accepts complete personal responsibility for the material contained within his or her chapter. There is no endorsement for this work (real or implied) by The Church of Jesus Christ of Latter-day Saints, the Church Educational System, or Brigham Young University.

© 2001 Deseret Book Company

All rights reserved. No part of this book may be reproduced in any form or by any means without permission in writing from the publisher, Deseret Book Company, P. O. Box 30178, Salt Lake City, Utah 84130. This work is not an official publication of The Church of Jesus Christ of Latter-day Saints. The views expressed herein are the responsibility of the author and do not necessarily represent the position of the Church or of Deseret Book Company.

Eagle Gate is a registered trademark of Deseret Book Company.

Visit us at www.deseretbook.com

Library of Congress Cataloging-in-Publication Data

Remember the promise.
    p.   cm.
  ISBN 1-57345-981-X (pbk.)
  1. Mormon youth—Religious life.   2. Mormon youth—Conduct of life.
3. Church of Jesus Christ of Latter-day Saints—Doctrines.   4. Mormon
Church—Doctrines.   5. Especially for Youth (Program) [1. Mormons.
2. Conduct of life.   3. Christian life.]   I. Title.

BX8643.Y6 R46 2001
248.8'3'088283—dc21

                                                                    2001001306

Printed in the United States of America   72082-6831

10   9   8   7   6   5   4   3   2   1

Richie,
Sup boy? I Hope
you had a great
week. You the coolest
cheerleader I've ever met
♥ much Love K.I.T
Kathryn Z.

Princess321@aol.com Brooke

Hey. Wuzzup! It was really awesome getting to know you. You will find a nice guy. don't worry. sorry it aren't work out the way you @Blanket19 wanted.

Remember
THE PROMISE

Richard,

Thanks for being so cool this week and for helping me out with everything. Now go back home + make us all proud.

I know you can do it. Remember to always

search the scriptures for answers to life's questions.   Love ya Bro,

Chris Wozniak

Hey Rich, you're a real ladies man! You are a cool guy and you have changed just a little bit. Keep in touch. Jacob Smith

Hey man, I'll cya on Sunday Peace,

HEY SWEET BOY you're the coolest! you're sooo muchfun and your a great dancer! Much

JULIA BATES

Hey well I'm really glad that we got 2 meet. :) Hope to see you at EFY again. Cami

CONTENTS

1

REMEMBER THE PROMISE

Randall C. Bird

In a powerful message to his three sons, king Benjamin said:

"My sons, I would that ye should *remember* that were it not for these plates [meaning the scriptures], which contain these records and these commandments, we must have suffered in ignorance, even at this present time, not knowing the mysteries of God.

"For it were not possible that our father, Lehi, could have *remembered* all these things, to have taught them to his children, . . . that thereby they could teach them to their children, and so fulfilling the commandments of God, even down to this present time.

"I say unto you, my sons, were it not for these things, which have been kept and preserved by the hand of God, that we might read and understand of his mysteries, and have his commandments always before our eyes, that even our fathers would have dwindled in unbelief. . . .

"O my sons, I would that ye should *remember* that these sayings are true, and also that these records are true. . . .

"And now, my sons, I would that ye should *remember* to search them diligently, that ye may profit thereby; and I would that ye should keep the commandments of God" (Mosiah 1:3–7; emphasis added).

Notice how often the word *remember* is used in these few verses. In the scriptures the word is used 337 times. The theme for the 2001 sessions of Especially for Youth is *Remember the Promise*, taken from Alma 37:15–17, which reads: "And now behold, I tell you by the spirit of prophecy, that if ye transgress the commandments of God, behold, these things which are sacred shall be taken away from you by the power of God, and ye shall be delivered up unto Satan, that he may sift you as chaff before the wind.

"But if ye keep the commandments of God, and do with these things which are sacred according to that which the Lord doth command you, (for you must appeal unto the Lord for all things whatsoever ye must do with them) behold, no power of earth or hell can take them from you, for God is powerful to the *fulfilling of all his words*.

"For he will *fulfil all his promises* which he shall make unto you, for he has *fulfilled his promises* which he has made unto our fathers" (emphasis added).

Several years ago while directing an Especially for Youth session in Alaska, I received a phone call from home informing me that my mother had been diagnosed with cancer. I can still remember the emotions and many thoughts that raced through my mind as I contemplated my mother's future. As I delivered the fireside talk that week, it was very difficult for me to teach these wonderful youth while I was still thinking of my mother. The Lord was good to me, however, and sent his spirit to comfort and inspire me at this point in my life. It was just about a year later, while leaving to teach an Especially for Youth in Provo, Utah, that the phone rang at my home informing me of my mother's death. Just the day before, I had had the opportunity to spend some time with her. As I had left Idaho to drive back to my home in Utah, she had mentioned that she didn't think she would be around much longer. I had given her encouragement and left for Utah not knowing that this would be the last time I would see my mother alive. A few days prior to her death, Mom had worked the entire day trying to do her hair, makeup, and clothing for a picture she would have taken that would be given to each of her children. Through pain, suffering, and trials, my mother had left me something that would allow me to always remember her the way she wanted to be remembered: as a woman of courage, beauty, and dignity. That picture now sits atop my piano, in our living room, as a constant reminder of my mother.

President Spencer W. Kimball once said: "When you look in the dictionary for the most important word, do you know what it is. It could be 'remember.' Because all of you have made covenants—you know what to do and you know how to do it—our greatest need is to remember. That is why everyone goes to sacrament meeting every Sabbath day—to take the sacrament and listen to the priests pray that they '. . . may always remember him and keep his commandments which he has given them; . . . ' Nobody should ever forget to go to sacrament meeting. 'Remember' is the word.

'Remember' is the program" ("Circles of Exaltation" [address to religious educators, June 28, 1968], 8).

Sister Joanne B. Doxey, former second counselor in the Relief Society General Presidency, gave a talk in a general women's meeting on 23 September 1989 entitled "Remember Him" (*Ensign*, Nov. 1989, 89–91). Some of the general categories I have used here come from that talk. Let's see how the promises of the scriptures, commandments, and the Lord can help us in our efforts to return to our Father in Heaven.

WE CAN REMEMBER THE LORD THROUGH THE SCRIPTURES

The scriptures have been written and preserved so that we can enjoy the blessings of the gospel. We have a responsibility to know what these scriptures contain. The Savior commanded us to search the scriptures and the words of the prophets. He taught: "Yea, a commandment I give unto you that ye search these things diligently" (3 Nephi 23:1). Nephi reaffirmed the value of scripture study when he taught: "Feast upon the words of Christ; for behold, the words of Christ will tell you all things what ye should do" (2 Nephi 32:3).

Elder Gordon B. Hinckley said: "I promise you that if you will read the words of that writing which we call scripture, there will come into your heart an understanding and a warmth that will be pleasing to experience. 'Search the scriptures; for in them ye think ye have eternal life: and they are they which testify of me.' (John 5:39.)" ("The Miracle That Is Jesus," *Improvement Era*, June 1966, 531).

President Hinckley later added: "We *can* read the scriptures, ponder their meaning, and develop familiarity with them for our everlasting blessing. We can do so in our family home evenings, and as we do there will grow within our children a love for the Lord and His holy word" ("Let Us Move This Work Forward," *Ensign*, Nov. 1985, 85).

A friend once jokingly asked me, "Do you know what will cause the sun to be darkened in the last days?" I responded, "No, what?" He answered, "Everyone blowing the dust off from their Bibles at the same time."

Sister Doxey said, "If we treat the scriptures lightly, letting them gather dust on the shelves, unopened and unread, they are unable to bless our lives as planned. We will be denied the sweet whisperings of the Spirit in guiding our lives and the lives of our families unless we pay the price of studying, pondering, and praying about the scriptures.

"If we immerse ourselves daily in the scriptures, particularly the Book of Mormon, we will have increased discernment. We will have power to do good and to resist evil, and our ability to solve problems will be expanded. Messages to help us in our day were foreseen by the Lord and were divinely placed on the pages of the scriptures to assist us and our families" ("Remember Him," 89–90).

The lyrics to the following Primary song can help us see the need of scripture study while we are young.

Seek Ye the Lord

I'll seek the Lord early while in my youth,
And he will help me to know the truth.
I'll search the scriptures and find him there,
Then go to our Father in fervent prayer.
I'll seek the Lord early, and I'll obey
His living prophets in all they say.
I'll keep his commandments; his love will abound.
I will seek the Lord early, and he will be found
(*Children's Songbook*, 108).

President Spencer W. Kimball said, "I find that when I get casual in my relationships with divinity and when it seems that no divine ear is listening and no divine voice is speaking, that I am far, far away. If I immerse myself in the scriptures the distance narrows and the spirituality returns" (*The Teachings of Spencer W. Kimball*, ed. Edward L. Kimball [Salt Lake City: Bookcraft, 1982], 135).

Elder Howard W. Hunter counseled: "When we . . . read and study the scriptures, benefits and blessings of many kinds come to us. This is the most profitable of all study in which we could engage" ("Reading the Scriptures," *Ensign*, Nov. 1979, 64).

I love the scriptures and testify that they are the word of God. Though there are times in our homes when it can be difficult to study the scriptures, it is well worth the effort to daily immerse yourself in them.

WE CAN REMEMBER THE LORD THROUGH KEEPING THE COMMANDMENTS

Jesus told us, "If ye love me, keep my commandments" (John 14:15). Keeping the commandments helps us to be happy and grow closer to him.

A favorite Primary song tells us,

> *Keep the commandments; keep the commandments!*
> *In this there is safety; in this there is peace.*
> *He will send blessings; He will send blessings.*
> *Words of a prophet: Keep the commandments.*
> *In this there is safety and peace*
> (*Children's Songbook*, 146).

Elder Robert L. Simpson wrote of a three-year-old boy who knelt down with his daddy to say his bedtime prayers. Eyes were closed, heads were bowed, but no words were spoken for several moments. Soon the little boy climbed into his bed. The daddy opened his eyes and said, "But what about prayers?"

And the boy answered, "I said my prayers."

"But I didn't hear you," said the daddy.

Then followed the child's classic comment, "But Daddy, I wasn't talking to you" (see *Proven Paths* [Salt Lake City: Deseret Book, 1974], 148).

We learn in the book of Alma that Helaman's two thousand stripling warriors remembered their mothers' teachings and did obey them. They were strict to remember the Lord their God, keeping his commandments continually, and therefore were delivered from the hands of their enemies (Alma 56:47–48; 57:20–21).

King Benjamin gives us further insight into the value of keeping the commandments: "And moreover, I would desire that ye should consider on the blessed and happy state of those that keep the commandments of God. For behold, they are blessed in all things, both temporal and spiritual; and if they hold out faithful to the end they are received into heaven, that thereby they may dwell with God in a state of never-ending happiness. O remember, remember that these things are true; for the Lord God hath spoken it" (Mosiah 2:41).

WE CAN REMEMBER THE LORD THROUGH KEEPING OUR COVENANTS

Baptism, the sacrament, and the temple sealing are all ordinances of the gospel. When we receive each of them, we show that we have made certain agreements, or covenants, with our Father in Heaven.

Every covenant and every ordinance of the gospel is for our good. Keeping the covenants and taking part in the ordinances helps prepare us to return to the presence of God. Making these covenants, receiving sacred ordinances, and being faithful in keeping our covenants is like climbing a ladder that will ultimately return us to our Heavenly Father.

Elder Marion G. Romney said: "When Jacob traveled from Beersheba toward Haran, he had a dream in which he saw himself on the earth at the foot of a ladder that reached to heaven where the Lord stood above it. He beheld angels ascending and descending thereon, and Jacob realized that the covenants he made with the Lord there were the rungs on the ladder that he himself would have to climb in order to obtain the promised blessings—blessings that would entitle him to enter heaven and associate with the Lord" ("Temples—The Gates to Heaven," *Ensign*, Mar. 1971, 16).

When we make covenants with the Lord, we make sacred promises to "always remember him and keep his commandments" (D&C 20:77). Once we have made covenants with the Lord, we then are responsible to remember our promises and to keep them.

Keeping our covenants should make a difference in the way we live, the way we act, the way we speak, the way we dress, the way we treat each other. If we "always remember him," we will "always have his Spirit to be with [us]" (Moroni 4:3).

WE CAN REMEMBER THE LORD THROUGH APPLYING MORONI'S PROMISE

Moroni 10:4 says, "And when ye shall receive these things, I would exhort you that ye would ask God, the Eternal Father, in the name of Christ, if these things are not true; and if ye shall ask with a sincere heart, with real intent, having faith in Christ, he will manifest the truth of it unto you, by the power of the Holy Ghost."

At some time in each of our lives we will find that we must put this promise to the test. Each of us who desires to know if this church and gospel are true must remember the promise that Moroni gave us. Elder Jay E. Jensen of the Seventy wrote of an experience he had with the scriptures during a period of days in which he was feeling discouraged and confused. He said, "When I read a verse, I often insert my name in it. I did so with [D&C 3:5] and found the help I needed to remove my gloomy feelings: 'Behold, you, Jay Jensen, have been entrusted with these things, but how strict were your commandments; and remember also the promises which were made to you, Jay Jensen. . . .'

"The words 'remember also the promises' struck me with unusual power. I identified with the Prophet Joseph Smith when he read James 1:5. The words 'remember also the promises' seemed to 'enter with great force into every feeling of my heart. I reflected on [them] again and again.' (JS—H 1:12.) During those four days I had focused on nothing but problems. I had not stopped to consider one single promise.

"I had with me on the airplane that day a copy of my patriarchal blessing. I read it, noting several marvelous promises. I reviewed in my mind the promises given to me when I was set apart as a mission president. I turned to additional scriptures and pondered the promises in each one. I learned then and have had reinforced to me again and again that when we search the scriptures, we will come to know that 'they are true and faithful, and the prophecies and promises which are in them shall all be fulfilled.' (D&C 1:37.)"

Elder Jensen went on to teach that there are two categories of promises and that the Lord promised us specific blessings for reading and studying the scriptures. He mentioned an exercise he did with the scriptures that aided him in identifying these two promises. He would make two columns on a sheet of paper and label one "Promises for This Life" and the other "Promises for the Next Life." He would then list under the appropriate column the reference and promise that he would read in the scriptures.

"I have found repeated in different places in the scriptures two major promises for reading and studying the scriptures that pertain to the next life: one is exaltation, and the other is eternal life. For example, Nephi said: 'Wherefore, if ye shall press forward, feasting upon the word of Christ, and endure to the end, behold, . . . Ye shall have eternal life.' (2 Ne. 31:20.)" ("Remember Also the Promises," *Ensign*, Nov. 1992, 80–81).

WE CAN REMEMBER THE LORD AS WE PARTAKE OF THE SACRAMENT

After Jesus was crucified he visited the Nephites in the New World and taught them many things, including the ordinance of the sacrament. He said to them, "And this shall ye always observe to do. . . . And this shall ye do in remembrance of my body. . . . And it shall be a testimony unto the Father that ye do always remember me. And if ye do always remember me ye shall have my Spirit to be with you" (3 Nephi 18:6–7).

Before the earth was created, Heavenly Father chose his Son, Jesus Christ, to be our Savior. Because Jesus loves us, he was willing to give his life to save us from death and to help us overcome our sins.

When Jesus lived on the earth, he loved his disciples (followers), and he taught them many things. He taught them to love one another and to forgive one another. He also asked them to keep the commandments of God and to repent of their sins.

Many people were blessed and healed by him. His disciples loved him very much and wanted to be close to him.

At the end of his ministry, Jesus gathered his apostles around him, for he knew that the time for his great sacrifice had come. He knew that his blood would be shed and that his body would die. To help his apostles remember him, Jesus took some bread, blessed it, broke it, and gave it to them, saying, "Take, eat; this is my body" (Matthew 26:26).

He then took a cup, gave thanks, and gave it to them, saying, "Drink ye all of it" (Matthew 26:27). He explained, "This is in remembrance of my blood . . . , which is shed for as many as shall believe on my name, for the remission of their sins" (JST Matthew 26:24).

Jesus' apostles partook of the sacrament and later taught the other disciples about this new ordinance.

If you try to follow the Savior, you are his disciple. He loves you, and you can remember this when you partake of the sacrament.

As you sing the sacrament hymn each week in sacrament meeting, listen carefully to the words. They will help you remember what the Savior has done for you.

Carefully listen to the sacrament prayers. When you partake of the bread and water, you promise to always remember that Jesus' body was given and his blood shed for you. You promise to take his name upon you and to keep his commandments.

When you keep these promises, which you make when you partake of the sacrament, Heavenly Father will bless you with his spirit.

WE CAN REMEMBER THE LORD IN OUR EVERYDAY ACTIVITIES (IN THE NAME OF JESUS CHRIST)

I remember listening quite a few years ago to a postgame radio broadcast of a Brigham Young University basketball game. Paul James, KSL radio sports announcer, was interviewing Devin Durrant. During the course of the interview I was impressed that Devin Durrant mentioned that everything he did in this life he did *in the name of Jesus Christ*. He mentioned that he played basketball *in the name of Jesus Christ*, that every time he stepped on the floor he was grateful for the talents God had blessed him with and wanted to be an example for Christ. Can you see what a wonderful place each of our homes, schools, and communities would be if we would remind ourselves that everything we do is in the name of Jesus Christ? Our dates, extracurricular activities, academics, family life, and church and community service would all take on new meaning if truly done in the name of Jesus Christ.

WE CAN REMEMBER THE LORD AS WE
READ OUR PATRIARCHAL BLESSINGS

I waited until my high school graduation to receive my patriarchal blessing. I was at a crossroad in my life and wanted additional guidance from the Lord. *Do I play college football and have my education paid for? Do I go on a mission?* (This was a time when a ward could only send out two missionaries per ward per year because the Vietnam War was being fought.) *What do I study in college?* and a host of other questions and decisions were floating through my mind. It was at this time that I felt I needed additional help from the Lord. I made an appointment with my stake patriarch to receive my blessing. He was an elderly man who knew very little about me, but knew a lot about the Lord. He prepared himself to give me a blessing from the Lord. Now, I know that a patriarchal blessing is not intended to answer every question you have or decision you must make, but it does give spiritual help and guidance from the Lord. Following my blessing I knew exactly what I needed to do with my life, and I often refer to my blessing to remember the promises of the Lord concerning me. I would encourage each of you to receive your patriarchal blessings at a time when you and your family feel it is appropriate and then read it often to remind you of the Lord's promises to you.

President Thomas S. Monson said: "The same Lord who provided a Liahona for Lehi provides for you and for me today a rare and valuable gift to give direction to our lives, to mark the hazards to our safety, and to chart the way, even a safe passage—not to a promised land, but to our heavenly home. The gift to which I refer is known as a patriarchal blessing. Every worthy member of the Church is entitled to receive such a precious and priceless personal treasure" ("Preparation Precedes Performance," *Ensign*, Sept. 1993, 71).

WE CAN REMEMBER THE LORD AS WE RETURN TO
OUR HOMES FROM ESPECIALLY FOR YOUTH

I frequently hear, following the closing ceremonies at Especially for Youth, comments like, "I wish I could feel like this forever," "I love this church and gospel," or "I'd love to have all these friends back at my high school." One of the great challenges of your experience at Especially for Youth is to take home with you all that you feel, learn, and experience, and thus make your home, school, church, and community a better place to be. I've always felt that one sign that your experience at EFY moved you in the right direction would be that you'd return home and be a better son or daughter, a better brother or sister, a better class member at church, a better student in school, and a better servant in your community. For that is what the gospel does to us. President Gordon B. Hinckley once said, "This is what the gospel is all about—to make bad men good and good men better" (*Be Thou an Example* [Salt Lake City: Deseret Book, 1981], 67–68).

A few years ago, the directors and counselors of Especially for Youth sang a song titled "Taking It Home with Me" (*Joy in the Journey* [CD] Salt Lake City: Deseret Book, 1998). The chorus of that song went as follows:

> *I know who I am,*
> *I'll take a stand for all I believe.*
> *I hope this feeling won't go away.*
> *If I let it stay,*
> *I'm taking it home with me.*

May each of us remember the promise made by our Father in Heaven: "For God so loved the world, that he gave his only begotten Son, that whosoever believeth in him should not perish, but have everlasting life" (John 3:16). What a wonderful promise! May we so live as to enjoy the blessings of our Father's promises.

Randall C. Bird is manager of seminary curriculum for the Church Educational System. He is a sports enthusiast, and during his high school years was named to the Idaho all-state teams in football and track. He has been a high school coach in both sports. He also enjoys fishing, collecting sports memorabilia, reading, and being with his family. He currently serves as stake president. He and his wife, Carla, are the parents of six children.

2

STAND TALL

Matthew O. Richardson

I once attended a college football game where the home team's student body was seated in the rows closest to the field. I sat with the non-students in the rows higher up the concourse. During the game, the students cheered with rabid enthusiasm hoping to encourage their team to victory. While I was impressed with their obvious spirit, I was particularly amazed by their stamina. These students not only cheered on their team but they *stood* while they cheered. Early in the game, a person seated in my section, who could not see over the standing students, yelled: "Down in the front!" I remember watching the last row of standing students turn and look toward our section in disbelief. One student cupped his hands to his mouth and yelled: "Up in the back!" Some of the fans in my section grumbled about the youthful enthusiasts and remained seated, while others rose to their feet and joined in with the cheering.

There have been many times in history where tides have been turned because individuals heard the call, "Up in the back!" and responded appropriately. I fondly recall such an experience from the Book of Mormon. A young military captain named Moroni had just returned home after rallying his troops and valiantly leading his people to a difficult victory over the Lamanites. It wasn't long before a group of Nephites, led by Amalickiah, was filled with pride, aspired to positions of power, and made designs to kill their own brethren. Sadly, Amalickiah's clever plans and his slick speech began to sway many of the Nephites to follow him.

Perhaps you can image how Moroni must have felt. He had bravely led Nephite soldiers to battle, many of which nobly lost their lives in the fray, to protect the freedom and religious way of life for all Nephites—including

Amalickiah and his thugs. Think how you would feel if you had spent all of your energy fighting in a war and some of your family members, friends, and neighbors died fighting to protect the lifestyle of those back home. Think how you might feel to return home, having paid such a terrible price, only to find those very people you fought for turning traitor and acting as your former enemy. It must have been unbearable. It is possible that some would react to this situation by throwing their hands in the air and giving up. Perhaps some would be persuaded to join the opposition. Some may not join them but might say, "I've done my part, it's someone else's turn now." President Gordon B. Hinckley said, "We cannot be indifferent to the great cause of truth and right. We cannot afford to stand on the sidelines and watch the play between the forces of good and evil" (*Standing for Something: Ten Neglected Virtues That Will Heal Our Hearts and Homes* [New York: Random House, 2000], 171).

This was the case of Moroni. He was not one to sit down—even when so many were telling him to. Moroni ripped his coat and wrote upon it— "In memory of our God, our religion, and freedom, and our peace, our wives, and our children" (Alma 46:12). He put on his armor, fastened the cloth on a pole, and bowed himself down in solemn prayer, entering into a covenant with God. He then went into the streets, waving his homemade flag and asking if there were any that would stand with him in this fight. In a way, he shouted, "Up in the back!" "Up in the back!" and it worked. "The people came running together with their armor girded about their loins" to join him (Alma 46:21). Moroni's personal stand influenced those sitting on the sidelines to join a royal army of destiny. He turned the tide of a situation that the Book of Mormon described as "precarious and dangerous" (Alma 46:7).

We too live in a precarious and dangerous time. In fact, the First Presidency described our day as a "day when the temptations, responsibilities, and opportunities are the very greatest. . . . This is a time for you not only to live righteously," the First Presidency admonished, "but also to set an example for your peers" (*For the Strength of Youth* [Salt Lake City: The Church of Jesus Christ of Latter-day Saints, 1990], 3). It seems that we are facing circumstances similar to those in Moroni's day. Like the nineteenth year of the judges in the Book of Mormon, our day too seems to be looking for someone to raise a title of honored values and boldly invite others to join in a valiant stand. Just as those in the Book of Mormon desperately needed Moroni, we too need modern-day Moronis to stand tall.

It is unfortunate, however, that most of us, when we begin to compare ourselves to scriptural heroes and heroines, feel pretty inadequate. We tend to place those who lived before us in a special "super" category, one where we would never belong. But we can be *like* these individuals. We can emulate the traits that made them unique. There are five traits we can learn from Captain Moroni when he made his courageous stand. I fully believe that these traits can help us stand a little taller. Each trait is something you can do—now. You don't have to be older, exceptional, or even extremely spiritual. You just have to be willing and be disciplined. In other words, each of us can be just like Moroni if we choose to be.

1. Define for *yourself* the things *you* will be willing to stand up for (Alma 46:12). It didn't take Moroni long to notice that things around him were not right. He was faced with what I often call a "defining moment." A defining moment is a time where we determine what type of people we really are. It is not what we think we are, or even what we have said or say we are that defines us. We are defined by what we believe and what we do. Amalickiah allowed himself to be defined by pride, sin, and self-conceit. As a result, he was selfish, shortsighted, and evil. Moroni had to decide if he would join Amalickiah's growing group or if he would choose otherwise. What Moroni did in that moment of choice defined his character as well as his future.

In a moment that truly mattered, Moroni tore his coat and wrote out those things that *he* felt were important enough for *him* to make a solemn stand. You see, Moroni didn't wait for someone else to tell him what he should fight for. *He* declared *his* own platform. There is little doubt that parents, righteous leaders, and others influenced his choices, but ultimately *he* defined *his* destiny. "Standing tall," Sister Sheri L. Dew reminds us, "begins with our own conversion" ("Stand Tall and Stand Together," *Ensign*, Nov. 2000, 96).

It is also important to realize that Moroni didn't wait around for someone else to get going. He didn't call his friends to see what they were going to do. He just did what he felt he had to do. Sometimes we will stand alone—at least in the initial stages. Those who expect to be surrounded by adoring fans or supportive friends will surely be disappointed at one time or another. When we personally set our individual battles, we will find courage to stand firm and tall. "There is something reassuring about standing for something, and knowing what we stand for," President Hinckley stated. "For men or women who are true to themselves and to the virtues and standards they have personally adopted," he said, "it is not difficult to be true" (*Standing for Something*, xxiv).

2. Be prepared to defend your values *before* you step onto the battle-field (Alma 46:13). It seems clear that Moroni expected to be confronted by those who would call out to him, "down in the front!" He seemed to realize that his battle would come from trying to find the courage to define his beliefs. His fight would require him to defend and practice his values. Why else would he put his armor on prior to leaving his home? Moroni was smart enough to enter the battle prepared. In a way, one of the best forms of protection is preparation. President Ezra Taft Benson often said, "It is better to prepare and prevent than it is to repair and repent" ("The Law of Chastity," in *Brigham Young University 1987–88 Devotional and Fireside Speeches* [Provo: Brigham Young University Press], 51).

During a difficult time for the early Saints, the Lord reminded them, "if ye are prepared ye shall not fear" (D&C 38:30). Being prepared for our defining moments is akin to wearing armor into battle. If we wait to adequately dress for the battle until after the battle has begun, we cannot expect to enjoy the protection of the armor. I remember a saying I heard often as a youth: "When opportunities arise, the time for preparation is past." Have you ever noticed that defining moments rarely come when we would like them to or, for that matter, when it is convenient. Typically, defining moments require immediate response without much time to think things over. That is why it is so important to be prepared to stand, defend, and act at a moment's notice. President Spencer W. Kimball often reminded the youth that "right decisions are easiest to make when we make them well in advance, having ultimate objectives in mind." He then said, "The time to decide on a mission is long before it becomes a matter of choosing between a mission and an athletic scholarship. The time to decide on temple marriage is before one has become attached to a boyfriend or girlfriend who does not share that objective. . . . The time to decide that we will settle for nothing less than an opportunity to live eternally with our Father is now, so that every choice we make will be affected by our determination to let nothing interfere with attaining that ultimate goal" ("Decisions: Why It's Important to Make Some Now," *New Era*, Apr. 1971, 2). There is confidence and protection in adequate preparation.

3. Pray "mightily" that your cause might be favored by God (Alma 46:13, 16). Although Captain Moroni was described as a strong and mighty man, with "perfect understanding" (Alma 48:11), he was also a man who fully understood his personal limitations. Therefore, he, being a man "firm in the faith of Christ" (Alma 48:13), relied on divine power. Before he left his home with the Title of Liberty and armor upon his body, he knelt in mighty prayer to ask God to favor his cause. President Gordon B. Hinckley taught, "You cannot make it alone. You cannot reach your potential alone. You need the help of the Lord" (*Teachings of Gordon B. Hinckley* [Salt Lake City: Deseret Book, 1997], 470). Bringing your cause to God in prayer forms a partnership between you and God. Unfortunately, in our excitement, anxiety, or even fear of the moment, we often forget to pray for divine strength. Yet, President Hinckley affirms that "prayer unlocks the powers of heaven in our behalf" (ibid.). When we act in accordance with God and our newly formed partnership, we are stronger than any imaginable power. Perhaps this is why it was later said of Moroni that "if all men had been, and were, and ever would be, like unto Moroni, behold, the very powers of hell would have been shaken forever; yea, the devil would never have power over the hearts of the children of men" (Alma 48:17). There is real power in divine partnership.

4. Stand as a witness at all times, in all places, and in all things (Alma 46:19). Moroni left the safety of his home and "went forth among the people, waving the rent part of his garment in the air, that all might see the writing which he had written upon the rent part" (Alma 46:19). This reminds me of the words of a familiar hymn: "Who's on the Lord's side? Who? Now is the time to show. We ask it fearlessly: Who's on the Lord's side? Who?" (*Hymns*, no. 260). Moroni was not ashamed of his values posted on his newly fashioned flag. Notice that Moroni waved the flag and cried out with a "loud voice" (Alma 46:19). Apparently there weren't many who were wondering what Moroni stood for. He made it clear in his speech, actions, manner, and dress.

Elder Neal A. Maxwell said, "We can be walking witnesses and standing sermons to which objective onlookers can say a quiet amen" ("The Net Gathers of Every Kind," *Ensign*, Nov. 1980, 15). The best examples are those who "stand as witnesses of God at all times and in all things, and in all places" (Mosiah 18:9).

5. Invite others to join in a just cause (Alma 46:19–20). After thorough preparation, Moroni now went to find others who would stand with him. It took courage to go into the street, not knowing who would be friend or foe, and bravely say: "Here is what I stand for. . . . Will you join me?" Yet he was confident in his situation and determined to succeed. I particularly enjoyed how Moroni enlisted his new army according to the same principles that he himself had employed when he first began this quest. "Behold, whosoever will maintain this title upon the land, let them come forth in the strength of the Lord, and enter into a covenant that they will maintain their rights, and their religion, that the Lord God may bless them" (Alma 46:20). There is a unique power that comes when individuals willingly join together to make a stand. There is a power felt by the individual, the group, and even those who come in contact with the group. We must learn to stand together.

When we understand these principles, it is easier to know how to act. "What remains to be seen," President Ezra Taft Benson pondered, "is where each of us personally, now and in the future, will stand in this fight—and how tall we will stand" ("In His Steps," in *Speeches of the Year*, 1979 [Provo: Brigham Young University Press, 1980], 59–60). Will you be able to follow the traits of Captain Moroni and his royal army? Is there hope for our day when the values of so many seem to be forfeited for things of little value? I believe we have soldiers among us—Latter-day Saints who stand up every day for their beliefs. I have often felt the power of those making their stand in a confused world. In that way, I think I might understand how Moroni and his new army felt as they stood together, in full armor, boldly taking a public stand. I can think of two specific occasions where I witnessed modern-day Moronis standing firm and tall.

On occasion, I have the opportunity to visit young women meetings in our ward. My favorite part of their meeting is when they recite the Young Women theme. I particularly like the way the young women in my ward go about this ritual. A single young woman will stand and call her sisters to their feet by asking, "Who will stand for truth and righteousness?" In unison, our young women stand together and say, "I will stand for truth and righteousness," and then they recite their theme. While there is power when a single young woman can declare her values, there is a unique power that comes from standing together. I hope there isn't a single young woman in the Church who hasn't felt that power. I hope they feel it, because I have felt it from them. It is a sweet feeling, yet it is powerful. It binds individuals together in purpose.

Recently, our stake presented a program as part of the worldwide celebration for the young women of the Church. A young woman stood and asked: "Who will stand for truth and righteousness?" It was interesting that many of the audience stood, not realizing that this was part of the program. Some were a little embarrassed and quickly sat down when they realized what was happening. I was touched, however. Sometimes we fail to see the power we have on others. These young women, like Moroni, stood and invited others to a noble cause—without even knowing they were having such an impact. Rather than snicker at those who stood mistakenly, I was touched that there were those in the audience that felt compelled to stand as an answer to the question. This experience was an "up in the front" experience for all those present.

My second experience occurred at a recent Especially for Youth, where my wife and I had the opportunity to stand with modern-day warriors who are, in many ways, similar to those young women in my ward and the warriors who stood defiantly at Moroni's side. While all the young men at EFY were gathered together, I told the story of Moroni and emphasized the importance of young men measuring up to their priesthood responsibilities. One responsibility I emphasized was that of serving a mission. It is said that only one of every three eligible Latter-day Saint young men serves a full-time mission. To demonstrate this point, I asked all the young men to stand up. Dressed in white shirts and ties, more than four hundred young men and their counselors stood in the room. I then pointed out two thirds of the audience and asked them to be seated. This left around 135 young men, a third of the group, standing near the front of the room. "If statistics hold true," I told the young men, "this is how many of you will go on missions." It was staggering to see how many young men were seated in comparison to those standing. The very sight made my heart groan.

Then I noticed two young men standing quietly toward the back of the room. Everyone else around them was seated, just as I asked them to be. These two boys hadn't said a word—they just stood there like soldiers. Looking at the two young men, I asked: "Didn't I ask you boys to sit down with the rest of the group?" Before they could answer, I followed with another question: "Why are you still standing?"

Without hesitation, one of the young men said: "Because I am going on a mission."

I couldn't help but notice the steady resolve in his voice.

The other young man, who was several rows away from the first, nodded in agreement.

"What if you get a scholarship to college?" I asked.

"It will have to wait," he said, "I'm going on a mission."

"What if you meet a pretty young woman who adores you and can't be without you?"

"I don't care," he said again, with the same amount of confidence, "I'm going on a mission."

I tried to think of every possible scenario where a young man might choose to forfeit his priesthood responsibility of serving a mission. After each attempt to test his resolve, I was given the same answer—with the same tone and determination.

"I don't care," he would say, "I'm going on a mission."

"When did you decide you were going on your mission?" I asked. "When I was twelve years old," he responded.

I was so proud of these two young men. I remember saying something about Captain Moroni making his unusual stand in the street and having other committed soldiers join him when I started to hear the noise. I looked around to find other young men in the room standing. First one here and then another there; then several more until the entire room was on their feet. I turned to look around and was awed by young men making their stand—together. I couldn't help but think of the stripling warriors, young men, united in cause, standing together. Without saying a word, the moment taught a great sermon.

We still had a fair amount of time left for our talk, so I returned to the podium to join my wife. We stood together at the pulpit and asked the boys to sit down so we could finish our assigned presentation. Reluctantly, they all sat down—save one row near the front. It must have been seven or so boys still standing while we were giving our talk. We decided not to say anything but continued with our comments. Then it happened—again. First one, then two, then large groups. As we continued talking, they continued to stand. These young men stood together, many of them linked arm in arm, with apparent resolve. They looked like soldiers. They seemed to be a little taller than before. The Spirit filled the room, and we spent the next half hour or so on our feet—standing together. Many of the boys were weeping, feeling a spiritual power. This was not merely teamwork; it was the power of fellowship. My wife and I concluded our remarks and thought the boys would sit down for the song practice that would follow. But not these young men. They stood through the practice and even during the closing prayer. Maybe this is what Moroni felt like when others joined him in his cause. I felt like Helaman when he called the stripling warriors his sons (Alma 56:46). I would have been proud to have any one of those boys at that moment as my son.

The time has come for all of us to stand for the cause. The time has come to stand a little taller. You make a stand each time you dress modestly, avoid pornography, and stay away from immoral practices. You stand a little taller when you use clean language, tell the truth, obey the prophet, and demonstrate good character. You are part of a royal army of great unity and cannot afford to sit on the sidelines. When so many are asking you to sit down, I hope you will have Moroni's courage to stand up. President Hinckley once received a letter where a young woman wrote: "I do want you to know that I am a darned good kid. I am so proud of my Church and my standards, which come from the Church. I am going the right direction. I don't know how much faith you have in the youth of the world today, but you can count on me. I will be on the front line when the time comes to fight the great battle, the final battle, because of my love for the Savior. I love you and all you stand for. I'll keep trying to do my best" ("'Choose the Right,' Prophet Urges Youth," *Church News*, Jan. 20, 1996, 4). I know you are probably like this young woman. I hope you will find yourself standing tall with the prophet on the front lines. We can be like Captain Moroni and make a courageous stand for a just cause. Therefore, take President Hinckley's advice and "turn around, stand tall, put your head up, and look forward to the marvelous opportunities that you have" (*Standing for Something*, 173).

Matthew O. Richardson is an assistant professor at Brigham Young University in the Department of Church History and Doctrine. He served a mission to Denmark and holds a doctoral degree in educational leadership. Matt enjoys sports, traveling, and making Mickey Mouse pancakes on Saturday mornings. He is passionate about his family and the gospel. He and his wife, Lisa, have four children.

3

TAKING IT HOME WITH ME

Randal A. Wright

Imagine that you have a life-long dream to attend law school at Harvard University. Beginning in elementary school and continuing through high school and college, you work diligently toward that goal. Knowing your entrance score is critical, you take multiple prep courses and practice exams to increase your chances of admittance. Finally, after a life-time of preparation, you receive a letter of acceptance to Harvard University for the upcoming fall semester. Then, being a goal-oriented person, you take on another personal challenge—never to make any written notes during your three years of law school. You plan to remember everything you hear and read without writing anything down. What do you think your chances of getting a 4.0 are? Surely no one would even think of attempting to pass difficult college classes without writing down important information.

If we fail to record important lessons, we quickly forget them in most cases. Consider the reason Nephi and his brothers had to go back to get the brass plates from Laban. Did Nephi have to have the terrible experience with Laban? Why didn't Lehi just teach his family the things of God from memory? Mosiah 1:3–4 answers this question:

"And he also taught them concerning the records which were engraven on the plates of brass, saying: My sons, I would that ye should remember that were it not for these plates, which contain these records and these commandments, we must have suffered in ignorance, even at this present time, not knowing the mysteries of God.

"For it were *not possible that our father, Lehi, could have remembered all*

these things, to have taught them to his children, except it were for the help of these
plates" (emphasis added).

The reason Nephi had to return and obtain the plates was that Lehi
could not have remembered all the things he needed to teach future generations. Without the plates, even the great prophets would have dwindled in
unbelief and suffered in ignorance.

Without records, our earthly experience resembles attending law school
without pen or paper and trying to remember what is truly important. If we
fail to record the wonderful experiences that teach valuable lessons, we soon
forget them, and the benefit is lost both to us and to our posterity.

I usually spend a portion of my summers working with the Church
Educational System's Youth and Family programs. Over the years I have
learned some of my greatest lessons at the Especially for Youth program. In
1995, I was very excited to serve as the session director of the EFY held at
Cornell University in New York. Most appealing to me was the chance to
visit the Peter Whitmer farm, the Sacred Grove, and to see the Hill
Cumorah Pageant.

The first day brought tremendous excitement as Latter-day Saint youth
from many parts of the United States and Canada began checking in.
During the afternoon, some outstanding youth speakers addressed the EFY
participants. Everything went well until Jason arrived at the dance that
night. One of the college-age counselors noticed that Jason was wearing an
earring and reminded him of the CES policy prohibiting young men from
wearing earrings. Jason, somewhat rebelliously, noted that he had recently
gotten the earring put in and was not going to take it out.

Program administrators would rather not deal with these kinds of situations. If Jason refused to follow the established rules, our only alternative
was to send him home. We dreaded calling his parents on the first day of
the program; we were fairly certain they hadn't made it back to their home
state. Jason was again asked to follow the rules he had agreed to by signing
his application. He refused.

J. D., an EFY coordinator, was called over to try to talk Jason into following the rules, but Jason still refused. He was escorted to a room and
reminded of his agreement to follow the program's policies. He said we could
send him home if we wanted to, because he "didn't care." Finally J. D. said,
"Jason, we really want you to be here this week. We are going to have a
great time. However, if you choose to break the rules, we will be required to

send you home. But we don't ever want you to say that we didn't want you here, because we do. It's your choice. What are you going to do?"

Jason wrote down his parents' phone number and said, "Send me home if that's what you want to do." J. D.'s reminder that Jason's money would not be refunded had no effect.

Finally he said, "Jason, I'm going to walk out of this room for five minutes. While I'm gone, I want you to ask yourself if you are going to let a ten-dollar earring keep you from having one of the greatest experiences of your entire life." Then he left Jason alone to think about his decision.

"Jason, what are you going to do?" J. D. asked upon returning.

"I think I'll stay," Jason replied. He removed the earring and agreed to keep all the rules. As he walked back into the dance that night, we all felt a tremendous relief.

Although Jason stayed, his attitude was not the best, and he had a negative impact on those around him. Thursday, charter buses arrived to take the 550 youth to Church history sites in the area. As we walked toward the Sacred Grove, I heard one young man ask a friend if he thought there would be a place where he could be alone and pray as Joseph Smith had done. A short time later, I heard another young man say, "So, are we just going to walk around in these woods or what?" What a contrast in attitudes and desires between those two young men that day!

Nearing the edge of the grove, I stopped to talk to three young men coming out. I asked them about their experience in the grove. Gabe, a six-foot, five-inch athlete from New York City, started to answer, but his eyes filled with tears, his lip started to quiver, and he couldn't speak. I knew by his countenance that he had received a testimony of what had transpired in that grove 175 years earlier. One of his friends spoke up, "I live in this area and have been in the Sacred Grove over a hundred times, and it still gets me every time I go in." I was touched. As I continued toward the grove, I saw another young man coming out alone. It was Jason. As I approached, I could tell he had been crying. "Jason, how was it?" I asked. He started to answer but became very emotional and unexpectedly threw his arms around me and began to sob. After he pulled away, I asked him again about his experience in the grove. He could not control his emotions enough to reply. Finally I commented, "It's all true, isn't it, Jason? God the Father and Jesus Christ really did appear to the Prophet Joseph Smith in that grove!" He looked me in the eye, slowly nodded his head, and then walked away.

I then walked into the Sacred Grove and had a marvelous experience myself. When I left the grove that day I wanted to take the memory of my encounter with Jason and my own experience in the grove home with me so I could reflect on it in the future. As soon as I got back to the car, I wrote the experience down in the journal section of my planner.

Do you record the valuable lessons you have in life? We have been counseled to do so by prophets of God. President Spencer W. Kimball said, "Every person should keep a journal and every person *can* keep a journal. It should be an enlightening one and should bring great blessings and happiness to the families. If there is anyone here who isn't doing so, will you repent today and change—change your life?" ("Let Us Move Forward and Upward," *Ensign*, May 1979, 84). On another occasion, President Kimball said, "By now, in my own personal history, I have managed to fill seventy-eight large volumes which are my personal journal. There have been times when I have been so tired at the end of a day that the effort could hardly be managed, but I am so grateful that I have not let slip away from me and my posterity those things which needed to be recorded" (as cited in JoAnn Jolley, "News of the Church," *Ensign*, Oct. 1980, 72).

One of the Prophet Joseph Smith's greatest regrets in life was his failure to record many important events in Church history, including the date of the restoration of the Melchizedek Priesthood. He said, "If I now had in my possession, every decision which had been had upon important items of doctrine and duties since the commencement of this work, I would not part with them for any sum of money; but we have neglected to take minutes of such things, thinking, perhaps, that they would never benefit us afterwards; which, if we had them now, would decide almost every point of doctrine which might be agitated. But this has been neglected, and now we cannot bear record to the Church and to the world, of the great and glorious manifestations which have been made to us with that degree of power and authority we otherwise could, if we now had these things to publish abroad" (*Teachings of the Prophet Joseph Smith*, sel. Joseph Fielding Smith [Salt Lake City: Deseret Book, 1976], 72). The lesson from the Prophet is clear: We should learn and record the lessons the Lord provides for us.

Bishop Orson F. Whitney explained the plan clearly: "We believe that in that pre-existent life, where the spirits of all men once dwelt, a Savior was prepared, pre-ordained to die for the salvation of the world. We also believe that other great and noble ones were selected—prophets, poets, philosophers, reformers, painters, sculptors, etc., and sent into the world to play their parts, to hold aloft the torch of God-given genius to illumine the pathway leading to perfection. All good gifts are from God, from him who sent us forth into this school to learn life's lessons, to assist each other to learn, and having gained our education, to return to Him perfected, and dwell in peace eternally" (in Brian H. Stuy, comp., *Collected Discourses Delivered by President Wilford Woodruff*, 5 vols. [Burbank, Cal.: BHS Publishing, 1987–92], 3:46). Many of us learn vital lessons from life, yet we often fail to record such lessons. What are the chances of remembering what we learn today one or ten years from now? Will our insights spare our posterity the heartache of making unwise decisions? We have been sent to earth not only to fulfill certain missions and learn important lessons but also to light the path for others.

Imagine that Nephi has passed his valuable small plates to you and instructed you to include only the things which you considered "most precious" in your writings. Which of life's lessons would you consider including on the plates? Without making a conscious effort to glean lessons from life's experiences, our plates would not resemble the powerful records of Nephi, but they might look like those of another Book of Mormon writer: "Now I, Chemish, write what few things I write, in the same book with my brother; for behold, I saw the last which he wrote, that he wrote it with his own hand; and he wrote it in the day that he delivered them unto me. And after this manner we keep the records, for it is according to the commandments of our father. And I make an end" (Omni 1:9). He didn't leave much of a message in the three sentences written to us. Every time we learn something significant, we should write down the details of the experience and what we specifically learned from it. Consider Alma's example: "And it came to pass when Alma had heard these words *he wrote them down that he might have them*" (Mosiah 26:33; emphasis added). Alma didn't rely on his memory alone to remember the counsel of the Lord. Because he wrote it down we can benefit from what this prophet learned more than twenty-one hundred years ago.

Recording the lessons that I have learned in a journal has truly changed my life. I am confident it will do the same for you. If you will record these valuable lessons, the Prophet Joseph Smith said, "You will find it of infinite worth, not only to your brethren, but it will be a feast to your own souls" (*Teachings of the Prophet Joseph Smith*, 73). If you will record the essential lessons learned in your lifetime, you will find in your possession a tremendous help for almost everything you do in life. Your personal testimony will grow, and life will become more meaningful because each day as you arise, you will be excited to see what new lessons you will learn.

Randal A. Wright was born and reared in Texas and serves as an institute of religion director for the Church Educational System. He holds a Ph.D. in family studies from Brigham Young University and has done extensive research on the impact of electronic media and adolescents. He has also written articles for several magazines and is the author of five books. He loves basketball, music, books, red velvet cake, and being at home with his family. He and his wife, Wendy, are the parents of five children and reside in Austin, Texas.

4

THE ASSURANCE OF PROTECTION

Todd Parker

The word *insulate* comes from the Latin word *insula*, meaning island. *Webster's* defines the word as such: "to place in a detached situation: isolate, . . . to separate from conducting bodies by means of nonconductors so as to prevent transfer of electricity, heat, or sound" (10th ed., Springfield, Mass.: Merriam-Webster, Inc., 1993). Often people insulate the warmth of their bodies from a cold windchill by using coats or jackets containing material that "separates" them or "isolates" them from the cold.

Apparently, Moroni used a principle of "insulation" to establish an "assurance of protection" (Alma 50:12) for his people, the Nephites. Through a careful examination of the principles used by Moroni in preparation for physical battles, we may be able to apply the same principles in our lives and thus prepare for the spiritual battles we face in the modern world. Many students of the Book of Mormon believe that Mormon specifically included the "war section" in the book (Alma 43–63) to teach us the principles of spiritual preparation. Indeed, we may be able through wise application of these scriptures to develop a modern "assurance of protection" that could prepare us in a "manner which never [before] had been known" (Alma 49:8). How was it that the Nephites had "all power over their enemies" (Alma 49:23)? Wouldn't it be nice to have "all power" over our adversary of the latter days when battling with temptation and evil? How did Moroni pull it off? Let's take a look.

The fiftieth chapter of Alma in the Book of Mormon lists for the latter-day reader seven things Moroni did to protect his people from the invading Lamanites. Following is an examination of each one, along with some suggestions that will help us use his strategies in our day.

1. "To defend his people against the Lamanites . . . they . . . commence[d] in digging up heaps of earth round about all the cities, throughout all the land" (Alma 50:1).

The heaps of earth were obviously used as a form of physical "insulation" from the attacks of the Lamanites. If our spiritual attacker is Satan, and he uses temptation and sin to wound or kill us spiritually, does it not seem reasonable that we should insulate ourselves from the spirit of temptation and the destructive forces of transgression? Jesus himself taught us to do so when he said: "If thy right eye offend thee [cause thee to stumble], pluck it out, and cast it from thee. . . . And if thy right hand offend thee, cut it off, and cast it from thee" (Matthew 5:29–30).

Jesus' teaching to his disciples in Galilee suggests that he cautioned them to "remove" their eyes from seeing things that would cause them to stumble spiritually. Likewise, when tempted to touch something that could cause them to sin, they were taught to remove their hands from the tempting situation. In other words, Jesus suggested that we should control our own environment, especially the things we see, hear, touch, or experience. That may be easy to say and easy to agree with in principle, but it can be difficult to do in practice. Mormon listed for us several of the precautions taken by Captain Moroni that kept his enemy from penetrating the Nephites' environment. Note that there was more than one line of defense. The Nephites used mounds of earth, walls of timbers, towers, pickets, places of security, and weapons of war to keep the enemy at bay.

2. "And upon the top of these ridges of earth he caused that there should be timbers . . . built up to the height of a man" (Alma 50:2).

Moroni's second line of defense was a wall of timbers surrounding each city. If our first line of defense (heaps of earth) is a controlled environment, to what should we liken the wall of timbers? I suggest that it could represent awareness and acknowledgment that multiple forms of defense are essential. In his prophetic counsel to members living in the latter days, the prophet Nephi said: "For behold, at that day [the last days] shall [Satan] rage in the hearts of the children of men, and stir them up to anger against that which is good.

"And others will he pacify, and lull them away into carnal security, that they will say: All is well in Zion; yea, Zion prospereth, all is well—and thus the devil cheateth their souls, and leadeth them away carefully down to hell" (2 Nephi 28: 20–21).

According to Nephi, one of Satan's main weapons in the latter days will be his ability to carefully persuade members of the Church to think that they are safe and secure—that there is no need for numerous lines of defense. Note that in the Book of Mormon, even when there was "continual peace among them, and exceedingly great prosperity in the church" (Alma 49:30), Moroni did not stop making preparations for war to defend his people in case the Lamanites should attack them (Alma 50:1). Moroni recognized the need to continually build up defenses even during times of peace, when the enemy was not attacking. At a later time, the Lamanites took possession of the city of Zarahemla because "[the Nephites] had not kept sufficient guards in the land of Zarahemla . . . and [the Lamanite's] march was with such exceedingly great speed that there was no time for the Nephites to gather together their armies" (Helaman 1:18–19). The message seems clear. If we become preoccupied with other things and let our guard down, the enemy can attack swiftly and overtake us.

3. "And he [Moroni] caused that upon those works of timbers there should be a frame of pickets built . . . ; and they were strong and high" (Alma 50:3).

The frame of pickets was above the timbers, which were above the mounds of dirt.

The fact that the pickets were "strong and high" lends itself to a comparison of strong and high standards of conduct. It should be noted that the pickets were pointed and sharp to prevent the enemy from climbing over them and entering the city. We too should build a set of high and well-defined (pointed) standards to be used to thwart our enemy from gaining entrance into our minds, our hearts, and our lives. The First Presidency of The Church of Jesus Christ of Latter-day Saints has provided just such a set of standards. They are contained in a pamphlet entitled *For the Strength of Youth.* In that pamphlet the First Presidency states: "You can avoid the burden of guilt and sin and all of the attending heartaches if you will but heed the standards provided you through the teachings of the Lord and His servants.

"We bear witness of the truth of these principles and promise you the blessings of the Lord as you keep the standards outlined in the scriptures and emphasized in this pamphlet. . . .

"Standards are rules or guidelines given to help you measure your conduct. . . . Standards help you know how well you are preparing to live with your Father in Heaven. . . . By comparing your behavior and thoughts with your Father's standards, you are in a better position to govern yourselves and make the right choices. God's commandments (standards) are constant, unwavering, and dependable. As you adhere to them, you will receive countless blessings from heaven—including the gift of eternal life" (1990, 4, 6).

The pamphlet describes the standards of the Church regarding dating, dress, friends, honesty, language, media, the Word of Wisdom, music, sexual purity, and the Sabbath day. Setting specific or well-defined high standards in each of these areas provides additional protection, as did the pointed "frame of pickets" in Moroni's day.

4. "And [Moroni] caused towers to be erected that overlooked those works of pickets" (Alma 50:4).

In the Old Testament, the Book of Mormon, and the Doctrine and Covenants, the Lord refers to his servants (apostles and prophets) as "watchmen" (Ezekiel 33:1–7; Mosiah 15:28–29; D&C 101:45). Just as Moroni's towers provided a place for watchmen to warn his people of impending danger, so too has the Lord provided watchmen on the tower to warn his people in the latter days.

Lucile C. Tate, who authored the biographies of apostles LeGrand Richards and Boyd K. Packer, wrote the following concerning these "watchmen": "The imagery of *watchman* is fitting for those fifteen men who have been called by the Lord as prophets, seers, and revelators, who have been sustained as such by the Church, who have been anointed of the Lord, and who serve as His special witnesses.

"They have been so designated by the Lord in the various dispensations of time. They are found in the Old Testament, the Book of Mormon, and the Doctrine and Covenants, identified as those who are to watch over His Church.

"The term *watch* helps to define their roles which, in part, are: to be attentive to trends, drifts, and conditions within and without the Church; to be vigilant and alert to dangers from the archenemy, Satan; to guard, tend, heed, and warn" (in *Boyd K. Packer: A Watchman on the Tower* [Salt Lake City: Bookcraft, 1995], vii).

In Moroni's day, people who failed to heed the warnings of the watchmen on the tower came face to face with physical death. Failure to heed our modern watchmen could yield consequences that are even more serious. President James E. Faust said: "I do not believe members of this Church can be in full harmony with the Savior without sustaining His living prophet on the earth, the President of the Church. *If we do not sustain the living prophet, whoever he may be, we die spiritually.* Ironically, some have died spiritually by exclusively following prophets who have long been dead. Others equivocate in their support of living prophets, trying to lift themselves up by putting down the living prophets, however subtly" ("Continuing Revelation," *Ensign,* Aug. 1996, 5; emphasis added).

Heeding our modern watchmen is truly a life and death matter. It is dangerous, however, to be like those who have varied reactions to the counsel of living prophets. Some people see their warnings as advice, others see their words as scripture, and yet others choose to ignore their warnings completely. President Ezra Taft Benson gave an address to students and faculty at Brigham Young University entitled "Fourteen Fundamentals in Following the Prophet." He said, "Our salvation hangs on them." His fourteen fundamentals were:

1. The prophet is the only man who speaks for the Lord in everything.
2. The living prophet is more vital to us than the standard works.
3. The living prophet is more important to us than a dead prophet.
4. The prophet will never lead the Church astray.
5. The prophet is not required to have any particular earthly training or credentials to speak on any subject or act on any matter at any time.
6. The prophet does not have to say "Thus saith the Lord" to give us scripture.
7. The prophet tells us what we need to know, not always what we want to know.
8. The prophet is not limited by men's reasoning.
9. The prophet can receive revelation on any matter—temporal or spiritual.
10. The prophet may be involved in civic matters.
11. The two groups who have the greatest difficulty in following the prophet are the proud who are learned and the proud who are rich.
12. The prophet will not necessarily be popular with the world or the worldly.
13. The prophet and his counselors make up the First Presidency—the highest quorum in the Church.
14. The prophet and the presidency—the living prophet and the First Presidency—follow them and be blessed; reject them and suffer.

President Benson further testified that "these fourteen fundamentals in following the living prophet are true. If we want to know how well we stand with the Lord, then let us ask ourselves how well we stand with His mortal captain. How closely do our lives harmonize with the words of the Lord's anointed—the living prophet, the President of the Church, and with the Quorum of the First Presidency?" (in *1980 Devotional Speeches of the Year* [Provo: Brigham Young University Press, 1981], 26–30).

5. "And [Moroni] caused places of security to be built upon those towers, that the stones and the arrows of the Lamanites could not hurt them" (Alma 50:4).

What should be our "places of security" as we fight our spiritual battles "to quench all the fiery darts of the wicked" (D&C 27:17)? Just as Moroni "did prepare strongholds against the coming of their enemies" (Alma 50:6), so should we have our own "strongholds." To what could we liken Moroni's strongholds? May I suggest that our homes and our circle of friends can act as strongholds of insulation against the evil influences of the world.

Let us consider first our homes. Many evil influences can potentially enter our homes through media and technology: television (cable), video-cassettes, DVDs, the Internet, and music. All of these have potential to influence us positively or negatively. To make our homes "strongholds" against the wicked we need to do some editing, screening, and discreet selection as we choose which materials can enter our homes. Consider, for example, this statement from Al Menconi in the *American Family Association Journal*: "A plague is sweeping across our country. It is destroying families, careers, ministries, and churches. The plague I am speaking of is pornography. . . . With easy access to the Internet today, almost every family in America is becoming vulnerable. A Nua Internet Survey [www.nua.ie] reports that 75 percent of hits on the Web are looking for a porno site. That means that more than half of all activity on the Web right now involves pornography" ("Pornography: Junk Food for Your Soul," June/July 2000, 20).

The preponderance of pornography sites on the Internet prompted one stake president to remark, "If you don't have a restrictive server on your Internet, it's spiritual suicide." His remark came as a result of several interviews with Church members who had become addicted to pornography through the Internet. As a bishop, I can add my witness that, if their homes aren't "strongholds," young men and women will struggle with this temptation at home. Standards for video ratings, TV shows, and appropriate music should be discussed in families, and well-understood standards should be established. To relax our standards puts us in the position of entering the "strongholds of the wicked." Moroni himself said, "we durst not go forth and attack them in their strongholds" (Alma 58:2).

Friends can serve either as righteous strongholds or become strongholds of the wicked. Most of the youth that I know who get into trouble don't do it alone. Almost without exception, teens in trouble have been influenced by friends. The Savior in his wisdom therefore counseled: "It is better for thee to enter into life without thy brother, than for thee and thy brother to be cast into hell; . . .

"And again, if thy foot offend thee, cut it off; for he that is thy standard, by whom thou walkest, if he become a transgressor, he shall be cut off. . . .

"Therefore, let every man stand or fall, by himself, and not for another; or not trusting another. . . .

"And if thine eye which seeth for thee, him that is appointed to watch over thee to show thee light, become a transgressor and offend thee, pluck him out. . . .

"For it is better that thyself should be saved, than to be cast into hell with thy brother" (JST Mark 9:41–42, 44, 46, 48).

The Savior's counsel is rather blunt and to the point. If you have a friend who is a transgressor, you are to "cut" him off or "pluck him out." Jesus' counsel is to discontinue your association with your "friend." Do not let inappropriate friends, television, videos, or Web sites invade your stronghold. Just as Moroni cut off the supply of provisions to the city of Cumeni to defeat the Lamanites (Alma 57:7–11), so should we cut off any supply of evil that might attempt to enter our strongholds.

6. "And they [the Nephites] were prepared that they could cast stones from the top thereof, . . . and slay him who should attempt to approach near the walls of the city" (Alma 50:5).

To this point, Captain Moroni's precautions have all been defensive measures. But here, Moroni adds an offensive element to his preparations—casting stones. Certainly Moroni must have had someone assigned to keep a constant supply of stones ready in the towers in case of a Lamanite attack. What sort of "spiritual stones" should we be stockpiling in our lives as spiritual weapons against our adversary? In the parable of the ten virgins (Matthew 25:1–13), Jesus exemplified this principle of preparation by using oil as the medium. Whether oil in lamps or stones in towers, the principle of being ready is the same. President Spencer W. Kimball interpreted the symbolism of the oil in the parable of the ten virgins as follows: "The foolish asked the others to share their oil, but spiritual preparedness cannot be shared in an instant. The wise had to go, else the bridegroom would have gone unwelcomed. They needed all their oil for themselves; they could not save the foolish. The responsibility was each for himself.

"This was not selfishness or unkindness. The kind of oil that is needed to illuminate the way and light up the darkness is not shareable. How can one share obedience to the principle of tithing; a mind at peace from righteous living; an accumulation of knowledge? How can one share faith or testimony? How can one share attitudes or chastity, or the experience of a mission? How can one share temple privileges? Each must obtain that kind of oil for himself.

"The foolish virgins were not averse to buying oil. They knew they should have oil. They merely procrastinated, not knowing when the bridegroom would come.

"In the parable, oil can be purchased at the market. In our lives the oil of preparedness is accumulated drop by drop in righteous living. Attendance at sacrament meetings adds oil to our lamps, drop by drop over the years. Fasting, family prayer, home teaching, control of bodily appetites, preaching the gospel, studying the scriptures—each act of dedication and obedience is a drop added to our store. Deeds of kindness, payment of offerings and tithes, chaste thoughts and actions, marriage in the covenant for eternity—these, too, contribute importantly to the oil with which we can at midnight refuel our exhausted lamps" (*Faith Precedes the Miracle* [Salt Lake City: Deseret Book, 1972], 255–56).

Whether viewed as oil or stones, we each need to secure our own stockpile of spiritual weapons against the wiles of the devil. It cannot be done in an instant. Preparation is a process. The Lord himself has said that if we are prepared we "shall not fear" (D&C 38:30).

7. "And [Moroni] also placed armies . . . in the borders of their possessions, . . . that they might secure . . . their people from the hands of their enemies" (Alma 50:10).

Who are those armies of today that surround our people and "secure" them from the hands of their enemies? If our apostles and prophet leaders are the watchmen on the tower, are not our local leaders the spiritual lieutenants who help us to fight our battles on a regular basis? They carry a responsibility to train us, to feed and nourish us, and to prepare us for battle. They help us put on the "armour of light" (Romans 13:12). They help us wield the sword of the spirit and the shield of faith. They help us to gird our loins with truth.

When speaking to a group of BYU students, Elder Harold B. Lee explained the spiritual symbolism for some major parts of the armor of God, as listed in both Doctrine and Covenants 27:15–18 and Ephesians 6:11–18. Elder Lee said: "We have the four parts of the body that . . . [are] the most vulnerable to the powers of darkness. The loins, typifying virtue, chastity. The heart typifying our conduct. Our feet, our goals or objectives in life and finally, our head, our thoughts" ("Feet Shod with the Preparation of the Gospel of Peace," *Brigham Young University Speeches of the Year* [Provo, Nov. 9, 1954], 2).

Our leaders help protect our chastity by girding our loins with truth or, in other words, by teaching us the word of God. They try to improve our conduct by changing our hearts that we have "no more disposition to do evil" (Mosiah 5:2). They help us set goals of missions and temple marriage, that our feet might be on the path of eternal life (2 Nephi 31:17–21). They train us to "let virtue garnish [our] thoughts unceasingly" so that our confidence will "wax strong in the presence of God" (D&C 121:45). As Moroni raised the standard or "title of liberty" (Alma 46:12) to symbolize the covenant his people made with their God (Alma 46:22), so today do our ward and stake leaders raise a standard of righteousness in challenges, activities, and programs to help strengthen the youth in living the covenants they have made at baptism. Each week thousands of young women recite a standard they hold dear in the Young Women theme. Many young priesthood holders also recite the purposes of the Aaronic Priesthood to remind them of the standard they must strive to maintain.

Moroni was wise in his preparation. His preparations astonished and frightened his enemies (Alma 49:8; 43:21). His lines of defense were numerous and strong at all times. Today we must be wise like Moroni. Our preparations should be so strong as to astonish the adversary. We must have multiple lines of defense. If we take the time to properly prepare, we can avoid sin instead of having to repent of sin. Mormon observed that Moroni knew this principle when he wrote, "it was easier to keep the city from falling into the hands of the Lamanites than to retake it from them" (Alma 59:9). President Ezra Taft Benson once said, "It is better to prepare and prevent than it is to repair and repent" (*The Teachings of Ezra Taft Benson* [Salt Lake City: Bookcraft, 1988], 285).

May we all be wise like unto Moroni in preparing defenses and fortifications that will act for us as an "assurance of protection" in the Lord's church.

Brother Todd Parker was born and raised in Ogden, Utah. He married Debra Harbertson, and they are the parents of six boys and three girls. He received his bachelor's degree from Weber State College, majoring in English. His M.Ed. degree in counseling and his Ed.D. degree in educational psychology are both from Brigham Young University.

He has taught seminary for fourteen years and institute for five years and is presently an associate professor at BYU in the Department of Ancient Scripture. Brother Parker has served in a variety of church positions. He has been an elders quorum president, executive secretary, den leader, a counselor in a ward bishopric, high priest group leader, a stake mission president, and a high councilor. He presently serves as bishop of the Orem Canyon View Fifth Ward.

5

BE A CHRISTIAN SOLDIER, NOT A WEEKEND WARRIOR

Curtis Castillow

Years ago, when Elder Rex D. Pinegar taught early-morning seminary, he reviewed with his students some important principles from the Book of Mormon. During the discussion, one young woman held up an illustration in her Book of Mormon of the two thousand stripling warriors. In all seriousness, she asked, "Tell me, Brother Pinegar, why aren't our young men built like this today?" Elder Pinegar said he didn't know if the stripling warriors were actually built like that. And then he asked, "Where did the *strength* of these young men come from?" (see "Faith: The Force of Life," in *Faith* [Salt Lake City: Deseret Book, 1983], 88). Isn't that an interesting question? It is one worth pondering.

The stripling warriors were young men distinguished for their courage and valor on the battlefield. Helaman, their prophet-general, described them by saying they "fought as if with the strength of God; yea, never were men known to have fought with such miraculous strength; and with such mighty power." Though outnumbered, their courage against the Lamanites was such that "they did frighten them; and for this cause did the Lamanites deliver themselves up as prisoners of war" (Alma 56:56).

What makes their victory miraculous is that they weren't the "Green Berets" of Mormon's day—they were young recruits fresh out of boot camp. The first time I saw the painting of those husky warriors, I seriously thought *stripling* meant *rippling*—like rippling muscles. I was mistaken, though. *Stripling* means "youthful." These were young men your age—they were just like you. They went to Zarahemla High, dreamed of prom, set goals to make the team, and aspired to success. Because they were just like you, you can be just like them. You can be just as strong as they were.

The kind of strength I'm speaking of doesn't come from massive triceps; it comes from a Titanic-sized testimony—one that can withstand evil. You need that kind of spiritual muscle and brawn to withstand Satan because he is in an all-out war against the youth of this church. Statistics show that most Church members who become less active do so between the ages of sixteen and twenty-five (see Stan L. Albrecht, "The Consequential Dimension of Mormon Religiosity," *Brigham Young University Studies*, Spring 1989, 73). This means that your age automatically places you in the trenches at the front line of a heated battle. It is a battle against a fierce enemy that "walketh about, seeking whom he may devour" (1 Peter 5:8). But Satan is not fighting with slingshots, paintballs, or BB guns. Bruce R. Hafen, who is now a member of the First Quorum of the Seventy, said that Satan has "dragged out the heavy artillery. . . . Now he is Darth Vader, with laser guns, light speeds, and the death star" ("The Gospel and Romantic Love," in *Brigham Young University 1982–83 Fireside and Devotional Speeches* [Provo: Brigham Young University Press, 1983], 31).

Elder Neal A. Maxwell warned: "Righteous desires need to be relentless . . . because, said President Brigham Young, 'the men and women, who desire to obtain seats in the celestial kingdom, will find that they must battle every day' (in *Journal of Discourses*, 11:14). Therefore, true Christian soldiers are more than weekend warriors" ("'According to the Desire of [Our] Hearts,'" *Ensign*, Nov. 1996, 22). In this chapter I will share with you insights from the story of the two thousand stripling warriors—certainly among the most valiant Christian soldiers ever—that will help you become more like a Christian soldier instead of a weekend warrior. As you discover the source of the stripling warriors' strength, it is my hope that you too will be able to triumph over evil.

CHRISTIAN SOLDIERS KEEP THEIR COVENANTS

One vital source of strength for the stripling warriors was the covenants they had made with the Lord. They had covenanted to follow Jesus Christ. In fact, they "covenanted that they never would give up their liberty, but they would fight in all cases to protect the Nephites and themselves from bondage" (Alma 53:17). Today, true Christian soldiers covenant to fight for their freedom and avoid the spiritual bondage that comes from alcohol, drugs, pornography, and immorality.

A friend of mine shared an experience from her mission which portrays the freedom that accompanies righteous choices and the enslavement that follows bad choices. When Kim served her mission in Dublin, Ireland, she and her companion knocked on the door of a belligerent man who sought to prove that the doctrines of the Church were stupid and senseless. As he puffed his pipe, he blurted out, "I know who you are, you're one of those Mormons. You're the people who have a pope who tells you what you can eat, drink, smoke, wear, and do. You're like a bunch of prisoners held captive by all your restrictive restraints!" After the man made some other sneering remarks, he paused just long enough for Kim to speak.

Now Kim was a girl who personified the word spunk. She wasn't one to cower in a corner when confronted—especially when it came to her religion. Kim said, "Sir, let me tell you something. When I get up in the morning, I don't have to have a cup of coffee to get me going; and after lunch, I don't need a cigarette to calm my nerves; and when I go out with my friends, I don't need to have a drink to 'loosen up' and have fun—we get high on life." With courage, she pointed to him and stated boldly, "Now you tell me, who's more free: *you* or *me?*" Do you see her point? We really are free when we make and keep covenants. We are free when we covenant each Sunday to remain clean and uncontrolled by anything that creates a habit for itself. The freedom that comes from keeping covenants is a tremendous source of strength.

CHRISTIAN SOLDIERS FOLLOW THE PROPHET

The book of Alma states that the stripling warriors "would that Helaman should be their leader" (Alma 53:19). At this point in the Book of Mormon, Alma the prophet had been translated. So who was the next prophet? Alma's son—Helaman. This means that the stripling warriors chose a prophet of God to lead them. Latter-day Christian soldiers should likewise choose to follow our prophet, President Gordon B. Hinckley, into spiritual battle. This is a wonderful choice, especially now when the world seems to be heading in a direction that leads us further and further away from the Lord. Let me illustrate. A poll taken in 1900 discovered that 78 percent of the youth's heroes were historical figures such as George Washington and Abraham Lincoln. Twelve percent chose literary figures such as Hercules, and 10 percent chose relatives and acquaintances. In 1950 the same study was performed, but the researcher discovered an interesting change. Thirty-three percent of those chosen as heroes were historical figures, none were literary, and 57 percent were sports, radio, and movie stars (Dorothy Barclay, "Youth's Heroes and Hero Worship," *The New York Times Magazine*, Nov. 4 1951, 42).

Randal A. Wright did a similar study across four states in 1993. He asked youth whom they idolized most. Whom do you think rated number one? Would you believe Cindy Crawford? Tom Cruise was second, Madonna was eighth, Garth Brooks placed tenth, Michael Jordan was seventeenth, and Mel Gibson ranked eighteenth (*Why Good People See Bad Movies* [Springville, Utah: National Family Institute, 1993], 13–14).

There is nothing wrong with appreciating the talents of some of the world's great athletes and performers, but it is even more important to develop an eternal perspective. It is the Savior's words, taught by his prophets, that will help you overcome the world—not a person's batting average or waist size. Draw on the strength that comes from making the prophet your leader. The stripling warriors did.

CHRISTIAN SOLDIERS OBEY ABSOLUTELY

Last April, one of my former students came to my office and asked, "Brother Castillow, can I talk with you?" It was a girl I nicknamed "Scooter" (her name is withheld to protect the righteous). I called her Scooter because of her spirited and spunky personality. She came to my office to ask if she could speak with me concerning a difficult decision she was trying to make. I could tell she was struggling because she wasn't her usual peppy self. She sat down, took a deep breath, and said, "I've been invited to prom."

"Cool!" I said.

"Not cool!"

"Why?" I asked curiously.

"Because I don't turn sixteen until two days after the prom."

"Not cool!" I replied. Grasping for inspiration, I said, "What did your parents say?" (This is the universal question we adults ask when our inspiration bucket has sprung a leak.)

"They said I could go," she replied.

"What?" I shot back.

I thought to myself, *Oh no, I'm toast! What do I say to that? She has wonderful parents.*

Knowing she had friends with high standards, I asked, "What did your friends say to do?"

She answered, "They said I should go."

I thought to myself, *Darn it! I hate those friends!*

I had one more match left in my "Emergency Counsel Kit" to light the fire of inspiration. Emotionally exasperated—yet trying to look as cool as a cucumber—I asked, "Scooter, do you *really* like this guy?"

If her feelings toward him seemed lukewarm, I would say "Is he really worth it?" But right at that moment, she began to blush and glow with excitement.

Scooter then exclaimed, "Oh yes, Brother Castillow, I've known him since grade school. He's the neatest guy!"

Oh great, I thought, *the winds of fate just snuffed out my last chance!*

I stared at her in desperation. She stared off toward heaven enraptured in a vision of sugar plum fairies and a cute guy dancing through her head. Then a scripture story came to mind—the story of the stripling warriors.

Helaman tells of a time when the stripling warriors had to defend themselves against a barrage of attacks from the Lamanites. He writes: "They were about to overpower us. But behold, my little band of two thousand and sixty fought most desperately; yea, they were firm before the Lamanites, and did administer death unto all those who opposed them. And as the remainder of our army were about to give way before the Lamanites, behold, those two thousand and sixty were firm and undaunted. Yea, *and they did obey and observe to perform every word of command with exactness*; yea, and even according to their faith it was done unto them" (Alma 57: 18–21; emphasis added).

After relating this part of the story to Scooter, I said, "Scoot, I don't have all the answers, but this much I know: absolute obedience brings absolute blessings." We then talked for about an hour, but I could tell she was still a little frustrated. Finally, I said, "If this guy told you to go, your friends told you to go, and your father told you to go, then why don't you go?" She paused, then with a little emotion she said, "Because my Heavenly Father told me not to go."

"There's your answer," I suggested.

"I know, Brother Castillow, but it's hard!"

"Sure it is," I said, "but I know you will make the right decision." Two days later, I found a letter on my desk with my name printed on it. Here's what it said:

"Dear Brother Castillow,

"Thank you for helping me make a very important decision. I will not go to Prom this year. I answered Scott as nicely as I could, and he reacted well.

He even told one of my friends that he's glad he's going after a 'good girl.' Some people can't figure out why I'm not going, but most people are proud of me. I have never felt such peace. I know I made the right choice and that my Savior is happy with me. Only 100 percent obedience brings happiness, like you told me, and the entire experience has boosted my character and changed my heart. I am inspired to be a better person. Thanks."

Scooter thanked *me*, but I'm thankful for her example. Scooter would have made a great stripling warrior. Like them, she knows that absolute obedience brings about absolute blessings . . . and great strength.

CHRISTIAN SOLDIERS ARE A GREAT SUPPORT

Another source of strength we find in the stripling warriors was their commitment to be a source of support. Helaman had this to say about his young soldiers: "They never had hitherto been a disadvantage to the Nephites, they became now at this period of time also a great support" (Alma 53:19). Similarly, Christian youth today should strive to be an advantage and great support to everyone they meet. Young women, your modest clothing would greatly support the young men of this church. Consider the following statement from the First Presidency: "Because the way you dress sends messages about yourself to others and often influences the way you and others act, you should dress in such a way as to bring out the *best in yourself and those around you.* However, if you wear an immodest bathing suit because it's 'the style,' it sends a message that you are using your body to get attention and approval, and that modesty is not important" (*For the Strength of Youth* [Salt Lake City: The Church of Jesus Christ of Latter-day Saints, 1990], 8; emphasis added).

I don't think that the young women in this church who dress immodestly do so with the intention of hurting our young men; but I sometimes fear that young women don't realize the effect their appearance has on young men. Let me illustrate. In my stake, our Young Women president was about to speak to a group of young women about immodesty, when she came across a group of young men she knew. When they found out she was speaking to their ward's young women about modesty, they started laughing.

She asked, "Want to share what's so funny?"

Finally one young man looked up and said with a smile, "Girls just don't get it!"

"What do you mean they don't get it?" she asked.

"They just don't get it!" The young man repeated.

Then he shared a story with her about a girl who came to church that very morning wearing a low-cut dress. With a serious tone in his voice he said, "How are we supposed to keep our minds on the sacrament with that going on?"

Elder Spencer W. Kimball stated, "I know I'm not going to be popular when I say this, but I am sure that the immodest dresses that are worn by our young women, and their mothers, contribute in some degree to the immorality of this age. . . . I wonder if our young sisters realize the temptation they are flaunting before young men when they leave their bodies partly uncovered" (A *Style of Our Own: Modesty in Dress and Its Relationship to the Church,* BYU Devotional, Feb. 13, 1951, 7). More recently, Sister Carol B. Thomas, first counselor in the General Young Women Presidency, echoed President Kimball's teaching. She taught the young women to remember that "'we stand as witnesses of God at all times and in all things'—and in *all prom dresses*" ("Spiritual Power of Our Baptism," *Ensign,* May 1999, 93).

Now, young men, Elder Richard G. Scott said you too can be an advantage to young women with your attitude toward their dress and appearance. He said that many young women "dress and act immodestly because they are told that is what you want. . . .

"Those young women who do embrace conservative dress standards . . . are often criticized for not being 'with it.' Encourage them by expressing gratitude for their worthy example" ("The Sanctity of Womanhood," *Ensign,* May 2000, 36).

Young men, you are also an advantage to young women when you honor your priesthood by keeping *yourself* morally clean. Young women should expect you to be clean. President Gordon B. Hinckley said so. He taught: "The girl you marry will take a terrible chance on you. She will give her all to the young man she marries. He will largely determine the remainder of her life. She will even surrender her name to his name." Therefore, he continues, she "can expect you to come to the marriage altar absolutely clean. She can expect you to be a young man of virtue in thought and word and deed" ("Living Worthy of the Girl You Will Someday Marry," *Ensign,* May 1998, 49). Do you want to have the strength of a stripling warrior? Consider making an effort to support gospel teachings and support others who wish to do the same.

CHRISTIAN SOLDIERS ARE TRUE AT ALL TIMES

You've heard the old saying, "When the cat's away the mice will play." That might be true of some people but not of Christian soldiers. The stripling warriors were not only "exceedingly valiant for courage . . . strength and activity" but they "were men who were true at *all times*" (Alma 53:20; emphasis added)—even when the "cat's" away. Let me explain. In 1998, one of my former seminary students went with her drama class to spend a couple of days at a Shakespeare competition in southern Utah. The night before the individual competitions, her roommates decided to watch an R-rated movie in the hotel room—her best friend was among them. She asked them to turn off the television, but they responded with, "The movie's not that long." At one point she was asked why she was making such a big deal about it. Then, they offered to turn down the volume, thinking that she might like to sleep instead of watch the movie. She told me later, "I declined the offer because I had learned that I couldn't be in that sort of atmosphere and remain unaffected." She finally resorted to pacing the hotel's parking lot and singing "Twinkle, Twinkle Little Star" six times. Then she sang other songs until 3:30 A.M. Later she wrote this to me:

"I wish I could say that I went on to place at the competition. But, I didn't. In fact, the next day, because I was so tired, I had a headache. The stress on my body coupled with my heart condition caused me to faint twice that day.

"Some people might wonder what 'inspired me' or gave me courage to face the peer pressure and my tiredness. Really, I don't have an answer to that. *I had merely made up my mind, at some point earlier in life, that I would never watch an R-rated movie.* That night I never thought twice about my decision. I'm not a perfect person, I'm not a prophet's daughter, or even a bishop's daughter. I'm just me trying to do what I know to be right" (emphasis added).

The stripling warriors were true at all times—with or without supervision. My former student was, too. Undoubtedly, that quality added strength to the stripling warriors, and it will to you as well.

So, my friends, can you see what made the stripling warriors so amazing? Can you see from where their strength came? It came because they kept their covenants, followed their prophet, obeyed absolutely, and supported gospel teachings and others. You too may have wondered why youth today aren't built like the stripling warriors. But remember, you don't have to be *built* like them to acquire their spiritual strength, you just have to *live* like them. As you live like them you will be stronger than a weekend warrior; you'll be a true Christian soldier.

Curtis Castillow was born in Phoenix, Arizona, where he grew up on a small farm and traveled the rodeo circuit as a bull rider. He converted to the Church when he was twenty-one and served a mission in Tacoma, Washington. He has a bachelor's degree in psychology from Brigham Young University and a master's degree in educational technology from Utah State University. He has taught seminary full time for eight years and currently teaches seminary at Pleasant Grove High School in Utah.

He says he loves his "gorgeously spiritual wife," his four lovable children, scriptures, classical literature, computers, fly-fishing, woodworking, home improvement, and playing his guitar.

6

SATAN'S TRAPS

Richard Staples

Have you ever done something that was really questionable? Perhaps you have taken a dare, or dared someone else to do something, and then asked yourself, "Why did I do that?" One warm, summer day, when I was about five years old, my friend and I decided it would be fun to run through the sprinkler and play in his wading pool. We put on our swimming suits and were really having a lot of fun for the first hour or two. But then I somehow got it in my mind to challenge him to see if he could throw a sand bucket from a distance and hit me with it. What a challenge! The sand buckets we played with when I was a boy were made of metal, not plastic like the ones we have today. He accepted my challenge and threw the bucket at me. Have you ever seen a flying sand bucket come at you at a great rate of speed? I jumped one way, but the bucket seemed to curve right at me. I couldn't move quickly enough, and it hit me. Ooh, did it hurt! Then, because he had hit me, and I was hurting and he was not, I went and bit him so that he could hurt also. His mother came out and spanked us both for our part in the conflict. My foolish challenge resulted in painful consequences.

Each of us needs to avoid situations that will get us into trouble, especially when we know better. The choices we make now will have eternal consequences in our lives. Satan wants us to disobey our Father. He doesn't want us to succeed in the eternal plan of happiness. I want each of you to know that Satan is real. In Joseph Smith—History 1:15–16 it reads:

"After I had retired to the place where I had previously designed to go, having looked around me, and finding myself alone, I kneeled down and began to offer up the desires of my heart to God. I had scarcely done so,

when immediately I was seized upon by some power which entirely overcame me, and had such an astonishing influence over me as to bind my
tongue so that I could not speak. Thick darkness gathered around me, and it
seemed to me for a time as if I were doomed to sudden destruction.

"But, exerting all my powers to call upon God to deliver me out of the
power of this enemy which had seized upon me, and at the very moment
when I was ready to sink into despair and abandon myself to destruction—
not to an imaginary ruin, but to the power of some actual being from the
unseen world, who had such marvelous power as I had never before felt in
any being—just at this moment of great alarm, I saw a pillar of light exactly
over my head, above the brightness of the sun, which descended gradually
until it fell upon me."

Satan is real, and he is always trying to stop the work of God. However,
we can take comfort in knowing that "God is faithful, who will not suffer
you to be tempted above that ye are able; but will with the temptation also
make a way to escape, that ye may be able to bear it" (1 Corinthians 10:13).

Just as the Prophet Joseph Smith was almost ready to give up in the
grove, Heavenly Father and his Son, Jesus Christ, appeared to him and
delivered him from temptation. What a blessing it is to know that God is
in control and will help us if we only ask him.

We need to make wise decisions that will not invite the adversary into
our lives. In Moroni 7:16–17 it teaches us how to make good choices:

"For behold, the Spirit of Christ is given to every man, that he may
know good from evil; wherefore, I show unto you the way to judge; for every
thing which *inviteth to do good*, and to *persuade to believe in Christ*, is sent
forth by the power and gift of Christ; *wherefore ye may know with a perfect
knowledge it is of God*.

"But whatsoever thing persuadeth men to do evil, and believe not in
Christ, and deny him, and serve not God, then ye may know with a perfect
knowledge it is of the devil; for after this manner doth the devil work, for
he persuadeth no man to do good, no, not one; neither do his angels; neither
do they who subject themselves unto him" (emphasis added).

Everything that is good is of God; and anything that takes us away from
him or his plan of happiness is of the devil. The foolish decision I made by
challenging my friend to throw the sand bucket at me resulted in pain and
suffering. To avoid becoming miserable in life, we must exercise good judgment and avoid making decisions that will later hit us with much greater

force than a metal sand bucket. In 2 Nephi 2:27, father Lehi teaches us that Satan wants us to be "miserable like unto himself":

"Wherefore, men are free according to the flesh; and all things are given them which are expedient unto man. And they are free to choose liberty and eternal life, through the great Mediator of all men, or to choose captivity and death, according to the captivity and power of the devil; for *he seeketh that all men might be miserable like unto himself*" (emphasis added).

After I had been hit with the sand bucket and was hurting, my next impulse was to pay back my friend by making him hurt too. Misery loves company.

Elder Henry B. Eyring, of the Quorum of the Twelve Apostles, said: "The world will become more wicked. You will need the help of heaven to keep the commandments. You will need it more and more as the days go on. Satan will expand the space that is not safe. He will try every way he can to persuade you that there is no danger in trying to come as close as you can to that dividing line. At the same time, he is trying to persuade people that there really is no line at all. Because he knows that you know it is there, he will say to you, 'Come closer to the line.'

"But you can bring the protective powers of heaven down on you by simply deciding to go toward the Savior, to wait on him. Satan will tell you, as he has done regularly for ages, that you will not be happy in safety, that you must come near his ground to live the happy life. Well, that is a clear choice, too. . . .

"I hope you will remember that when you see some beautifully packaged, cleverly advertised invitation to go into Satan's territory. It will be funny or pleasant or charming or glamorous; but remember, he wants you to be as miserable as he is himself" (*To Draw Closer to God: A Collection of Discourses by Henry B. Eyring* [Salt Lake City: Deseret Book, 1997], 98–99).

A few years ago I was going up a mountain road with my nephews when we came across a bobcat that was caught in a trap. We were approximately fifteen yards away from the bobcat when we stopped to watch the cat for a few moments. I noticed a tremendous fear in his eyes. He would run back and forth as far as the trap and chain would allow, then he would just lie down in a tense position, crouched and waiting, watching and wondering what we were going to do to him. Never before had I seen such fear in a creature's eyes.

It wasn't long after this experience that a young lady expressed her heartache and sorrow to me. She had made some choices that were against the Lord's will. Her boyfriend had said that he loved her and that he thought she was everything to him. She fell for the old line, "If you love me, you will . . ." Now she was expecting a child and did not know what to do. The fear I had seen in the bobcat's eyes was very similar to the fear that I saw in this young lady's eyes. She was miserable, just like Satan wanted her to be. I counseled her to go see her bishop and get started on the steps to repentance so that the Lord's atonement could take effect in her life. She took the advice and is now doing quite well. The fear she once had in her eyes has now been replaced with hope and a renewed desire to do whatever it takes to be forgiven. "Wickedness never was happiness" is wise counsel for us today (Alma 41:10). Doing the Lord's will always brings the peace and joy each of us is striving for.

Korihor's story in the Book of Mormon is a perfect example of Satan's ability to deceive us into following him and then leave us alone and deserted in our sin. After he is brought before the chief judge on charges of being an antichrist, Korihor challenges Alma to prove to him that there is a God by giving him a sign from the heavens:

"I do not deny the existence of a God, but I do not believe that there is a God; and I say also, that ye do not know that there is a God; and except ye show me a sign, I will not believe.

"Now Alma said unto him: This will I give unto thee for a sign, that thou shalt be struck dumb, according to my words; and I say, that in the name of God, ye shall be struck dumb, that ye shall no more have utterance" (Alma 30:48–49).

The next verse fulfills the prophesy: "Now when Alma had said these words, Korihor was struck dumb, that he could not have utterance, according to the words of Alma" (v. 50).

At that point, Korihor admits his wrongdoing and explains that Satan trapped him and misled him:

"And Korihor put forth his hand and wrote, saying: I know that I am dumb, for I cannot speak; and I know that nothing save it were the power of God could bring this upon me; yea, and I always knew that there was a God.

"But behold, the devil hath deceived me; for he appeared unto me in the form of an angel, and said unto me: Go and reclaim this people, for they have all gone astray after an unknown God. And he said unto me: There is no God; yea, and he taught me that which I should say. And I have taught his words; and I taught them because they were pleasing unto the carnal mind; and I taught them, even until I had much success, insomuch that I verily believed that they were true; and for this cause I withstood the truth, even until I have brought this great curse upon me" (vv. 52–53).

After all of this, Korihor is left to suffer the consequences of falling for Satan's trap.

"And it came to pass that as he went forth among the people, yea, among a people who had separated themselves from the Nephites and called themselves Zoramites, being led by a man whose name was Zoram—and as he went forth amongst them, behold, he was run upon and trodden down, even until he was dead.

"And thus we see the end of him who perverteth the ways of the Lord; and thus we see that *the devil will not support his children at the last day, but doth speedily drag them down to hell*" (vv. 59–60; emphasis added).

As you can see, the devil will not support his followers and will speedily drag them down to hell; he wants us to be "miserable like unto himself" because misery loves company.

What a sad ending to a tragic story! It appears that Korihor would have had tremendous potential for good if he had not listened to the deceiving lines of the devil. We need to rely on what we have been taught by our prophets and leaders and follow closely the teachings in the scriptures so we will not be misled.

Satan's traps are very subtle and realistic. Bishop Richard C. Edgley, first counselor in the Presiding Bishopric stated: "There are certain clues to guide us as to what to avoid. . . . You would recognize these clues because they are common and they are familiar—clues such as:

"'Everybody is doing it.'

"'Nobody will know.'

"'It is not really hurting anyone.'

"'It won't hurt just this once.'

"'So what?'

"'You can repent later and still go on a mission and be married in the temple.'

"'Christ atoned for your sins; he will forgive you'" ("Satan's Bag of Snipes," *Ensign*, Nov. 2000, 43).

Elder Neal A. Maxwell also made reference to the same idea when he said: "The perks of discipleship are such that if we see a stretch limousine pulling up, we know it is not calling for us. God's plan is not the plan of pleasure; it is the 'plan of happiness.'

"The tugs and pulls of the world are powerful. Worldly lifestyles are cleverly reinforced by the rationalization, 'Everybody is doing it,' thus fanning or feigning a majority. Products are promoted and attitudes engendered by clever niche marketing" ("The Tugs and Pulls of the World," *Ensign*, Nov. 2000, 35).

Often, worldly enticements can cloud our minds and prevent the spirit of discernment from helping us to make wise choices. Because we are constantly making choices, we are constantly choosing between the things of the world and the things of God. It really is amazing how the things we think are important often turn out to be not so important. Sometimes they actually cause us to be taken in by Satan. President Spencer W. Kimball shared this story to explain how our unwise choices can trap us:

"I am reminded of an article I read some years ago about a group of men who had gone to the jungles to capture monkeys. They tried a number of different things to catch the monkeys, including nets. But finding that the nets could injure such small creatures, they finally came upon an ingenious solution. They built a large number of small boxes, and in the top of each they bored a hole just large enough for a monkey to get his hand into. They then set these boxes out under the trees and in each one they put a nut that the monkeys were particularly fond of.

"When the men left, the monkeys began to come down from the trees and examine the boxes. Finding that there were nuts to be had, they reached into the boxes to get them. But when a monkey would try to withdraw his hand with the nut, he could not get his hand out of the box because his little fist, with the nut inside, was now too large.

"At about this time, the men would come out of the underbrush and converge on the monkeys. And here is the curious thing: When the monkeys saw the men coming, they would shriek and scramble about with the thought of escaping; but as easy as it would have been, they would not let go of the nut so that they could withdraw their hands from the boxes and thus escape. The men captured them easily" ("The False Gods We Worship," *Ensign*, June 1976, 5).

It is simply amazing to me that the monkeys would allow themselves to be captured and never let go of the nut. Do not allow yourself to become trapped by giving in to temptations that the prophet has counseled us to avoid. Don't hold on tight to small things that will compromise your desire to be righteous, to dress modestly, to not date until the age of sixteen, to stay away from R-rated movies, and so on. We continually receive wise counsel from the brethren. We can choose to follow their counsel or hang on to the nut and get captured.

Elder Boyd K. Packer said: "All of the training and activity in the Church has as its central purpose a desire to see you, our young people, free and independent and secure, both spiritually and temporally.

"If you will listen to the counsel of your parents and your teachers and your leaders when you are young, you can learn how to follow the best guide of all—the whisperings of the Holy Spirit" ("Spiritual Crocodiles," *Ensign,* May 1976, 31).

We need to be very careful with our choices. Always remember to put the Lord first, and things will fall into place in your lives according to his will. Choosing godly things will help us in our efforts to avoid the traps that are laid out to catch us.

One trap that almost caught me, and I didn't even recognize it until my bishop approached me, was that of pride. Thinking that I had it all, I almost missed the opportunity to serve a mission. Let me share that experience with you.

I had always planned to go on a mission. As the time approached, I began to feel that my life was going quite well. I became very comfortable. The bank and I owned a nice car; I had unlimited access to my father's green 1952 Chevrolet truck; I was enrolled in college and dating a very nice, good-looking young lady; I had a good-paying job with shifts set up around my schedule; I was still living at home so I didn't have any bills except a car payment and gas money; and I had my sister's horse to ride and take care of. My bishop, who was my next-door neighbor, casually asked me over the fence if I had recently thought much about going on a mission. I hadn't really been seriously thinking about mission preparations because I was only eighteen at the time and was just enjoying life. My bishop asked me to meet with him in his office the following week.

Always make up your mind early to do what the Lord wants you to do. Remember, President Ezra Taft Benson said: "God will have a humble people. Either we can *choose* to be humble or we can be *compelled* to be humble. Alma said, 'Blessed are they who humble themselves without being compelled to be humble.' (Alma 32:16)" ("Beware of Pride," *Ensign,* May 1989, 6; emphasis added).

Wow, what a week was ahead! That week my father asked me to bring back one of his cows from our summer pasture. I took my sister's horse and rode for approximately one hour to get to the two-hundred-acre pasture where our cow usually spent the summer. After another hour of riding, I found the cow. She was very disobedient and did not want to go home. After chasing her on my sister's horse for quite some time, I finally got her headed towards home. At this moment, my horse collapsed and almost rolled over me. Later that afternoon, the horse died. The veterinarian said she had had an infection and the poison had entered her bloodstream just as I was riding her. A small voice inside my heart quietly echoed the bishop's question of a mission.

A few days later, my friend and I decided to go on a double date up the canyon for a picnic. We were traveling up a mountain road, driving my father's green '52 Chevy truck, when the right front wheel hit a badger hole and pulled the truck over to the edge of an embankment. I hit the brakes, and the pedal went clear to the floor. The truck rolled over and landed upside down in a little stream of water. My friend, his date, and my date were all pushing me deeper into the mud because I was on the bottom. I could smell and hear dripping gasoline, and I was getting scared that the truck would blow up, just like the movies. We all climbed out the top window to safety. Even though the truck did not blow up, it was totaled. We walked the long road home, and needless to say, my dad was not well pleased. Now, I had lost a horse and a truck; yet, the Lord was very kind to me to protect me with all that was happening. Once again, the small voice inside me told me how much I needed to go on a mission.

I was really humbled by these experiences and was determined to do whatever the bishop asked. Sunday approached, and the bishop asked me if I would like to serve a mission. I said yes. Then he asked me if I had a girl-friend. He knew I had a girlfriend because he was my next-door neighbor and had seen us together! I said, "Yes, I have a girlfriend." He then asked me to break up with her so that I had no attachments except my family. So with a deep breath, I agreed to break up our relationship. Within one week I had lost my horse, my truck, and my girlfriend. I was beginning to see how close I'd been to falling into Satan's trap. He'd led me to believe I had it all and that I was happy. The blessings I would have lost by not going on a mission would have been eternal.

When I met with the bishop for my mission interview, he gave me a beautiful promise. My parents were nearing retirement age, and I was a little concerned that they might not be here when I got back. He said, "I promise you that if you serve faithfully, your parents will be here when you return."

I told my girlfriend that I wanted to be obedient to the bishop's counsel.

I wanted to avoid any more traps. It was hard on both of us, but by being obedient, we were blessed. When I returned from my mission, my parents were both there but the girl was not. That too was a blessing because I met my wife-to-be a few years later and realized the Lord really knows what is best for each of us.

I testify that if we will rely on the Lord and his great plan of happiness and make choices based on obedience to the guidelines he has set, we will find the joy and peace we are all seeking. May the Lord's choicest blessings be upon you.

Richard Staples was born and raised in Coalville, Utah. He is the youngest of seven children. He served in the Tennessee Nashville Mission. He graduated from Brigham Young University with a bachelor's degree in education and later received a master's degree from Utah State University. He married Melinda Read in the Manti Temple, and they have seven children, four boys and three girls. He taught seminary for thirteen years. Currently, he is a Church Educational System coordinator in Marysville, California, where he directs institute and supervises three stakes of early morning seminary.

7

HANGING AROUND WITH THE BOOK OF MORMON

Brad Wilcox

My lands!" That's what a girl in my touring group said as she boarded the bus. I thought, *My lands? What rest home did you just crawl out of?* I was fresh off my mission and had never heard anyone younger than ninety use that expression. Over the next few days the girl and I happened to spend a lot of time together. She kept saying "My lands!" I kept thinking it was hilarious. Then one day I got on the bus and said, "My lands!" I couldn't believe it! I was actually saying the words I had thought were so funny just a few days before. Right then I realized that the things we hang around with rub off on us.

That's why it is so important to hang around with the things we want to rub off on us—like the Book of Mormon. Can you imagine spending enough time with the book that the people, places, and teachings of those ancient prophets came to life? I remember feeling down and depressed one day. My wife, Debi, asked me what was wrong, and I said, "Alma died."

She said, "You are so weird."

"I know," I responded. But I couldn't help it. I had been reading in the Book of Mormon about that prophet and had come to appreciate him so much that when I read of his death (Mosiah 29:45) thousands of years ago it affected me.

The Prophet Joseph Smith called the Book of Mormon the "keystone of our religion" (*Teachings of the Prophet Joseph Smith*, sel. Joseph Fielding Smith [Salt Lake City: Deseret Book, 1976], 194). President Ezra Taft Benson taught that along with being the keystone of our religion, the Book of Mormon is the keystone of our witness for Christ, our doctrine, and our testimonies (see "The Book of Mormon—Keystone of Our Religion," *Ensign,* Nov. 1986, 5–6). Elder Bruce R. McConkie summed it up when he taught that the teachings of the Church stand or fall with the truth or falsity of the Book of Mormon. He said, "The truth of the message of the restoration is established in and through and by means of the Book of Mormon" (in Conference Report, April 1961, 40).

We all need to hang around more with the Book of Mormon. Moroni tells us how: Read, ponder, and pray (Moroni 10:3–5). Like the legs that support a stool, these three activities provide the foundation for our testimonies of the Book of Mormon. If we read, but fail to ponder and pray, the stool stands on only one leg and is not going to stay up. If we ponder and pray, but refuse to read, our testimonies, like the stool, will be shaky. We need to do all three to stay firm and strong.

READ

When I taught sixth grade, there was a Latter-day Saint boy in my class named Spencer. He was handsome and athletic with lots of friends. Toward the end of the year I called each student to my desk one by one to complete some final evaluations and fill out forms for the upcoming parent-teacher conferences. When Spencer's turn came, I asked, "How many books have you read?"

Spencer thought for a minute and replied, "None."

I said, "You must have misunderstood. I'm not talking about recently. I'm talking about the whole year. How many books have you read?"

Again, he responded, "None."

"You mean to tell me that you have been in sixth grade for one year in *my* class and you haven't read *any* books?" I must have asked the question too forcefully because tough, football-playing Spencer began to puddle up. I felt terrible. It's not cool for a teacher to make his student cry. I apologized, rubbed his head, and pulled him closer to my chair.

Then he said, "Mr. Wilcox, does the Book of Mormon count?"

"Yes. It counts," I responded. "It counts double! Have you been reading in the Book of Mormon?"

He looked at me intently. "I just finished it," he said.

"Spencer, that's difficult reading. For a sixth grader that's a hard book."

He said, "No, Mr. Wilcox. It's the best book I've ever read."

I was tempted to say, "It's the only book you have ever read," but I restrained myself. Here was a sixth grader who had read the entire Book of Mormon cover to cover. I know many young men and women who enter the Missionary Training Center without ever having done that. I know lots of teenagers who skim parts for seminary so they can get their stars on the chart or earn their ice cream sundaes. Still, they have never done what Spencer did. They have never read the whole thing all the way through. They have begun the book so many times they have the first verses memorized. They know all about Laban and the brass plates. They aren't quite as familiar, however, with the characters and stories that come later in the book.

I once taught a group of young men in a priesthood class and said, "Open your scriptures to Third Nephi."

One of the boys said, "Oh, oh, oh, so you're trying to trick us. Third Nephi, huh? *Third* Nephi?"

I felt so sorry for this poor priest who had never gotten beyond Second Nephi. He didn't know there was a third. I didn't have the heart to tell him there's a fourth.

If Spencer can read the Book of Mormon all the way through, so can we. Let's turn off the TV, Nintendo, and computer games a little bit more and turn on to reading the Book of Mormon.

PONDER

Along with reading the words in the Book of Mormon, we must also think about what they mean and how they apply to us in our lives. Some young people have learned the value of discussing scriptures with others. Some enjoy reading commentaries by Latter-day Saint teachers and General Authorities. Others have discovered the effectiveness of keeping a journal close to their scriptures, where they can write about the insights, impressions, and connections they make as they read the Book of Mormon.

Have you ever stopped to think about what it really would have been like to live among the Nephites or how you would have felt to be in Bountiful when Christ came? Have you ever felt lonely, like Moroni did? Have you ever been rejected because of your beliefs and standards? How can we learn to seek companionship and comfort from God as Moroni did? What does king Benjamin's address mean to us? Why were Korihor's teachings so damaging and dangerous? Are there people today who teach similar things?

In addition to pondering questions like those just asked, we must also consider what we actually hold in our hands when we pick up the Book of

Mormon. Carl Sagan's novel, *Contact* (New York: Simon and Schuster, 1985), tells the story of an astronomer who has the opportunity to venture to the center of the universe in a uniquely constructed spacecraft. Her suit is equipped with built-in video cameras that are programmed to record everything she hears and sees during her journey. Amazingly, she ends up meeting God and is sent back to earth with the message that God exists and that we are not alone in the universe. She returns to earth to deliver her message but finds that no one believes her because they claim the spacecraft never worked. According to them, she never left earth, even though she says her travels took her away for approximately eighteen hours. She swears she is telling the truth, but all are incredulous because there is no evidence to substantiate her claims—no evidence except the fact that the video equipment ran for eighteen hours. Nothing she saw or heard actually shows up on the tapes when they are viewed; but it is evident that the cameras *did* run for eighteen hours. People find they can't, therefore, dismiss her story completely because of those eighteen hours of blank videotape that no one can explain away.

The Book of Mormon is similar to those eighteen hours of videotape. It is, in fact, even more compelling because it is not blank. It is full—more than five hundred pages witnessing the fulness of the gospel. It is tangible evidence that we can hold in our hands and read to discover that Joseph was indeed a prophet and that God and Christ direct this church today. The Book of Mormon is proof positive that there is life after death, purpose in our existence, and meaning amid chaos. The Book of Mormon exists. It can be seen, read, studied, analyzed, and scrutinized. And then, after doing so, it can lead us to a witness that cannot be explained away.

The body of scholarly writing and research concerning the Book of Mormon is impressive, and yet many young people are completely unaware of it. In May 1997, Brigham Young University professor Noel B. Reynolds delivered a forum address at the university in which he reported on mounting evidence that the Book of Mormon is truly of ancient origin (see "Shedding New Light on Ancient Origins," *Brigham Young Magazine*, Spring 1998, 37–45). He spoke of studies dealing with demographics, warfare, literary structures, and ancient typologies.

For years many have wondered how the large numbers of people described in the Book of Mormon could have descended from the few original settlers who came across the ocean with Nephi. Yet recent research shows the high numbers reported in the text to be very plausible.

Descriptions of the wars detailed in the Book of Mormon correspond to what scholars are now learning about ancient warfare. Most of the weapons mentioned in the Book of Mormon are similar to ancient Mesoamerican implements of war. Joseph Smith could never have known such things.

Scholars have also shown that the Book of Mormon contains many Hebrew poetic structures called parallelistic patterns. One such complex pattern is called Chiasmus, in which ideas are presented in a certain order and then repeated in reverse order. Check out Alma 36. It focuses on the turning point in Alma's life when he called out for Jesus Christ to forgive him. The first half of the chapter outlines the negative attributes of Alma's experience, while the second half presents the positive opposites (see John W. Welch, "A Masterpiece: Alma 36," in John Sorenson and Melvin Thorne, eds., *Rediscovering the Book of Mormon* [Salt Lake City: Deseret Book and F.A.R.M.S., 1991], 114–31). How could Joseph Smith have known of such ancient forms of writing? Even if he had, how could he have successfully introduced so many beautifully crafted examples throughout the entire book? Similarly, scholars have shown how the typology of the account of the tree of life and other passages in the Book of Mormon show up in many different forms in ancient Egypt within a time frame that could easily connect with Lehi and his family.

Brother Reynolds also spoke to the BYU students about comprehensive word-print studies that have been conducted using the Book of Mormon. Latter-day Saint researchers used computerized text and powerful statistical techniques to establish that the Book of Mormon had multiple authors; that is, the different sections of the Book of Mormon were actually written by different people. They then compared each section to the writings of Joseph Smith, Sidney Rigdon, and Oliver Cowdery and found that none of them could have authored any part of the Book of Mormon. Their nineteenth-century writing styles were too different from the text of the Book of Mormon. Do you realize what that says about every anti-Mormon claim that the book was written by Joseph Smith or any of his contemporaries? Non-LDS scientists using a different and more conservative technique have now replicated this word-print analysis. Interestingly, they have reported the same conclusions.

LDS scholars have identified a site on the southern coastline of Oman that appears to match the Book of Mormon's description of Lehi's camp by the sea. They have even found iron deposits there that would have been available to Nephi so he could make metal tools for the building of a ship.

As we ponder the Book of Mormon, we must consider that none of the original eleven witnesses who were shown the plates from which the Book of Mormon was translated ever altered or denied his testimony. LDS scholars have done extensive historical investigations into the lives of each of the witnesses. Although some had differences with Joseph Smith and even left the Church, they were all true to their witness that the Book of Mormon was of divine origin.

Consider also the fact that all accounts of how Joseph Smith translated the Book of Mormon from the gold plates agree that he never reviewed a page or sentence before continuing. Furthermore, he never used notes, books, or reference materials. The Book of Mormon introduces hundreds of individual characters and place names without any confusion. The book has three independent dating systems that are maintained accurately. Yet Joseph Smith and his scribes completed about seven to nine pages of the translation daily for about sixty-three days. Can you imagine writing such a detailed and complex book in just two months? I have written several books and I couldn't possibly do it. It goes against everything that is known about the composing process authors use.

Even if Joseph Smith had completed his formal education (which he had not), and even if he had acquired access to many books (which he had not), he simply would not have had the background knowledge necessary to create such an intricate piece of work. The Book of Mormon is full of many interesting words and phrases that help to legitimize the Latter-day Saint belief that the book is of ancient origin. In the late 1820s, Joseph Smith could never have known that *Jershon* (the word in Alma 27:22 that designates a place that was given to the people of Anti-Nephi-Lehi as a "land . . . for an inheritance") actually means "a place of inheritance" in Hebrew.

A similar example is the Book of Mormon's use of the word *deseret*. This fascinating word, which has become quite common in modern LDS circles (Deseret Book, *Deseret News,* Deseret Industries), first appears in Ether where we read of the provisions the Jaredites took with them as they prepared to journey to the promised land. Ether 2:3 says, "And they did also carry with them deseret, which, by interpretation, is a honey bee."

Can you imagine Joseph Smith just making up the Book of Mormon as he went along? Can you imagine him saying, "*And they did also carry with them* . . . Wow, I need a word here. I need a really good word. How about—I don't know—let's just say *deseret?*" Can you imagine that? Take it one step further. Imagine Joseph Smith saying, "*Which, by interpretation, is* . . . Gosh, I need a definition. I just made up a cool word. I ought to be able to come up with a nifty definition. Let's just say—for lack of anything better—*a honey bee.*" I simply can't imagine such a thing happening. However, even if it had, how would we explain the fact that many years after Joseph Smith, philosopher-scholar Hugh W. Nibley wrote, "It is a remarkable coincidence that the word *deseret,* or something very close to it, enjoyed a position of ritual prominence among the founders of the classical Egyptian civilization, who associated it very closely with the symbol of the bee?" (*Lehi in the Desert and the World of the Jaredites* [Salt Lake City: Deseret Book, 1988], 189). Brother Nibley's research was done in the twentieth century, making that "remarkable coincidence" something Joseph Smith could never have known during his lifetime.

Daniel C. Peterson wrote an article in the *Ensign* called, "Mounting Evidence for the Book of Mormon" (Jan. 2000, 18–24), in which he pointed out many additional connections between the Book of Mormon and the ancient Near East. For example, the Book of Mormon name *Sariah* has now been found in ancient Jewish documents, and *Nephi* has been shown to be a name that belongs to the same era in which the Book of Mormon Nephi lived. Critics have noted for years that *Alma* is a woman's name and comes from a Latin root. Yet recent documentation has been found to show that *Alma* was used in the ancient Near East as a masculine personal name just as it is used in the Book of Mormon. The systems of exchange, execution, and the oaths of allegiance taken by soldiers in the Book of Mormon all have roots in ancient Israel. As do also the curse of speechlessness placed upon Korihor, king Benjamin's final address to his people, and the allegory of the olive tree.

Such research is powerful and certainly provides readers of the Book of Mormon plenty of reasons to ponder, but it does not replace the need for a spiritual witness of the truthfulness of the Book of Mormon. Research alone does not provide a foundation for our testimonies. Pioneers and other early Church members did not have access to such knowledge and yet their testimonies were strong and enduring. Along with reading and pondering, we must also pray.

PRAY

Many feel the Spirit bear witness to the "truth of all things" (Moroni 10:5) long before they verbalize a prayer. They feel the power of the Holy

Ghost as they read and ponder the Book of Mormon. Still, we are instructed to "ask God, the Eternal Father, in the name of Christ, if these things are not true" (Moroni 10:4). The answer we receive may simply be a quiet assurance that what we have felt as we have read and studied has indeed been of God—that we have known the truth all along. Nevertheless, we still need to pray "with a sincere heart, with real intent" (Moroni 10:4).

One young future missionary was very discouraged when he shared a copy of the Book of Mormon with a religious friend who promised she would read, ponder, and pray about the book. Later when they met, the friend claimed she had read and pondered and found parts of the book to be very interesting. Still, when she prayed, God told her the book was of the devil. The young man didn't know how to respond. That was not what he expected.

Elder Dallin H. Oaks has said, "Moroni did not promise a manifestation of the Holy Ghost to those who seek to know the truth of the Book of Mormon for hypothetical or academic reasons, even if they 'ask with a sincere heart.' The promise of Moroni is for those who are *committed in their hearts* to act upon the manifestation if it is received. Prayers based on any other reason have no promise because they are not made 'with real intent'" (*Pure in Heart* [Salt Lake City: Bookcraft, 1988], 20; emphasis added).

When I was on my mission in Chile, my companion and I met an outstanding and well-educated young man whom I will call José. He came from a wealthy family and had a good job. As we taught him about the Church, we encouraged him to read and ponder the Book of Mormon, which he did eagerly. However, he refused to pray about the book. He said, "Truth is truth and it should just be obvious. The sky is blue. That's obvious. I shouldn't have to kneel down and pray to find out if the sky is blue."

His reasoning baffled us, but we continued to teach him. It was actually quite challenging to keep ahead of him. He read the book, used the cross references with the Bible, and came to each discussion with long lists of observations and questions he was excited to talk over with us. Still, despite his enthusiasm, he refused to pray and finally quit progressing toward baptism. We had to stop teaching him.

Occasionally, we would see José on the street downtown or in a store. He would greet us warmly and assure us that he was still reading and studying.

"Have you prayed?" we would ask.

"No," he would answer. "Because truth is truth and it should just be obvious." It was always the same response.

Finally one day when we were waiting for a bus, we happened to run into José again. We exchanged greetings and I cut straight to the question that I knew we would end with sooner or later. "So, have you prayed yet?"

"No. Because truth is truth and . . ."

"José," I said, "Don't give me that. Just pray. It's not that hard. What's the big deal?"

He suddenly became very serious and said, "I'll tell you what the big deal is. If that book is true, I will have to change my whole life. I will lose my job. I will lose my family. I'll lose everything."

"But think of what you'll gain, José," I smiled at him. "Think of what you'll gain." Our bus arrived and we said quick good-byes.

A few days later, my companion and I were surprised to hear a knock at our door late at night. When I opened the door, it was José. He had tears in his eyes. I said, "You finally prayed about the book, didn't you?" All he could do was nod. He had asked God if it was true—not for hypothetical or academic reasons. José was finally committed in his heart to act on the manifestation if it was truly received, and it was indeed received. As he prepared for his baptism over the next few weeks, he lost his job and his family kicked him out, just as they told him they would. But think of all he eventually gained.

President Ezra Taft Benson spoke often of flooding the earth with copies of the Book of Mormon (see *Ensign*, Nov. 1988, 4–6), but perhaps he was also referring to a different kind of flood—the flood of life-changing tears I saw on José's cheeks once he prayed and received his answer. Of course we want the Book of Mormon in everyone's hands, but even more we want the Book of Mormon in everyone's hearts.

Reading, pondering, and praying—that's how our testimonies will gain a firm foundation. That's how we can hang around with the Book of Mormon and let it rub off on us. That's when the Book of Mormon can affect us and make a difference in our lives. I have felt the power of that book. I know it was written for our day and is truly another testament of Jesus Christ.

Brad Wilcox served his mission in Chile and is now married with four children. He is an associate professor in the Department of Teacher Education at Brigham Young University, where he helps future educators prepare to teach reading and writing. He also supervises the BYU students who go to Mexico to complete their student teaching and will soon be moving to New Zealand to direct a BYU semester abroad program. He has served as the bishop of a BYU student ward and loves speaking and writing to the youth.

8

LOST AND FOUND

Kim M. Peterson

You probably have a long list of things you've lost. Maybe you have a comparable list of things you've found. Which list represents things of a greater value? Have you lost or found more?

A few years ago, I bought a new briefcase. Excitedly, I emptied the contents of my old worn case into the new one. I placed my folders, books, and laptop in the new bag just to see if they'd fit. By coincidence (so I thought) I lost my checkbook about the same time. The first place I looked was in the new case . . . no luck. The second place I looked was in the old case . . . also no luck. I went to the store where I bought the bag . . . no luck. By the fourth day, I had frantically torn apart my truck, my desk, and my closet. I was quite convinced that someone was spending my money; I even blamed the store where I had purchased the bag. Two weeks later I was looking through my new bag and happened to open a pocket that I hadn't previously noticed. There was the checkbook. Not only was it in the last place I looked, it was also in the first!

I've met young people who have lost significant spiritual things. Some claim they've lost interest in the scriptures. Others have lost the desire to attend seminary. A few even claim they've lost their testimonies. What horrible things to lose! If you've felt like you've lost your testimony (or that your testimony has lost strength), why not look in the last place first?

THE OLD TESTAMENT

What could you possibly find in the Old Testament . . . after all, it's old? The Old Testament tells the story of the first testament, or covenant, that God made with man. It is filled with wonderful hints about how to gain and strengthen a testimony. In the story of the Creation (Genesis 1–3), for example, you can find many things to strengthen your testimony and many things of which to testify. You could gain a testimony that God created the heaven and the earth (Genesis 1:1), that you were created in the image of God (Genesis 1:26–27), and that the Sabbath is a special day (Genesis 2:2).

The story of the Creation can even teach you about being lost. After God created Adam and Eve, he commanded them not to eat of the tree of knowledge of good and evil (Genesis 2:17). You probably know that Adam and Eve did eat of the fruit. What happened next? They discovered that they were naked and they hid because of their nakedness. From whom did they hide? Can I suggest that it would probably have been a pretty short game of hide-and-seek? God knew where they were, but he allowed Adam to reveal his hiding place. Similarly, when you sin, you may wish that you could hide or at least not tell anyone what you have done. In reality, you would be attempting to hide from God. If you are lost, God will find you.

THE NEW TESTAMENT

What exactly is new about the New Testament? It witnesses of the same God that created the world (John 1:1–3), it speaks about the promises made to Abraham (Luke 1:72; Galatians 3:17), and it testifies of the law given to Moses (Matthew 5:18). This "new" testament is new because its teachings embody those of the Old Testament and add upon them. Christ testified that he had come not to destroy those things that had been prophesied and taught in the Old Testament but to fulfill them (Matthew 5:17). Christ used an old testament, or covenant, to lay an important foundation for a new one. In his teachings, Christ frequently quoted from the Old Testament (see Bible Dictionary, sv. "quotations," 756–59).

Let me tell a story to help illustrate. When I was about eight years old, my father entrusted me with an old baseball mitt. He wrote my name and phone number on it and instructed me to make sure I didn't leave it in the rain or out where someone could steal it. I was so excited to be able to play baseball during lunch recess. But soon, to my horror, I lost my mitt. Like Adam and Eve, I tried to hide the truth from my father. But eventually he found out. I knew I was in trouble. Later, a man called to say that he had found my mitt. My dad made me talk to him on the phone and then in person. I was grateful for the mitt despite my embarrassment.

Isn't it interesting that my father gave me instructions to take care of my mitt and not misplace it, but still wrote my name and number on it anyway? Your Heavenly Father has also given you instructions. Just in case you get lost, he has provided a way to return. While I had that mitt, I learned to keep my eye on the ball, to catch with two hands, and to stay in front of grounders. Eventually, the mitt was too small for my growing hands. I think I passed it on to my brother. I worked and saved to buy a new one. Even though I replaced my old mitt, I still remembered the things I had learned while playing with it. I'm glad I didn't have to start from scratch just because I got a new glove.

In a somewhat similar manner, God's testaments didn't start over with the New Testament; they built on the Old Testament. Consider the Sermon on the Mount. In Matthew chapter 5, the Savior says five different times, "ye have heard that it was said by them of old time" (vv. 21, 27, 33, 38, 43). He then recounts one of the laws or commandments given in the Old Testament. Subsequently, he says another five times, "but I say unto you" and adds new provisions to old commandments (vv. 22, 28, 34, 39, 44). These additional teachings prove that the Lord's people had fulfilled, or completed, the old law and were ready for a greater law.

Your testimony operates in the same way. When you gain new realizations and practice new applications of things you've known to be true, your testimony will only be strengthened. Your new realizations, however, don't eliminate old ones. I didn't have to start over when I got a new mitt. Similarly, your first testimony is still true.

ANOTHER TESTAMENT

If we have an old and a new testament of the Savior and his gospel, why do we need another testament? Remember that the word *testament* means covenant. You probably already know that a covenant is a promise. And you probably recognize that the Book of Mormon is subtitled *Another Testament of Jesus Christ*. This additional testament witnesses to the truthfulness of both the Old and the New Testaments.

Let's suppose you had an expensive car and a good friend. If your friend asked to borrow your car, wouldn't you make them promise you a few things before you handed over the keys? Maybe you'd have them promise to park it in a garage, drive slowly, fill it with gas, and lock the doors. You might even make them promise to replace it if it were stolen or damaged. Each of the promises you receive from your friend would be a sort of insurance that your car would be safe and you wouldn't lose it.

Heavenly Father doesn't want to lose you! For that reason, he has made multiple promises with you. The Book of Mormon reviews and strengthens the promises made in both the Old and the New Testament. Nephi spoke of Christ, wrote of Christ, prophesied of Christ, and taught of Christ. He also kept the law that was taught in the Old Testament (2 Nephi 25:24–27). Abinadi taught that the law in the Old Testament was to help the people remember God (Mosiah 13:30). Jesus Christ quoted an Old Testament prophet (Malachi) to demonstrate that all of us should keep the law found in the Old Testament (3 Nephi 25).

Moroni kept us from being lost by guarding the plates and finishing that record. With his family and friends all gone, his only motivation for sacrificing so much was that you and I would benefit from his efforts. Consider the following passage in Moroni 1:3: "And I, Moroni, will not deny the Christ; wherefore, I wander whithersoever I can for the safety of mine own life." If you look at the bottom of each page throughout the book of Moroni, you will notice that the text on those pages encompasses twenty years. Moroni likely carried eighty pounds of scriptures for more than twenty years! I will never complain again that my scriptures are too heavy to take to seminary or church. You also know that Moroni buried the plates and trusted that God would take care of them.

FINDING WHAT WAS LOST

Like my mitt, a lost testimony can be embarrassing, awkward, or even troubling. Finding that testimony, rejuvenating the desire to be active, and discovering the joys of having the Spirit may take a miracle. The coming forth of the Book of Mormon contains marvelous miracles that testify of its own truthfulness and the truthfulness of the Old and New Testaments. These miracles teach us that we can find and keep our testimonies.

After the First Vision, Joseph struggled with temptations and weakness (JS—H 1:28). Do you recognize the significance of this problem? He had seen God, and still struggled to do what is right. Maybe your testimony was once stronger than it is right now, or maybe you used to avoid the temptations that currently cause you grief. Joseph Smith also struggled. In fact, he even felt weak (JS—H 1:29). Joseph did not quit, become depressed, or give in to temptations. Joseph prayed! "After I had retired to my bed for the night, I betook myself to prayer and supplication to Almighty God for forgiveness of all my sins and follies, and also for a manifestation to me, that I might know of my state and standing before him; for I had full confidence in obtaining a divine manifestation, as I previously had one" (JS—H 1:29).

Joseph Smith, a seventeen-year-old, believed he could have another tes-timony (manifestation). If you have ever felt the confirmation that Heavenly Father loves you, you can feel it again! Even if you've lost the feel-ing, you haven't lost the opportunity to feel again.

Moroni visited Joseph as an answer to his prayer. Moroni's message con-tained wonderful references to both the Old and New Testaments. He quoted Malachi: "But who may abide the day of his coming? and who shall stand when he appeareth? for he is like a refiner's fire, and like fullers' soap" (Malachi 3:2). Fire and soap both purify. Joseph prayed for forgiveness and discovered that God would cleanse the earth. Moroni subsequently quoted from Joel chapter two and Isaiah chapter eleven. Both of these chapters talk about what will happen to those who are not clean when Christ returns. In answer to Joseph's prayer to repent, God helped him see how important it was to be clean.

Moroni also quoted from the New Testament: "For Moses truly said unto the fathers, A prophet shall the Lord your God raise up unto you of your brethren, like unto me; him shall ye hear in all things whatsoever he shall say unto you. And it shall come to pass, that every soul, which will not hear that prophet, shall be destroyed from among the people" (Acts 3:22–23).

Joseph may not have realized this scripture was referring to him! Moroni (a prophet from the other testament) quoted Malachi (a prophet from the Old Testament) and Peter (an apostle from the New Testament), bringing together in Joseph's tiny bedroom three witnesses of the Savior, Jesus Christ. If Joseph felt lost prior to this vision, he certainly couldn't now.

At length, Joseph met Moroni at the Hill Cumorah. Joseph received instruction for the next four years. When he was twenty-two, he received the plates. During those four years, Joseph worked, he moved, and he mar-ried. On 22 September 1827, Joseph borrowed a wagon, drove the three miles to the Hill Cumorah, and left his wife, Emma, in the wagon while he met with Moroni. Moroni warned Joseph Smith to protect the plates. In the coming days, Joseph discovered why Moroni's warning was so important. He wrote: "I soon found out the reason why I had received such strict charges to keep them safe, and why it was that the messenger had said that when I had done what was required at my hand, he would call for them. For no sooner was it known that I had them, than the most strenuous exertions were used to get them from me. Every stratagem that could be invented was resorted to for that purpose" (JS—H 1:60).

Finding and keeping these lost records wasn't easy. Joseph was attacked by his neighbors, ambushed by treasure hunters, and threatened by mobs (see *Church History in the Fulness of Times*, 2d ed. [Salt Lake City: The Church of Jesus Christ of Latter-day Saints, 2000], 45). Through all of it, he was protected. Your precious testimony must also be preserved and protected. But it may not be easy.

Once the record was found, it needed to be preserved. Joseph guarded it with the utmost care. Frequently he was warned to move the plates just prior to people discovering them. In addition to protection, God provided a way for the record to be translated. Martin Harris worked with Joseph from December 1827 to June 1828. After six months, they had completed 116 pages (the book of Lehi). Perhaps you know the story. Martin begged Joseph to let him take the manuscript and, at length, Joseph agreed. Through disobedience, Martin Harris lost the translated pages. When Joseph discovered that the manuscript was lost, he exclaimed, "All is lost! all is lost! What shall I do? I have sinned—it is I who tempted the wrath of God. I should have been satisfied with the first answer which I received from the Lord" (in Lucy Mack Smith, *History of Joseph Smith by His Mother* [Salt Lake City: Bookcraft, 1958], 128). Joseph learned an important lesson: to be satisfied with God's first answer. Subsequently, he lost the plates and the ability to translate. Joseph had the First Vision, the visit by Moroni, four years of instruction, and still had to learn how not to lose the things God had given him.

Many of us have received testimonies from God. At first it is thrilling to know there is a God, that he answers prayers, and that the Church is true. Then, like the wanderers in Lehi's dream, we can become restless and dissatisfied with our knowledge. Maybe we even become "ashamed" or fall away (1 Nephi 8:28) because of the cares of the world. During this challenging time in the Prophet's life, he received this counsel from the Lord: "Remember, remember that it is not the work of God that is frustrated, but the work of men; . . . you should not have feared man more than God. Although men set at naught the counsels of God, and despise his words— Yet you should have been faithful; and he would have extended his arm and supported you" (D&C 3:3, 7–8).

Even if you stop believing, God is still there. Even if you doubt that he exists, God is still there. Even if you don't want to obey, God is still there. Just like Joseph, when we are lost, God will find us and bring us back.

I felt bad when I lost my mitt. I was distressed when I lost my checkbook. Can you imagine how you'd feel if you lost the book of Lehi? Joseph repented and the plates were returned to him in the fall of 1828. In the spring of 1829, Oliver Cowdery miraculously met the Prophet and became his scribe. Oliver described his experience with these words: "These were days never to be forgotten—to sit under the sound of a voice dictated by the inspiration of heaven, awakened the utmost gratitude of this bosom! Day after day I continued, uninterrupted, to write from his mouth, as he translated with the Urim and Thummim" (JS—H, n., 58).

Oliver Cowdery had a front row seat to the first verbal reading of the Book of Mormon in at least fourteen hundred years! He was one of the first to hear the record that had been lost to the world.

Joseph began translating from the book of Mosiah through to the end of the Book of Mormon before he finished the translation of First Nephi. God knew, twenty-four hundred years before it happened, that 116 pages would be lost. Nephi made the plates and recorded not only the words of his father, but also his own summary of the words of his father. Near the end of their experience translating the Book of Mormon, Joseph and Oliver would have encountered Nephi's testimony that the Lord had commanded him to make this additional record for "a wise purpose in him, which purpose I know not" (1 Nephi 9:5). Imagine how humbling it would be to realize that Lehi taught, Nephi recorded, Mormon abridged, and Moroni protected a duplicate record of Lehi's teachings, all in the foreknowledge that 116 pages would be lost.

Your Heavenly Father also knows that you might wander and get lost. He has prepared for you to be found. Once I was on a hunting trip with a close friend. We walked into the middle of a beautiful valley. After sitting and talking for about an hour, we got up to return to our camp. Surprisingly, my friend began to walk in the opposite direction. He was convinced he was going back to camp. If he had continued on that course he would have become hopelessly lost. Even after talking to him and laughing at him, he didn't believe the camp was where it was. I literally had to bid him farewell and begin walking the opposite direction before he would agree to follow me. I think he followed initially because he thought he was going to take care of me. Maybe he just wanted to be there when I finally figured out he was right. In the end, he was extremely grateful that I knew where the camp was.

FOUND FOREVER

Even if you are spiritually lost, your Heavenly Father knows where you are. You can't hide from him (remember Adam and Eve)! Just like Heavenly Father knew that 116 pages would be lost, he has prepared a way for you to stay close to him. Covenants will allow you to be "found" at the right hand of God (Mosiah 5:8–9). During the translation of the Book of Mormon, Joseph and Oliver discovered that baptism was essential to be saved. Maybe they were translating 3 Nephi 11:33–34, where the Lord teaches that only those who are baptized will be saved. Surely, this would have troubled Joseph and Oliver since they were not baptized. Accordingly, they went into the woods to pray. John the Baptist appeared to them and ordained them to the Aaronic Priesthood. The authority that had been lost for centuries had been restored, and Joseph and Oliver were baptized! Within weeks Peter, James, and John visited them and restored the Melchizedek Priesthood. By April 1830, the Church was organized, and God's children could once again be baptized through proper authority, receive the Holy Ghost, and partake of the sacrament.

The Book of Mormon was the catalyst to the restoration of important ordinances. Today, the Book of Mormon can be a catalyst for your testimony of these same ordinances. If you have been baptized, you would still benefit from Alma's teachings to the people near the Waters of Mormon. He asked if they were willing to mourn with those that mourn, comfort those who need comfort, and to stand as witnesses (Mosiah 18:9). Nephi, too, taught the importance of these ordinances: "Wherefore, my beloved brethren, I know that if ye shall follow the Son, with full purpose of heart, acting no hypocrisy and no deception before God, but with real intent, repenting of your sins, witnessing unto the Father that ye are willing to take upon you the name of Christ, by baptism . . . then shall ye receive the Holy Ghost" (2 Nephi 31:13).

These doctrines are not lost! The Book of Mormon can help you never to be lost. It is another witness of Jesus Christ. Why not let it help you look in the last place first—and find the desire, the strength, and the knowledge that will help you follow the Son with full purpose of heart?

Kim Peterson has taught at Especially for Youth sessions for the past eighteen years. He loves his wife, Terri, and his children Bryn and Sarai. Together, they ski, snowboard, backpack, and read the Book of Mormon. Brother Peterson is currently the director of the Boulder Institute of Religion in Colorado.

9

ALWAYS

Lisa Heckmann Olsen

Years ago I stood in front of a wiggly group of Primary children. They were not paying attention to my carefully planned and rehearsed sharing time lesson, and so I asked the children to try something new with me. I turned to a large picture of Christ and asked them to think about Jesus for one minute. As I followed the second hand on my watch, the room went silent. Heads, one by one, were quietly bowed. The Spirit filled our little Primary room. It had actually changed their behavior. I quietly asked the children to share a story they had remembered as they were thinking about Jesus. One child mentioned that he knew he was loved because "Jesus loves the children." Another child said that Jesus died on the cross for her. As their teacher, I was grateful that these children knew Christ and could feel his Spirit. It was an unforgettable teaching moment, like that described in Doctrine and Covenants 50:22. "Wherefore, he that preacheth and he that receiveth, understand one another, and both are edified and rejoice together."

I explained to the children that our experience was over and it was time to go to class. I thanked them for being so reverent. A four-year-old Sunbeam, clearly frustrated, raised her hand and asked, "Sister Olsen, is it okay if I think about Jesus all of the time?" Her concern was sincere. I assured her that always thinking of Jesus would be *his* greatest wish. I will never forget the lesson she brought to my remembrance: to think about Jesus all of the time.

The Book of Mormon prophet Alma always remembered Christ. Do you recall Alma's dramatic and powerful first appearance in the Book of Mormon? He was one of the priests in wicked king Noah's court. He had been present on several occasions in which the prophet Abinadi had called the king and his people to repentance. Alma had caught a spark of the gospel light that Abinadi was working so hard to ignite. When king Noah condemned Abinadi to death by fire, Alma pleaded for Abinadi's life. He knew in his heart that the testimony Abinadi bore was true. "But the king was more wroth, and caused that Alma should be cast out from among them, and sent his servants after him that they might slay him" (Mosiah 17:3). The king's command, however, backfired, and Alma fled from amongst the servants.

"Now, there was in Mormon a fountain of pure water, and Alma resorted thither, there being near the water a thicket of small trees, where he did hide himself in the daytime from the searches of the king" (Mosiah 18:5). The word spread among the believers in the land that Alma was teaching and baptizing. In a powerful passage of scripture, Alma invited the believers to be baptized: "Behold, here are the waters of Mormon (for thus were they called) and now, as ye are desirous to come into the fold of God, and to be called his people, and are willing to bear one another's burdens, that they may be light; Yea, and are willing to mourn with those that mourn; yea, and comfort those that stand in need of comfort, and to stand as witnesses of God at all times and in all things, and in all places that ye may be in, even until death, that ye may be redeemed of God, and be numbered with those of the first resurrection; that ye may have eternal life" (Mosiah 18:8–9).

To stand as a witness of God is evidence that we always remember Christ.

AT ALL TIMES

My maiden name will always be Heckmann. Like Nephi, I was "born of goodly parents" (1 Nephi 1:1), who had equally wonderful parents, my grandparents. I loved visiting Grandpa Heckmann's fruit farm in Providence, Utah. I vividly remember passing out ice cream to the fruit pickers, helping my grandpa weigh cherries, hanging upside down on the swing set, exploring the run-down chicken coop, making bread with my grandma, sleeping in the sunken-in "yellow bed," and many other choice memories. My grandpa was a hard worker, one who watched Lawrence Welk while eating a TV dinner, who loved cookies and ice cream, and who lovingly cared for my grandmother during her illness. My favorite store in Providence was Tires, a small family-owned grocery store. Once I was short a little change to buy a treat. The clerk simply asked, "Are you Will Heckmann's grandchild?" "Yes," was my proud response. "Go ahead and take the treat, Will is good for the rest!" The best gift that my grandpa ever gave me was his name. It is a name associated with honor, respect, and dignity. I am proud to be a Heckmann.

When I married, I added a new name: Olsen. I have come to love all the Olsens. I now represent this family and have the power to cause this honorable name to be respected or disrespected.

At baptism, we received the name of Christ, which is as important, if not more so, than our surnames. Read the following verses of scripture that focus on the name of Christ:

> "That they are willing to take upon them the name of thy Son" (D&C 20:77).

> "That ye are willing to take upon you the name of Christ, by baptism— yea, by following your Lord and your Savior down into the water" (2 Nephi 31:13).

> "Yea, blessed is this people who are willing to bear my name; for in my name shall they be called; and they are mine" (Mosiah 26:18).

> "Have they not read the scriptures, which say ye must take upon you the name of Christ, which is my name? For by this name shall ye be called at the last day" (3 Nephi 27:5).

Taking upon us the name of Christ is an act of association with honor, respect, dignity, and truth. We covenant to honor his name always. We never get a break or have time off. It is a twenty-four-hour-a-day covenant.

Picture this. You are traveling on a long, deserted stretch of highway. In the distance you observe a car speeding recklessly. The car crosses the median. Suddenly the car jerks in the opposite direction. The driver has attempted to correct his mistake, but as a result of the impulsive action, the car rolls and comes to a screeching halt. As you pass the scene, it is obvious that the driver is injured. Did I mention that you are a doctor with a cell phone? What do you do? It seems absurd that you would continue to drive, pretending the accident didn't happen. Just because you are not at the hospital or the office in your doctor's uniform with your official badge pinned on does not change the fact that you have lifesaving knowledge. You would stop to offer help until the ambulance arrives.

We don't have to be at church, or at Young Men or Young Women activities, or seminary, or wearing a missionary badge to be a witness. Our actions should always reflect the name of Christ. When the resurrected Savior visited the Nephites he commanded them to "let your light so shine before this people, that they may see your good works and glorify your Father who is in heaven" (3 Nephi 12:16).

IN ALL THINGS

In 1990 the First Presidency issued a pamphlet to the youth of the Church. *For the Strength of Youth* warns, "You are at a critical time in your lives. This is a time for you not only to live righteously but also to set an example for your peers" (Salt Lake City: The Church of Jesus Christ of Latter-day Saints, 1990, 3). At this "critical time," it is important that, like Alma, you live righteously and stand as a witness in "all things." *For the Strength of Youth* asks you to consider the ways in which you can stand as a witness in your dating, dress and appearance, friendshipping, honesty, language, media choices, mental and physical health, music and dancing, sexual purity, and Sunday behavior. All youth will face these issues at some point in their growing-up years. Likewise, there will be a great need for spiritual help and repentance. The First Presidency knows this, and uses the pamphlet to help you understand that. They conclude the pamphlet by discussing worthiness and service. I invite you to carefully and prayerfully review *For the Strength of Youth*. You will never outgrow its guidelines and standards. They will teach you how to stand up!

I have a favorite former student who had the courage to stand up in a public situation. She sat at a table with her friends, three girls and two boys. As they worked on an art project, the conversation turned to recently viewed movies. They began to talk about a movie with "incredible computer graphics." They were impressed with the morphing and realistic interpretation of obvious fantasy. The movie was rated R. She sat quietly for a while until one of the boys asked, "Did you like the movie?" She looked him squarely in the eye and said confidently, "I didn't see the movie." (The Spirit brings confidence—what a great feeling! You have the Spirit when you're choosing the right!)

"WHAT?" was the shocked response "EVERYONE has seen (name of the movie)!"

The boy was baffled and totally unprepared for her next unsolicited statement: "I have never seen a rated-R movie!"

The entire group almost fell out of their chairs. "NEVER?" they asked unbelieving.

"Never," she returned.

One girl hollered across the classroom, "She has never seen a rated-R movie!"

The girl sat with a smile on her face, not embarrassed in the least. Other doubting students swarmed to the table to continue the interrogation. She patiently answered their questions. The conversation turned positive as students one by one expressed regret for the movies they had seen. Many committed to follow her example.

Standing as a witness in all things does not always have to happen in public. It can happen in other, more subtle ways. I have a nephew, Alma, who just turned one. In his baby blessing, his father, Jim, pronounced that Alma would be a "friend to the friendless." This little boy already has a smile that could melt any heart. It is easy to see that this is one of his gifts. He will be able to reach out to others. Isn't that exactly what Christ did? He was always a friend to the friendless.

I believe that every teenager at one time or another has felt as if they have no friends and that no one cares. It may be our witness of Christ's love that helps others change this feeling of insecurity. The way we treat others can have a powerful or devastating effect.

I've learned a lot from my art students. Camille (name changed) had an impact on a socially struggling student, Mac (name changed). It was obvious that Mac was different from the other students. His clothes were unkempt, his hair was a mess, and he had odd mannerisms. As a teacher I struggled when Mac would make comments out loud that had nothing to do with the subject at hand. It was an obvious cry for attention and help. He struggled just to have conversations with others. He sat at the back of the classroom, alone. However, Mac was a talented artist, a gift passed down from his mother. One day he approached me at the same time as Camille. Camille was beautiful and also kind. Both wanted feedback on their printmaking project. Mac was first, and I had no suggestions for improvement—his print was beautiful. Apparently Camille felt the same way. She reached for Mac's hand and said, "Mac, your print is beautiful! It's the best one in the class!" He couldn't even look her in the face. Instead he just melted. It didn't end with that compliment. She yelled across the room to a friend, "Come and see Mac's print—it's awesome!" From the moment of her speaking up, Mac was established as the best artist in the class. Mac slowly integrated himself back into the classroom, and Camille continued to be friendly and compliment him. She made the difference.

IN ALL PLACES

A few years ago our little family had a stopover in Mesquite, Nevada. We stayed in a family hotel but went to eat at an "all you can eat" breakfast buffet. Getting to the buffet was complicated and involved navigating through endless concourses of slot machines. Cole, who was then three, sensed something different. We proceeded to the buffet and loaded our plates with our favorite high-calorie, high-fat breakfast foods. Cole's plate was filled with pancakes and "chicken" (bacon). I assumed that he would quickly dig in. He didn't. His little spirit was upset and agitated. As we started to eat, Cole stood up in his seat and sang, "Follow the prophet, follow the prophet, follow the prophet; don't go astray!" (*Children's Songbook*, 110). It was difficult to make him stop singing. I was embarrassed and proud at the same time. Embarrassed because he was singing loudly and causing a scene, but proud because he had to let everyone know what he felt. I wondered if anyone understood what he sang and if it actually made someone think.

The scriptures are filled with examples of witnesses in all places. Some witnessed in their home (Nephi), some with friends (Alma the Younger), and others at the end of their lives (Mormon). In some places they feared for their own lives. Abinadi was such a prophet. Abinadi testified of Christ and exposed many of the people's iniquities. They were not happy with him. "Now it came to pass that when Abinadi had spoken these words unto them they were wroth with him, and sought to take away his life; but the Lord delivered him out of their hands." Then king Noah heard of Abinadi and said, "I command you to bring Abinadi hither, that I may slay him, for he has said these things that he might stir up my people to anger one with another, and to raise contentions among my people; therefore I will slay him" (Mosiah 11:26, 28).

King Noah was angry, not only because Abinadi exposed his sins, but because he also prophesied his death. Abinadi spent time among the people in disguise for two years. He continued to teach and to prophesy. The people were angered and took him forcefully to the king. He was sent to prison until the priests could gather for a council. Once convened, "they began to question him, that they might cross him, that thereby they might have wherewith to accuse him; but he answered them boldly, and withstood all their questions, yea, to their astonishment; for he did withstand them in all their questions, and did confound them in all their words" (Mosiah 12:19). The king commanded his priests to take Abinadi away because "he is mad" (Mosiah 13:1). However, they were unable to put their hands on him because of divine intervention.

Abinadi's final message included the Ten Commandments and a powerful testimony of the Savior. Once again Noah commanded the priests to take Abinadi away and put him to death. But his testimony was so powerful that it affected Alma. Alma pleaded for Abinadi's life. Even so, Abinadi suffered death by fire. In the face of death, he stood as a witness to the end. Do you ever wonder if Abinadi felt like a successful missionary? I wonder if he was discouraged because the priests and the king didn't listen. But one did. That one soul became a prophet.

It is unlikely we will ever face a situation like Abinadi's. But we might someday find ourselves in an unusual place with an opportunity to testify of the Savior.

In 1989 my parents had an amazing adventure. My father had been invited to communist Russia to perform some scientific research. They stayed in the country for six months, living like ordinary Russian citizens. They had no special privileges. When they were briefed on the trip, they were advised never to proselyte. However, if someone approached them and asked about their beliefs, they were told they could speak freely, but only as long as they were asked questions. In accordance with the law, they took with them one Russian Book of Mormon, just in case someone asked.

Everything about my parents—their dress, their actions, their speech—had to reflect the gospel of Jesus Christ. They carried with them the hope that someone would ask them about their beliefs. While in Moscow, a young scientist quizzed my parents. He wanted to know about their religion. They testified of Christ and his gospel here on earth. Then they presented to him their one Russian Book of Mormon. He took the book and held it to his chest. He had never owned scriptures before. With tears, he thanked them for the gift. He opened the book, read a passage, and said, "Such a beautiful book, such perfect Russian." He repeated over and over, "Such a beautiful book." He complimented my parents, who were not the first Americans he knew. "You are different. You have a peculiar energy about you." To their surprise, he pulled out a key and opened a locked desk drawer. He carefully placed the Book of Mormon inside. Their gift was precious. He then surprised them with the old Russian bow of deep respect; he stood up, raised his hand, bent halfway over, and swept the ground with his right hand. They were astonished.

Alma is specific about the gift we receive when we stand as a witness of God. It is the most valuable gift we could possibly receive here on earth, the Spirit of God. "Serve him and keep his commandments, that he may pour out his Spirit more abundantly upon you" (Mosiah 18:10). Each week, when we renew our baptismal covenants through the sacrament, we receive the same promise that Alma spoke of at the Waters of Mormon. We witness unto God that we "are willing to take upon [us] the name of thy Son, and always remember him and keep his commandments which he has given [us]; that [we] may always have his Spirit to be with [us]. Amen" (D&C 20:77). It is a perfect cycle—when we stand as a witness of Christ we are blessed with his Spirit. Then, in turn, his Spirit will give us courage, strength, and inspiration to become a more perfect witness.

May you remember the promise that you made at baptism: a covenant to stand as a witness of God "at all times in all things, and in all places." Each week while taking the sacrament, I hope that you will be filled with hope, courage, and renewed strength to continue the good work. Always take hope in the words of our prophet, President Gordon B. Hinckley, who loves you: "I believe we have the finest generation of young people that this Church has ever known. They are better educated; they are better motivated; they know the scriptures; they live the Word of Wisdom; they pay their tithing; they pray. They try to do the right thing. They are bright and able, clean and fresh, attractive and smart. These are very substantial in number. More of them go on missions than ever before. More of them marry in the temple. They know what the gospel is about, and they are trying to live it, looking to the Lord for His guidance and help" ("Your Greatest Challenge, Mother," *Ensign*, Nov. 2000, 97–98). The Lord loves his children, and our Savior needs us to testify of his perfect life and example. May your example reflect his life always.

Lisa Heckmann Olsen served a mission in Geneva, Switzerland, and later taught French at the Missionary Training Center in Provo. She graduated from Brigham Young University with a degree in art and French education. Lisa taught art at Timpview High School in Utah for ten years. She started working for EFY as a counselor in 1983. She loves painting, drawing pictures for her children, traveling, gardening, cooking, and being home. She and her husband, Brent, have three children, Cole, Sierra, and Maya.

10

TRAPPED WITH THE LUKEWARM

Andy Horton

President Brigham Young once stated, "It was revealed to me in the commencement of this Church, that the Church would spread, prosper, grow and extend, and that in proportion to the spread of the Gospel among the nations of the earth, so would the power of Satan rise" (*Journal of Discourses*, 26 vols. [London: Latter-day Saints' Book Depot, 1854–86], 13:280). As these two great powers have risen, it has become necessary for Latter-day Saints to be able to distinguish the kingdom of God from the kingdom of Satan. Individuals who cannot make that distinction lack absolute commitment to the kingdom of God and are more likely to make bad decisions and occasionally find themselves wedged between both kingdoms. The Lord said, "I know thy works, that thou art neither cold nor hot: I would thou wert cold or hot. So then because thou art lukewarm, and neither cold nor hot, I will spue thee out of my mouth" (Revelation 3:15–16).

As youth of the Church it is especially vital to be firm in your resolutions to live the gospel. It is risky to be "lukewarm" at this decision-making time of life. Being lukewarm makes it easy to give in to temptation when the world offers such enticing disguises for the kingdom of the devil— disguises that are specifically designed to lead us away from the Lord's kingdom. Sister Sharon G. Larsen, second counselor in the Young Women General Presidency, aptly described the duplicity inherent in those who are lukewarm: "Some would like to live in that eternal city and still keep a 'summer home' in Babylon" ("Agency—A Blessing and a Burden," *Ensign*, Nov. 1999, 12). We must be careful and committed. Otherwise it is easy to be tricked into believing that we can draw on the benefits of living in the kingdom of God and still make that trip out to Babylon, coming and going as we wish. This belief is inconsistent with the teachings of the Church and only leads to trouble and discouragement.

The following poem by Dr. Seuss may illustrate:

Ode to a Zode

Did I ever tell you about the young Zode
Who came to two signs at the fork of a road?
One said: TO PLACE ONE. And the other: PLACE TWO.
So the Zode had to make up his mind what to do.
Well . . . the Zode scratched his head, And his chin, And his pants.
And he said to himself, "I'll be taking a chance."
"If I go to Place One . . . now, it may be too hot.
And so, how do I know if I'll like it or not?"
"On the other hand though, I'll be sort of a fool,
If I go to Place Two and I find it too cool."
"In that case I may catch a cold and turn blue!
So maybe Place One is the best—not Place Two."
"So Place Two may be best! On the other hand though . . .
What might happen to me, if Place Two is too low?"
"I might get some very strange pain in my toe!
So Place One must be best." And he started to go.
Then he stopped and he said, "On the other hand though . . .
On the other hand . . . other hand . . . other hand though?"
For 36 hours and 1/2, that poor Zode
Made starts and made stops at that fork in the road.
Saying, "Don't take a chance. No! You may not be right."
Then he got an idea that was wonderfully bright!
"Play safe!" cried the Zode. "I'll play safe! I'm no dunce!
I'll simply start off for both places at once!"
And that's how the Zode, who would not take a chance,
Got No Place at All, with a split in his pants.

The Lord told Joseph Smith, "For Zion must increase in beauty, and in holiness; her borders must be enlarged; her stakes must be strengthened; yea, verily I say unto you, Zion must arise and put on her beautiful garments" (D&C 82:14). Before challenging the Prophet to gather the Saints and work to strengthen Zion, the Lord warned him that as the borders of Zion increase, so too will the borders surrounding the adversary's reign: "Therefore, what I say unto one I say unto all: Watch, for the adversary spreadeth his dominions, and darkness reigneth" (D&C 82:5). As darkness spreads, it becomes increasingly dangerous to remain uncommitted to either kingdom—to be stuck in the danger zone of mediocrity—sometimes choosing good and other times evil. Jesus stated, "No man can serve two masters: for either he will hate the one, and love the other; or else he will hold to the one, and despise the other. Ye cannot serve God and mammon" (Matthew 6:24).

In the book of Joel in the Old Testament, the Lord prophesies of his own second coming and declares that multitudes of people will linger in the "valley of decision" as the Day of Judgment nears. Then, the "heavens and the earth shall shake: but the Lord will be the hope of his people, and the strength of the children of Israel. So shall ye know that I am the Lord your God dwelling in Zion, my holy mountain: then shall Jerusalem be holy, and there shall no strangers pass through her any more" (Joel 3:14, 16–17). Is it possible that the strangers Jesus speaks of could be those who occasionally drop by the good side but aren't committed enough to stay there permanently—those who just "pass through here" as they waver between one side and the other? Elder M. Russell Ballard said: "It appears to me that the most important thing *every* one of us can do is to examine our own commitment and devotion to the Lord Jesus Christ. We must carefully guard against spiritual apathy and work to maintain the full measure of our loving loyalty to the Lord" ("'How Is It with Us?'" *Ensign*, May 2000, 31).

A year or so ago, while visiting the Hogle Zoo in Salt Lake City, Utah, I encountered an individual that appeared to be wandering in this "valley of decision." She was a young lady, probably about sixteen or seventeen years old, who was wearing a red T-shirt that displayed an ad on the front for Coors Light. I didn't think this was anything out of the ordinary until I saw the sun reflect off the ring on her finger. She was wearing a CTR ring. Can you see the predicament? If she is a member of the Church, then she knows that drinking alcohol is against the commandments. So, while she wears a shirt that obviously advertises alcohol, she also wears a CTR ring that tells her not to drink alcohol. Will she "choose the right?" or will she "choose the beer?" There she is, in the bottom of the valley, trying to be good, yet advertising for the bad at the same time.

Blair G. VanDyke, a seminary teacher in Orem, Utah, refers to this valley as the "big but zone." He says that a person caught between kingdoms will almost always use the word *but* as they rationalize their way into the lukewarm area. Listen to some common phrases of those caught in the "big but zone":

> "I need to say my prayers . . . *but* I'm so tired."
> "Sorry I'm late, Mom . . . *but* we got talking."
> "I should forgive him . . . *but* he was so rude."
> "It's not very modest . . . *but* it's the style now."
> "We shouldn't be alone like this . . . *but* we'll be real careful."
> "I should stop doing drugs . . . *but* I just need one more fix."
> "I should stay for the rest of church . . . *but* it's so boring."
> "I know I'm not sixteen . . . *but* he is so cute."
> "I know we shouldn't steady date . . . *but* we've set limits."
> "I know there will be drinking at the party . . . *but* I won't drink."
> "Yeah I cheated . . . *but* so did everyone else."
> "I need to read my scriptures . . . *but* I'm so tired."
> "It's R-rated . . . *but* it's only for violence."
> "I want to be good . . . *but* it is so hard."

Did any of those sound familiar? Have you ever used one (or two, or three) of those phrases? Are you stuck in the "big but zone"?

I recently had in my office a sixteen-year-old young man and his mother. The young man had had some problems with skipping seminary. He had skipped so much that his privilege to even be in seminary was now threatened. He needed to make up his mind: was he going to be in class every day or not? I explained the importance of agency and told him that he had to be the one to make the decision. When I asked what his plan was, his response was a muffled, halfhearted grunt. "Well, what would you like to do?" I asked again, his reply was another grunt, with a very definite "I don't know" thrown in behind. He was literally stuck in the "big but zone." He couldn't make up his mind. He said, "I want to be in seminary, *but* I don't like getting up that early." Make a choice!

Are there real consequences for those in the "big but zone"? For the Zode, it was simply a split in his pants, but it gets worse than that. "If we are not consciously and deliberately choosing the kingdom of God, we will in fact be moving backwards as the kingdom of God moves forward 'boldly, nobly, and independent' . . ." (Sharon G. Larsen, "Agency—A Blessing and a Burden," *Ensign*, Nov. 1999, 13). Elder Neal A. Maxwell said, "It is so easy to be halfhearted, but this only produces half the growth, half the blessings, and just half a life, really, with more bud than blossom" ("'Willing to

Submit,'" *Ensign,* May 1985, 71). Elder Bruce R. McConkie said, "Lukewarm saints are damned; unless they repent and become zealous the Lord promised to spue them out of his mouth. (Rev. 3:14–19.) Only the valiant gain celestial Salvation; those saints 'who are not valiant in the testimony of Jesus' can ascend no higher than the terrestrial world. (D. & C. 76:79.)" (*Doctrinal New Testament Commentary,* 3 vols. [Salt Lake City: Bookcraft, 1965–73], 3:405). Another consequence is clearly defined by President George Albert Smith, who said, "If you will stay on the Lord's side of the line you will be under his influence and will have no desire to do wrong; but if you cross to the devil's side of the line one inch, you are in the tempter's power, and if he is successful, you will not be able to think or even reason properly, because you will have lost the spirit of the Lord" (*Sharing the Gospel with Others,* sel. Preston Nibley [Salt Lake City: Deseret Book, 1948], 42–43).

It would seem that any member of the Church, with righteous goals, would want to avoid mediocrity at all costs. Losing the Spirit, or even worse, being denied a celestial abode, doesn't coincide with the Lord's work. The Savior said, "Behold, this is my work and my glory—to bring to pass the immortality and eternal life of man" (Moses 1:39). He also promised: "I, the Lord, am bound when ye do what I say: but when ye do not what I say, ye have no promise" (D&C 82:10). If you keep the commandments, then the Lord is bound to bless, sustain, strengthen, help, and support you, *but* if you don't keep the commandments, you have no promise of such help.

Elder Marvin J. Ashton once recounted the following: "I'm thinking of a five-year-old boy who fell out of bed during the night and came crying to his mother's bedside. To her question, 'Why did you fall out of bed?' he replied, 'I fell out because I wasn't in far enough!'

"It has been my experience over the years that, generally speaking, those who fall out of the Church are those who aren't in far enough." How do you know if you're in far enough? At the conclusion of the same talk, Elder Ashton said, "The word is *commitment.* To be something, we must be committed. God is our Father. Jesus is our Savior, and this is His Church. May we commit ourselves to living Christlike lives regardless of the environment or opposition" ("The Word Is Commitment," *Ensign,* Nov. 1983, 63).

In the kingdom of God, going halfway is not an option. In a parable, the Lord said, "For which of you, intending to build a tower, sitteth not down first, and counteth the cost, whether he have sufficient to finish it? Lest haply, after he hath laid the foundation, and is not able to finish it, all that behold it begin to mock him, Saying, This man began to build, and was not able to finish" (Luke 14:28–30). The Lord asks for nothing but complete dedication and commitment. If you are going to build a tower then finish the tower; if you are going to make covenants, then keep those covenants; if you are going to be a member of the kingdom of God, then be a member, 100 percent.

The Lord's kingdom is growing. And at a similar rate, the kingdom of the Devil is growing. Many will encounter the desire to choose the right, yet ultimately fall to the "dark side" when the choices arrive. This places them in the hands of the adversary and rids them of the Spirit of the Lord, threatening their eternal happiness. There are no benefits or blessings found when we loiter between kingdoms. "No man can serve two masters" (Matthew 6:24). Elder Ashton continued, "It is not too late to commit ourselves to living the gospel totally while here on earth. Each day we must be committed to lofty Christian performance because commitment to the truths of the gospel of Jesus Christ is essential to our eternal joy and happiness. The time to commit and recommit is now" ("The Word Is Commitment," 63). The secret to success is to be valiant in our testimonies, for "they who are not valiant in the testimony of Jesus . . . obtain not the crown over the kingdom of our God" (D&C 76:79). We have to be valiant in our testimonies. We bear testimony of Christ by the decisions we make. By choosing the right and following his example, we become valiant and avoid the burdens of mediocrity. This will enable us to further the Lord's work and glory as we labor in the Lord's mission "to bring to pass the immortality and eternal life of man."

Andy Horton graduated from Brigham Young University with a bachelor's in zoology. He is currently working on his master's degree and lives in Orem, Utah, where he teaches seminary full-time at Mountain View High School. He has a beautiful wife named Stephanie, two little girls, a little boy, and a table saw. In his spare time he makes log furniture, loves working in the yard, and kissing his wife right on the lips. He loves the youth and hates R-rated movies.

11

YOU HAVE TO BE DIFFERENT IN ORDER TO MAKE A DIFFERENCE

Dwight Durrant

Have you ever heard that Latter-day Saints are a little weird? Perhaps the world thinks that about us, and maybe they have a good argument. We do eat the highest per capita amount of green Jell-O with carrots shredded into it. We hold church at stake houses. (I'll take my steak [stake] medium rare with some green Jell-O on the side.) We also don't eat for twenty-four hours and then have a meeting we call fast meeting. It's the slowest meeting in the Church. The same families have been sitting on the same rows in church for three generations. We have more children than we can find biblical names for, and we consider peanut butter on our car seats an accessory. We have heroes named Moroni and Johnny Lingo, and we have two gallons of ice cream in our freezers at all times. I'll just bet that no other group of young women in the world call themselves Beehives. Really, where else can you hear about BYU football in testimony meeting and have a basketball hoop just above your head. I'll tell you, it thrills *every fiber of my being* to be part of such a wonderful church.

Do these things make us weird? When Mike Wallace interviewed President Gordon B. Hinckley on *60 Minutes*, President Hinckley said Latter-day Saints aren't weird, and I'm certainly not going to argue with a prophet. Weird has a negative connotation. Better words to describe us would be "different" or "unique."

Elder Neal A. Maxwell, in an October 1974 conference address, concluded by saying, "May we be different in order to make a difference" ("Why Not Now?" *Ensign*, Nov. 1974, 13). Different is good. We want to stand out. We should not be embarrassed about who we are. The apostle Paul in his epistle to the Romans said, "I am not ashamed of the gospel of Christ" (Romans 1:16).

If we are going to make a difference in this world, we must be different. Peter made a statement that I believe can be applied directly to the wonderful youth of the Church today. He said, "But ye are a chosen generation, a royal priesthood, an holy nation, a peculiar people" (1 Peter 2:9). In Greek, the word *peculiar* means purchased or preserved, and in Hebrew it signifies a special possession or property. Think about those words. We have been *purchased* and *preserved*; we are a *special possession, property*. Think about how these words apply to us in our relationship with the Savior. We are truly blessed. We have the gospel. We have the priesthood. We must set a higher standard. We must be different in order to make a difference.

Many youth come from high schools where they are one or two of only a few Latter-day Saints. Their classmates know they are LDS. The word gets out. People watch them. People watch all Latter-day Saint youth, even in places where your numbers are many. You must set a good example. You must be able to see the difference if you are going to make a difference. In the Sermon on the Mount, Jesus said, "Ye are the light of the world. A city that is set on an hill cannot be hid" (Matthew 5:14). What does it mean to be a city on a hill? I just happen to live in a city up on a hill. From all over the valley below you can see our little city up on the mountainside, beautiful Elk Ridge, Utah. We cannot hide ourselves. Even at night the lights of our little community can be seen from miles away. We stand out. You are like that in your high schools. People know who you are. Whether you like it or not, you stand out. You cannot hide the fact that you are a member of the Church, nor should you want to.

In his sermon, Jesus goes on to say, "Neither do men light a candle, and put it under a bushel, but on a candlestick." (It would be ridiculous to light a candle and then hide it under a basket.) You are that light. Don't try to hide it.

The verse continues, "and it giveth light unto all that are in the house" (Matthew 5:15). As you let your light shine it will provide light for the people around you, like your family and friends. Imagine, for example, what would happened if you were in a car with a group of your friends and one of them suggested you go to an R-rated movie. Would you hold up your candle and suggest an appropriate alternative? By so doing you would give light unto all that are in the car. Or perhaps if you let your light shine by being more kind to family members, they would see your light and in turn be kinder also.

Jesus concludes this part of the sermon by saying, "Let your light so shine before men, that they may see your good works, and glorify your Father which is in heaven" (Matthew 5:16). We can't be afraid to let our light shine, to live the gospel and thus set a good example. As members of the Church we have a great responsibility to set an example. We must be different from the world. Our behavior reflects on the whole Church. This very principle helped me meet a wonderful couple while serving a mission in Ohio.

It was my first area. I was serving in a university town. Frankly, we were not having a lot of success. It was difficult and a bit frustrating. One day as we entered sacrament meeting, we noticed a new couple seated near the front. We thought perhaps that they were already members just visiting from out of town. After the meeting, a member of the branch brought this couple to us and introduced us by telling us their names and mentioning that they were not members of the Church. They had just dropped in to see what an LDS church was like. We perked up as missionaries and asked if they were interested in finding out more. They were very interested, and so we set up an appointment for the next night. We were so excited. This was a wonderful young couple who were attending graduate school at the university. The next night as we began the discussion, I couldn't erase from my mind the question that had been eating at me all day. Why had they come to church? They knew no one in the branch. They had just sort of shown up to see what an LDS service was like.

Their answer stunned me. They were active members of another faith. As a couple they had decided to live a very healthy lifestyle. As part of this commitment they had decided to never drink alcohol. One night at a party they were attending, they were offered alcoholic beverages. When they declined, the person offering asked, "Are you Mormons?" They weren't even sure what a Mormon was and sort of forgot about it. Then within a very short period of time they had two very similar occurrences. The third time they decided to find out what they were being accused of. They got out a dictionary and looked up "Mormon." They found out it was a church headquartered in Salt Lake City, Utah. They didn't think there would be a Mormon church in this small town but they got out the Yellow Pages and found one listed. It also gave an address and a meeting time. The next Sunday, instead of going to their church, they drove to the address in the

Yellow Pages. Can you imagine the courage it took for them to get out of their car and step into our church without any knowledge of our beliefs and without knowing a single soul? They did it because of the high standards that people like you have set. They came to church because they wanted to know why, when they wouldn't drink, they had been accused of being Mormons. Isn't it wonderful to be a member of a church that has such high standards and such a great reputation? This wonderful couple joined the church and have since been sealed in the temple.

Because we are different, we make a difference in this world. What if you decided one day that you were going to drink alcohol? It won't hurt anyone, you say. Wrong! Just think about all those people who are watching. You are a city on a hill. What you do will reflect upon the whole Church. People will say, "Well, I guess Mormons do drink." Or "I guess Mormons do swear," or lie, or cheat, or steal, or go to R-rated movies. And then people like my friends would quit being attracted to the Church because we would be like the rest of the world.

Elder John A. Widstoe said, "So we need, in this Church and Kingdom, for our own and the world's welfare a group of men and women in their individual lives who shall be as a light to the nations, and really standards for the world to follow. Such a people must be different from the world as it now is. There is no opportunity for Latter-day Saints to say we shall be as the world is, unless the world has the same aim that we have. We are here to build Zion to Almighty God, for the blessing of all the world. In that aim we are unique and different from all other peoples. We must respect that obligation, and not be afraid of it. We cannot walk as other men . . . or do as other men, for we have a different destiny, obligation, and responsibility placed upon us, and we must fit ourselves for that great destiny and obligation" (in Conference Report, Apr. 1940, 36).

Sometimes being a good example and standing up for what is right brings ridicule and persecution from our peers. It can be very difficult, especially for some who are struggling to make friends or to fit in. Peer pressure is a powerful force in a young person's life. A story entitled "Be Yourself" makes this point (source unknown).

"Ever since I was a little kid, I didn't want to be me. I wanted to be Billie Widdleton, and Bill Widdleton didn't even like me. I walked like he walked, and talked like he talked, and I signed up for the same high school he signed up for. Which was when Billie changed. He began to hang around Herby Vanderman; he walked like Herby, and talked like Herby. He mixed me up. I began to walk like Billie Widdleton, walking and talking like Herby Vanderman. And then it dawned on me that Herby Vanderman walked and talked like Joey Haverlin, and Joey walked and talked like Corkey Sabinson. So here I am walking and talking like Billie Widdleton's imitation of Herby Vanderman's version of Joey Haverlin, trying to walk and talk like Corkey Sabinson. And walking and talking like? Of all people, Popey Wollington. That little pest who walks and talks like me."

Let me tell you about a seminary student I taught. His name was Garrett. He was on the high school wrestling team. He was also on our seminary council. The wrestling team went to the state tournament in a distant town. This required that they spend several nights in a hotel. As they checked into their rooms and turned on the TV, many were excited to see that they had several channels that carried R-rated movies. Garrett quietly left the room and went down to the hotel management and asked if they could block out those particular channels, which they did. This did not make Garrett very popular with some of his teammates, and he took a lot of ridicule for it. But he stood firm, as did his decision. (Did I mention that he was a very big kid? Not just in body but also in spirit.) Garrett made a difference for good that week. He cared more about what God would think than what his friends would think.

Jesus taught, "If the world hate you, ye know that it hated me before it hated you. If ye were of the world, the world would love his own: but because ye are not of the world, but I have chosen you out of the world, therefore the world hateth you" (John 15:18–19). Sometimes we care so much about what the world is going to think of us that we forget that what God thinks of us is most important. We want people to be our friends so we give in to negative peer pressure. It is much more important that Christ be our friend. Jesus also said, "Greater love hath no man than this, that a man lay down his life for his friends. Ye are my friends, if ye do whatsoever I command you" (John 15:13–14). Christ is our friend. He has paid the supreme price for us. He has purchased us. We are his special possessions. We must do as he wants and not what the world wants. The apostle James wrote, "Know ye not that the friendship of the world is enmity with God? whosoever therefore will be a friend of the world is the enemy of God" (James 4:4).

We have many great examples from the scriptures of people who were different and thus made a huge difference. Nephi was certainly one of these people. Without him we might not have had the Book of Mormon. Many of the things he said and did made him unpopular, but he stood firm. He wrote, "Wherefore, the things which are pleasing unto the world I do not write, but the things which are pleasing unto God and unto those who are not of the world" (1 Nephi 6:5). For Nephi, it was far more important to please God than to gain worldly popularity.

Think about Noah. His neighbors probably thought he was a little weird for building an ark on dry ground. But did he make a difference? We wouldn't be here if it weren't for Noah. How about the two thousand stripling warriors? These young boys listened to their mothers, they loved and served their families. Their lives were certainly different from those of their Lamanite counterparts. Because they were different, they survived two major battles without a single death. Then there is Ammon and his brethren. These young men *wanted* to serve a mission in enemy territory. Did they make a difference? Thousands of Lamanites owe their eternal salvation to the efforts of these great missionaries. The list goes on. Our missionaries today differ greatly from the rest of the world. They are young men willing to give up all worldly pursuits for two years to serve the Lord wherever he calls them. What a great difference they make!

The person who has made the biggest difference, however, is the Savior. Let's examine some of the ways he differed from the world during his thirty-three years of life.

Never once did Jesus give in to temptation. This is particularly incredible considering the fact that he was tempted more than any of us combined. King Benjamin said: "And lo, he shall suffer temptations, and pain of body, hunger, thirst, and fatigue, even more than man can suffer, except it be unto death" (Mosiah 3:7). The great Christian philosopher and writer C. S. Lewis said: "A silly idea is current that good people do not know what temptation means. This is an obvious lie. Only those who try to resist temptation know how strong it is. After all, you find out the strength of the German army by fighting against it, not by giving in. You find out the strength of a wind by trying to walk against it, not by lying down. A man who gives in to temptation after five minutes simply does not know what it would have been like an hour later. That is why bad people, in one sense, know very little about badness. They have lived a sheltered life by always giving in. We never find out the strength of the evil impulse inside us until we try to fight it: and Christ, because He was the only man who never yielded to temptation, is also the only man who knows to the full what temptation means—the only complete realist" (*Mere Christianity*, rev. and enl. [New York: Macmillan Publishing, 1952], 109–10).

Another significant way that Jesus differed from the world is in the way he loved all those around him, even his enemies. He may not have loved their behavior, but he certainly loved them. He loved those men who delivered him to the cross to be crucified and who nailed spikes into his hands. He loved the man who spit in his face. Can you imagine being this poor man at the judgment bar and realizing that it was the Savior whose face you had spit in? And yet Jesus loved him.

I once taught seminary with the father of a two-year-old boy. One day, this young father brought home a video from the seminary to preview. It was a video about the last few hours of the Savior's life. As he began to watch it, his little son Jacob sat down beside him, just to be with Dad. Soon the video progressed to the scene in which Jesus' murderers drove the spikes into his hands. The video showed the hammer being raised, but then the camera cut away from the Savior's hands and focused only on the hammer as it pounded in the nails. At this terrible point in the movie, Jacob jumped off the couch and approached the television set. He took his little index finger and waved it up and down as he shouted, "No, no, no, no!" You see, even a two-year-old could recognize the terrible injustice in that moment. The Savior likewise recognized the injustice, yet he loved those men who so cruelly nailed him to the cross.

What an example of love and mercy! Jesus expects us to follow his great example. He said: "A new commandment I give unto you, That ye love one another; as I have loved you" (John 13:34). This means we must love everyone, even our enemies. There are no exceptions. We must love as the Savior did.

As we learn to love and follow Jesus' example, we will recognize another area of the Savior's life in which he differed from the world. Jesus was forgiving. Even as he was being placed on the cross, he cried, "Father, forgive them; for they know not what they do" (Luke 23:34). He didn't hold grudges. He wasn't offended by the big things, let alone the little things. He taught us to turn the other cheek. When Jesus heard about the death of his good friend John the Baptist, he could have called down legions of angels to destroy Herod. He did attempt to be alone, likely to mourn the loss of his friend. But Matthew records that the people "followed him on foot out of the cities. And Jesus went forth, and saw a great multitude, and was moved with compassion toward them, and he healed their sick" (Matthew 14:13–14). Instead of seeking revenge or even spending time in mourning,

Jesus' heart was tender, and he sought out people he could serve. What a great lesson for us!

Jesus was also different in the sense that he didn't judge people unfairly. He didn't gossip or backbite. He would never tease those who didn't meet his standards. The scribes and Pharisees wanted to stone her, but Jesus protected the woman caught in adultery and counseled her to "Go, and sin no more" (John 8:11). Can you even imagine Jesus judging someone by what brand of clothes they wore, or how skinny they were, or how rich, or how pretty, or whether or not they were a cheerleader, or an athlete, or a skater, or a brain! Jesus was not concerned about outward appearances but about the shape and nature of our hearts.

Another significant difference in the life of the Savior is that he sought after spiritual rather than earthly treasures. Never once do we read about how big his house was, what kind of chariot he drove, or how he owned stock in IBM (Israelite Boat Manufacturers). Jesus seemed only to be concerned with those things which are eternal, those things that make us rich after death.

Jesus lived a life of serving others. He not only gave his life on the cross, he gave his everyday life to others. Many of us are so concerned about ourselves and our own struggles that we forget those who are less fortunate and could use a helping hand or a smile or a friend. I have learned that the way to true happiness is to stop being concerned about myself and focus on what I can do for others.

Jesus was different because he stood up for truth and right. He was the world's greatest example. He didn't back down to the Pharisees. On two occasions he cleansed the temple. He taught the truth, even when doing so made him very unpopular. He shared the truth. He was not embarrassed to speak out.

Jesus was different in so many ways. And because he was different, what did the world do to him? They nailed him to a cross. Because they did not want to change their own lives, to live as he taught and be different themselves, they crucified the Lord. In this, too, he was different. Surely if we had the power to call down angels and prevent our own deaths, we would do so. The Savior, however, *gave up* his life. He did so for us. Never has any one life impacted mankind more than our Savior's. My prayer is that each of us will strive to be more like him, to be different, and undoubtedly make a difference in this world.

Dwight Durrant teaches seminary in Payson, Utah, and is a part-time instructor at the Institute of Religion at Utah Valley State College in Orem, Utah. He and his wife, Marci, have five children: Eliza, Annie, Cami, Will, and Sam. He currently serves as the Gospel Doctrine teacher in his ward in Elkridge, Utah. He loves to run and has completed six marathons. He ran 2000 kilometers (1240 miles) in the year 2000 and has set a goal to run 2001 kilometers this year. He served in the Ohio Columbus Mission, graduated from Brigham Young University, and received a master's degree from Utah State University. This is his eighth year working for EFY.

12

THE INFLUENCE OF
THE HOLY GHOST

Dean Kaelin

While I was growing up I really looked up to my older brother. He was good looking, drove a motorcycle, worked on cars, played the piano, grew a beard, and was adored by all the girls. I wanted to be just like him. So I learned to play the piano, rode a motorcycle, tried to work on cars, and even tried to walk like him. (But I never could grow a beard, no matter how hard I tried.) The thing I admired most about my brother, however, was his ability to receive answers from his Heavenly Father.

You see, during those growing-up years, my Heavenly Father and I had a system: I would pray and he wouldn't say anything. This arrangement seemed to work quite nicely, and I got rather used to it (if not frustrated). I would have problems and pour my heart out to the Lord, and all I ever received was silence. My brother, on the other hand, seemed to simply be able to ask a question and immediately receive his answer. I told Heavenly Father, "I will do ANYTHING you want me to, please just tell me!" But there would always be silence.

When I left on a mission I felt more than ever that I needed my Heavenly Father's guidance. So I earnestly began to study the scriptures and other materials about receiving answers to prayer and hearing the voice of God through the Holy Ghost. I discovered that the Holy Ghost "knoweth all things" (D&C 35:19), and that he will manifest to us "all things which are expedient" (D&C 18:18). I knew that I desperately wanted to tap into the source that knows all things and would tell me all things that I needed to know!

I read about Nephi in the Book of Mormon and how he was "led by the Spirit, not knowing beforehand the things which [he] should do" (1 Nephi 4:6). I too wanted to be led. I learned of Alma and Amulek who "were filled with the Holy Ghost. And they had power given unto them, insomuch that they could not be confined in dungeons; neither was it possible that any man could slay them," and I wanted to have the power of God so that I too could go "forth and [begin] to preach and to prophesy unto the people, according to the spirit and power which the Lord had given" me (Alma 8:30–32).

And so my search began to discover the answer to the question, "How can you tell when the Holy Ghost is speaking?" I have come to the conclusion that the Holy Ghost speaks to us almost constantly if we are living worthily. Our biggest problem is that we don't know what he sounds like.

When we are baptized we are given the gift of the Holy Ghost. This means that if we are doing what our Heavenly Father wants us to do the Holy Ghost will be our "constant companion" (D&C 121:46). Imagine how incredible that is! When we are living worthily, we have the constant companionship of someone who knows all things. If we could only tune our ears to hear his voice, we could be led as Nephi, Alma, Amulek, Joseph Smith, and others were.

As I studied, I began to try to understand what the Holy Ghost sounds like so that I could recognize his voice. The Doctrine and Covenants refers to this voice as "the still small voice, which whispereth" (D&C 85:6). I came to recognize that his voice really does whisper, and that we don't hear him because we hear so many other voices that seem to drown out the Spirit. There is the voice of music, of television, movies, books, friends, entertainers, Satan, athletes, rock stars, movie stars, parents, and so on. So how can we hear the "still small voice" with all this noise constantly going on all around us?

When I was five years old I began learning how to play the piano. I really loved music and I really loved the piano, but I didn't want to play all the old, boring songs that my teacher would give me. I wanted to play the songs that I heard on the radio. So I began trying to figure out how to play these songs. At first it was an incredibly long and difficult struggle. I would tape a song off the radio and then play a very short section over and over and try to match the notes on the piano with those that I heard on the tape. It would take me two hours just to get the introduction of one song learned the first time I tried it. As I continued doing this, however, I became faster and faster until I finally got to the point when I was about thirteen that I could listen to a song once and then play it.

Later on in high school I began arranging music for my high school band and I found that I could listen to an orchestra or a band and pick out the notes that each individual instrument was playing. I could block out all other instruments except for the one I was trying to hear.

I then discovered that I could also do this with singers. I could listen to a harmony group like Boyz II Men and write out the parts they were singing so that others could sing their songs.

So, I wondered, *if I could do this with music, why not with the Holy* Ghost? I realized that I had *worked to develop* the talent for listening to music and notes, but I had not taken the time or put forth the effort to develop the talent of hearing the Holy Ghost! I decided that this was a talent more desirable than all others, and I likewise began to apply myself.

The Holy Ghost speaks "in your mind and in your heart" (D&C 8:2). In other words, when the Holy Ghost speaks, you might hear something quiet in your mind, as if someone is speaking to you. You might have a thought enter your mind. Or you may not hear actual words at all but instead feel something inside you. Some people have described this as a "burning," while others have called it "a feeling of peace." One of my favorite passages of scripture is Doctrine and Covenants 6:22–23: "Verily, verily, I say unto you, if you desire a further witness, cast your mind upon the night that you cried unto me in your heart, that you might know concerning the truth of these things. Did I not speak peace to your mind concerning the matter? What greater witness can you have than from God?"

Elder Boyd K. Packer has said that the Holy Ghost is in constant communication with us and that we will learn to hear his voice when we start following the promptings that we receive (see *That All May Be Edified* [Salt Lake City: Bookcraft, 1982], 15). So often we are waiting for a marvelous manifestation to our prayers that we don't notice the voice of the Spirit gently guiding us. We are waiting for the roof of our house to rip off and a bolt of lightning to come down accompanied by a loud voice! To my knowledge this has never happened. The Lord speaks through the Holy Ghost with peace and quiet, and as we begin to follow the promptings we receive we will begin to recognize his voice more clearly, just as I was able to hear specific instruments hidden within an orchestra.

Several years ago my family and I moved to a new home. It had the potential to be a beautiful home, but it was badly in need of flowers. I had never before purchased flowers, and so I sent my wife off (she has a much better eye for these sorts of things than I do) with two hundred dollars in cash to buy us some beautiful flowers that would make our home lovely. I was in great hopes that this would not cost more than fifty dollars, but I didn't want to use a credit card so I gave her some extra money just to be safe. My wife never carries more than twenty dollars in cash around with her, so this was unusual.

On the way to the nursery, our children, who had accompanied her, began asking for some sort of refreshment such as ice cream; and she, being the wonderful mother that she is, decided to stop and get them some. She got the ice cream and was putting all the kids back into the car when she set her wallet on the roof as she put the baby in her car seat. She then hopped in the car and drove off. Later, at the nursery she selected many beautiful flowers to make our home lovely. When she went to pay for them, however, she realized that her wallet was missing.

She got the children quickly back into the car and raced to the market where the ice cream had been purchased. She looked all over the store, inside and out, but did not find the wallet. Fearing that I would be extremely upset, she returned home without any flowers or money. I heard the sad story and, being a man, of course proclaimed, "I will go and find the wallet."

I jumped in my car and went to where the ice cream had been purchased. As I pulled into the parking lot, this thought came to me: *We used to live only a couple of blocks from here. Perhaps someone found the wallet and returned it to our old home.* Of course, I then thought, *No, don't be ridiculous! Who would go to the trouble of returning a wallet a few blocks away?* I looked for some time around the parking lot, asked the store clerk, and watched carefully as I drove down the street, but did not find any wallet. As I began to drive home the thought returned, *Go to your old home.* I thought, *Why not, what have I got to lose?* and I drove to my old home. On the front door was a note that said, "I found your wallet and have left it with your neighbor because you weren't home." I went to my old neighbor's house and retrieved the wallet!

It has been my experience that the Holy Ghost speaks most often with these simple, quiet, peaceful, and even logical thoughts and feelings. Usually these thoughts are not very miraculous; in fact, they sometimes seem almost commonplace and it is easy to pass them off as just a crazy idea or a passing thought. This is because the Holy Ghost speaks to us constantly. Often we are so used to hearing his voice that we don't think it was anything special. Remember, we have the gift of the Holy Ghost. He is our constant companion when we live worthily.

My brother lived for a time in the San Francisco area but was about to move back to Salt Lake City. He didn't want to leave California, however, without having visited Yosemite National Park. So he loaded up the van and the family and began driving back to Utah by way of Yosemite. At the campground entrance he stopped and asked the park ranger if they could camp there for the night. The ranger asked if they had a reservation. My brother replied that no, they did not, they didn't realize that they needed one. The ranger laughed at him and told them that there was no way they'd be able to camp there. Reservations are made months in advance, and the campsites were totally full. My brother then asked if he could at least drive around a while.

After looking at the sights, he and his family decided that they better get back on the road so that they could find some place to stay before it got too late. As he was about to drive past the ranger station he had a thought, *Ask the ranger if they've had any cancellations.* His first reaction was, *No way! The first time he laughed at me, what will he do now?* But then he decided, *What could it hurt?* So he stopped and asked if there had been any cancellations. With a surprised look, the ranger told him that he had indeed received a cancellation moments before and my brother could stay the night.

After setting up camp my brother decided to go for a walk. As he walked he noticed a boy about the age of fifteen walking on the cliff above him. He watched the boy off and on as they walked and noticed that the boy seemed quite close to the edge of the cliff. Suddenly a bit of ground gave way, and the boy fell some two hundred feet down the cliff. My brother raced to the boy, whom no one else would have seen. When he reached the boy he was still alive, although they would later find out that most of the bones in his body had been broken. My brother asked what he could do for the boy, who said in a very faint whisper, "I need a priesthood blessing." My brother was able to lay his hands on this boy and command that he remain alive until he got help. He asked the boy where his camp was and found that it was the camp right next to the site where my brother and family were staying. My brother ran and got the father of the boy, and they were able to order emergency help.

Approximately five years later my brother was at his home in Alpine,

Utah, and answered a knock at the door. He was greeted by a young man in a suit who told him that he was the same boy that had fallen from the cliff. He was on his way to the Missionary Training Center in Provo in preparation for leaving on his mission and he just wanted to come by and say thank you. All because my brother had a thought, *Ask the ranger if there's been a cancellation*.

I could tell you many more experiences when I or others I've known have followed a thought, just as President Packer has encouraged us to, with wonderful results. I wish I could say that I recognize and follow the Spirit all the time, but I must admit that I still miss it sometimes. I learn from these experiences, however, and am hopeful that I am becoming better at recognizing the voice of the Holy Ghost as he leads me in the correct paths.

Sometimes it is easier to recognize the Spirit when you've missed it, when in hindsight you are able to see that the Spirit was trying to lead you, but you failed to follow. Oftentimes when we follow the Spirit we take all the credit and think, *Whoa, I sure made a good move on that one!* or *What a lucky coincidence that was*. Take the time to learn from these experiences and to give credit to the Lord and the Holy Ghost so that your talent can be perfected.

Sometimes, when it is necessary, the Holy Ghost will speak more loudly and clearly, but even when he speaks in his quiet tone we can learn to hear him without doubt or question. Remember, you will feel it in your mind and in your heart. It feels right, it is peaceful. Sometimes there is emotion that comes when you hear or feel the Spirit, but most often the Spirit is simply calm and peaceful and there is not an overabundance of emotion. Getting "worked up" is not the Spirit. "Be still and know that I am God" (D&C 101:16; Psalm 46:10).

It is my testimony that God loves us and that he has not left us here entirely alone. He seeks to help us, but we must learn to block out the louder voices and tune in to his still, small voice that leads us toward peace, joy, and happiness. I hope that we can all better follow those small, quiet promptings that the Holy Ghost sends to us and allow those moments to bless our lives and then recognize them as guidance from our Heavenly Father through the Holy Ghost. As we do this we will develop what I feel is the greatest of all talents, the talent of hearing and understanding the Holy Ghost.

I will close with this powerful promise from the Lord to each of us who seek and find the Spirit: "Let him be humble before me, and be without guile, and he shall receive of my Spirit, even the Comforter, which shall manifest unto him the truth of all things, and shall give him, in the very hour, what he shall say. And these signs shall follow him—he shall heal the sick, he shall cast out devils, and shall be delivered from those who would administer unto him deadly poison; And he shall be led in paths where the poisonous serpent cannot lay hold upon his heel, and he shall mount up in the imagination of his thoughts as upon eagles' wings" (D&C 124:97–99).

Dean Kaelin is an assistant professor at Westminster College in Salt Lake City, Utah. He served a mission to South Africa and is a seminary and institute graduate, Eagle Scout, former released-time seminary teacher, and high school football, basketball, and baseball coach. He is a professional musician with vocal and recording studios in Salt Lake. He graduated with honors from the University of Utah and received a master's degree in business from Brigham Young University. He has released several CDs, tapes, and songbooks and has performed throughout the world with his wife, Susan, and five children.

13

INTEGRITY: BEING TRUE TO OURSELVES

Mark D. Ogletree

A few years ago we were preparing to have a typical Saturday afternoon lunch: hot dogs, chips, and drinks. My wife mentioned to the children that she had bought a gallon of their favorite ice cream and, as soon as they ate all of their lunch, they could have a few scoops of "Cookies and Cream." Everyone started digging in except for our only son, Brandon. He informed us that he no longer liked hot dogs (Can you really blame him for that?) and would just prefer to have ice cream for lunch. I let him know that personally I would rather have steak for lunch, but we don't always get what we want. Well, Brandon didn't care for my "steak" analogy, but he continued to beg for ice cream. After about fifteen minutes of deliberation, I firmly said, "Brandon, you cannot have ice cream for lunch, and if you want any ice cream at all, you're going to have to eat your hot dog first, just like everyone else, and that's final." A line had been drawn in the sand.

At that point my son realized that we had read too many parenting books and were not going to budge. He eventually caved in as he sheepishly said, "OK, I'll eat the hot dog." I felt good about the victory as my wife handed Brandon his paper plate filled with the goods. However, for some odd reason, instead of eating with the rest of the family, he chose to take his plate out to the garage. In less than thirty seconds, he was back in the house with his plate cleaned, ready for ice cream. I thought it was a bit strange (In actuality, I felt that I had been totally ripped-off, but had no way to prove it.) that Brandon (1) had decided to eat out in the garage, and (2) had been able to eat something he detested so quickly. I thus began the interrogation he so richly deserved. I attempted to get Brandon to admit that he really didn't eat the hot dog at all, but no luck. He stuck to his story like glue. I then checked the obvious locations for a hidden Oscar-Meyer— in the tailpipe of the car, under the lawnmower, and in the vice—but I found nothing. I hung my head in defeat as I handed my son his bowl of "Cookies and Cream." As Brandon gobbled down his reward, I decided to go work in the yard to try to forget the incident.

About thirty minutes later, as I was weed eating around the front flowerbed, I came across a perfect hot dog. It was obviously Brandon's because it hadn't even been touched. Now it was payback time! Brandon was across the street playing basketball with a friend, and I called him over. I said, "Brandon, is this your hot dog?"

"Nope," he responded. (This is called a "lie.")

I then followed with, "Brandon, don't lie to me. Just admit it."

His response was classic: "I didn't lie to you. I just tricked you."

Well, we had a long talk that afternoon about the difference between lying and tricking. As he sat in his room pondering the true meaning of tricking, I couldn't help but laugh. In his five-year-old mind, there was a difference between lying and tricking. "I just tricked you" has become a favored line in our family.

A short time later, in a family home evening lesson, we taught again the importance of honesty. We even made an honesty pact; each child made a promise that he or she would never lie again. As parents, we knew that such a promise was somewhat unrealistic, but we hoped our pact would last at least a month. Not too long after our lesson the Girl Scouts visited our home to deliver several packs of those thin mint cookies. Our children were secretly hoping to eat the cookies for dinner that night. (OK, since we're discussing honesty, I'll admit that I couldn't wait to eat them either.) As parents, we saw this as a great opportunity to get some work done around the house, so we announced: "Whoever can get their chores done will get a handful of cookies!" All of our children went scurrying to their rooms and around the house, making their beds, taking out garbage, vacuuming rooms, and so on. That is, all but one of our children. I couldn't find three-year-old McKenzie anywhere. After a thorough search, I noticed her behind the big chair in our family room. She was sitting down eating an entire box of thin mint cookies.

As I approached her, I said, "McKenzie, what do you have in your mouth?" She said, "Nothing." Now, if you can visualize this, it looked like

McKenzie had about ten cookies crammed into her cheeks. In fact, when she answered, "nothing," little cookie chunks went flying out of her mouth onto the carpet. I said, "McKenzie, why did you lie to me?" Like her brother before, except this time with tears, she cried: "I forgot." How do you argue with that? So much for the honesty pact. Nevertheless, we have continued to work with our children on honesty. (A few of them can quote 2 Nephi 9:34.)

INTEGRITY: A DEFINITION

When I was a teenager, I often thought of integrity as a synonym for honesty. There is much more to integrity, however, than mere honesty. Integrity comes from the Latin *integer,* which means whole or complete. President Spencer W. Kimball taught that "integrity is one of the corner-stones of character. . . . It is purity and moral soundness. . . . It is courage, a human virtue of incalculable value. It is honesty, uprightness, and righteousness. Take these away and there is left but an empty shell" (*The Teachings of Spencer W. Kimball,* ed. Edward L. Kimball [Salt Lake City: Bookcraft, 1982], 192).

Integrity is living true to what we know is true. We possess integrity when our actions are congruent with our beliefs. Perhaps this principle is what motivated Shakespeare to write, "To thine own self be true" (*Hamlet,* 1.3.78). It would be worthwhile to study in more depth some of the attributes that President Kimball used to describe integrity, such as purity, courage, and honesty.

PURITY

Elder Vaughn J. Featherstone said: "Synonyms for the word pure include chaste, virtuous, pure-hearted, pure in heart, clean, immaculate, spotless, stainless, taintless, white, unsoiled, unsullied, and undefiled. Wouldn't it be marvelous if all of us could be described by these adjectives?" (*Purity of Heart* [Salt Lake City: Deseret Book, 1982], 2). The apostle Paul declared, "Unto the pure all things are pure" (Titus 1:15). When we have pure hearts, we can eliminate the negative and see the good in everything, which includes those around us, our enemies, our surroundings, and even ourselves.

At a recent general conference, Elder Featherstone shared a story. It seems that when Elder Henry B. Eyring's father was a young man, he was crossing the border from Mexico into the United States. At that point, Elder Featherstone recounted, "the customs man said, 'Son, do you have any pornography in your suitcase or trunks?' He responded, 'No sir, we don't even own a pornograph'" ("One Link Still Holds," *Ensign*, Nov. 1999, 14).

Elder Eyring's father didn't even know what pornography was; he was as pure and innocent as a five-year-old. A mission president shared another example. His granddaughter was riding on a bus and sitting by her mother. Down the aisle was a man smoking up a storm. The little girl watched until she could not stand it any longer. At first, she simply stared him down. When that didn't work, she confronted him by saying, "'You should not smoke.' The man took the cigarette out of his mouth and firmly said to this little girl, 'Says who?' She responded, 'Smokey the bear and Holy the Ghost'" (in Vaughn J. Featherstone, *More Purity Give Me* [Salt Lake City: Deseret Book, 1991], 116–17). Isn't it great to be innocent and pure?

Purity is also reflected throughout the scriptures. For example, Alma taught: "For our words will condemn us, yea, all our works will condemn us . . . and our thoughts will also condemn us; and in this awful state we shall not dare to look up to our God; and we would fain be glad if we could command the rocks and the mountains to fall upon us to hide us from his presence" (Alma 12:14; see also Mosiah 4:30). If our words, works, and thoughts can condemn us, then they can also bless us. In fact, our pure words and pure works can edify all who come into our presence as we learn to speak with the tongues of angels (2 Nephi 32:2–3). To have integrity is to be pure and clean; it is to do and say what the Savior would do and say.

COURAGE

Elder Spencer W. Kimball said, "One of the strongest ingredients of integrity is courage. As Robert Frost has said: 'Courage is the human virtue that counts most'" (*Integrity*, Brigham Young University Speeches of the Year [Provo, Feb. 25, 1964], 2). In that same talk, President Kimball also said, "Sometimes it is easier to explain what integrity is by showing what it is not" (9). Consider the following experience shared by Brother Keith Merrill. Brother Merrill related how he and his friends used to dive off cliffs near the East Canyon Dam. As is common among teenage boys, a competition ensued one day as they decided to see who could jump from the highest point along the rugged canyon wall.

One boy bragged that he could dive from a higher point than anyone else. Most of the young men who took the challenge dove from the fifty- sixty- and seventy-foot mark. Eventually, however, most of the young men dropped out of the contest except for the young man who issued the challenge and Keith Merrill. Keith knew that if he simply jumped from the very top, the eighty-foot mark, his challenger could only "tie" him at best. Reflecting back, Brother Merrill explained:

"I stood there all alone, everybody waiting down below. The water was so far away it looked like crinkled tinfoil in the sun. I was just terrified. I was committed, but I had not even based my decision on what I wanted to do or what I felt was right. I had based it on about a half dozen guys whose names I don't even remember who were yelling, 'Hey, chicken, are you going to do it?'

"I realized that in order to make the jump I would have to run a distance to get enough momentum to carry me over the rocks below. So I backed up and ran as hard as I could toward the edge. . . . I don't know how long it takes to fall 80 feet, but for me it took about a week. On the way down I remembered distinctly how my parents and teachers had taught me to be careful when making decisions because I could kill myself with a wrong one. I said to myself, 'You have done it; you have killed yourself, because when you hit the water you'll be going so fast that it might as well be concrete.' And when I hit the water, I was sure it was concrete. . . . I was a grateful lad when my head finally popped above water. I took a quick inventory to make sure that the throbbing pain in my right thigh didn't designate the loss of anything important.

"Well, why did I jump? Did I prove myself to the guys? You think they cared? You think they're sitting at home tonight saying, 'Remember old Merrill, brave old Merrill, jumping off the. . . . ' They don't even remember! They don't care! But for me that moment was as important as my life. I made what could have easily been a fatal decision.

"I was subjected to pressure that was hard to withstand, the pressure of friends expecting things of me that I didn't want to do because I knew better. But I yielded to the pressure" ("Deciding about Decisions," *New Era*, June 1976, 12–13).

Like Brother Merrill, many of us do not live true to our consciences, or the promptings of the Holy Ghost, or those "gut" feelings that warn us of pending danger. Elder Kenneth Johnson of the First Quorum of the Seventy shared an experience similar to Brother Merrill's. On a warm summer day in Great Britain, a friend invited sixteen-year-old Brother Johnson to ride on the back of his motorcycle. Although they wore no protective gear, the friend driving leaned back and asked, "Have you ever traveled at one hundred miles an hour?" Brother Johnson timidly replied, "No." The friend then responded, "Well, you're going to." Brother Johnson said, "We don't have to." Nevertheless, his friend pulled back on the throttle and soon they were going over one hundred miles per hour. Years later, speaking of that experience from the podium at general conference, Elder Johnson said: "I determined that day that never again would I let somebody else control my life" ("The Motorcycle Ride," *Ensign*, May 1990, 42).

Perhaps you are familiar with Lehi's dream as found in First Nephi chapter 8. Verses 24 through 25 describe a group of people who were progressing in the kingdom. They were on the path, holding to the iron rod, and even made it to the tree and tasted of the fruit. (Or in other words, they were partaking of the goodness of God and the atonement of Christ.) We then read, however, that "after they had tasted of the fruit they were ashamed, because of those that were scoffing at them; and they fell away . . . and were lost" (v. 28). Why were they lost? They were doing so well. Footnote 28c provides us with the telling answer: They succumbed to peer pressure. These individuals feared their friends more than they feared God. Or, to paraphrase Elder Marion G. Romney, they were "trying to serve the Lord without offending the devil" (*The Price of Peace*, Brigham Young University Speeches of the Year [Provo, Mar. 1, 1955], 7). We cannot serve God and those who follow the devil at the same time. Sometimes it is difficult to do what is right and not offend your friends. However, remember that any friend who would encourage you to compromise your standards is not a true friend. When times get rough, such friends usually "jump ship," so to speak, and leave you stranded. The Savior, the one you should be following, will always be there for you, forever. That I promise.

HONESTY

We live in a world where honesty is rarely valued; in fact, honest people are often ridiculed. President Kimball told the story of a man who returned a large sum of money, which fell from an armored car onto the street. Many people in the community made fun of him, called him stupid, and even harassed him for being honest (see *Faith Precedes the Miracle* [Salt Lake City: Deseret Book, 1972], 240).

Such actions remind me of the verse in the Book of Mormon which states: "Wo unto them that call evil good, and good evil, that put darkness for light, and light for darkness, that put bitter for sweet, and sweet for bitter!" (2 Nephi 15:20). Using that "Woe" word again, President Brigham

Young taught, "Be Honest—Woe to those who profess to be Saints and are not honest. . . .

"Honest hearts produce honest actions. . . .

"Fulfill your contracts and sacredly keep your word" (*Discourses of Brigham Young*, sel. John A. Widtsoe [Salt Lake City: Deseret Book, 1941], 231–32).

We should be honest and fulfill our words. If we say that we are going to do something, then we should do it. Unfortunately in our culture today, giving your word or making a promise doesn't mean much. Perhaps you are the generation that could change that ideology. Consider the words of Karl G. Maeser:

"I have been asked what I mean by word of honor. I will tell you. Place me behind prison walls—walls of stone ever so high, ever so thick, reaching ever so far into the ground—there is a possibility that in some way or another I may be able to escape, but stand me on that floor and draw a chalk line around me and have me give my word of honor never to cross it. Can I get out of that circle? No, never! I'd die first!" (as quoted in Alma P. Burton, *Karl G. Maeser: Mormon Educator* [Salt Lake City: Deseret Book, 1953], 71).

Thus, one aspect of honesty is keeping your word. Another part of honesty is rejecting lies, and not lying yourself. In the book of Proverbs, Solomon tells us that one of the things the Lord hates is "a lying tongue" (Proverbs 6:17). Wilford A. Cardon shared the following story:

"Personal honesty is a most ordinary subject. It is often taught. I can tell when the subject is being stressed at BYU because I usually get an envelope with five dollars in it along with a note that reads, 'Dear Mr. Cardon: While I worked with you three years ago, I took two paper clips and four pencils and now have determined that I was dishonest in taking those. Here is an appropriate amount to cover the cost of the items which I took.' The size of dishonest acts ranges from small to large. Just recently in our company through the dishonest act of a supposedly 'good' person, six million dollars disappeared. Mark Twain said that after he had spent some time with the 'good' people in the community, and he had quotation marks around good, he understood why Christ spent most of his time with the sinners" (Wilford A. Cardon, "Honesty and Ethics in Life," BYU Commencement, Marriott School of Management, April 1987).

Perhaps a third aspect of honesty is to denounce cheating. In giving an examination one day, a trigonometry teacher said, "Today I am going to give you two examinations; one in trigonometry and one in honesty. I hope you will pass them both. But if you must fail one, let it be in trigonometry, for there are many good men in the world today who cannot pass an examination in trigonometry but there are no good men in the world today who cannot pass an examination in honesty" (in Cardon, "Honesty and Ethics in Life").

In a similar vein, President Gordon B. Hinckley declared: "Being true to ourselves means being honest. It means being honest in school. We cannot afford to cheat or do anything of that kind. Suppose that you needed a life-saving operation. You would not want that operation performed by a surgeon who had cheated in medical school, would you? Of course not" ("Stand True and Faithful," *Ensign*, May 1996, 92).

Indeed, this life is the most important test we will ever take. Joseph Smith taught: "No one can ever enter the celestial kingdom unless he is strictly honest" (as cited in Truman G. Madsen, *Joseph Smith the Prophet* [Salt Lake City: Bookcraft, 1989], 104). Unless we are honest, we are not going to get the grade we were expecting. Perhaps this is why the English poet Alexander Pope penned, "An honest man's the noblest work of God" (*An Essay on Man, Epistle III*, line 248).

As you might remember, Joan of Arc became general of the French Army at the age of seventeen. By the age of nineteen she had saved her country. She was later betrayed and condemned to be burned at the stake. There was hope, however. If Joan would simply renounce her faith in God, she would be spared. From Maxwell Anderson's play, here are her final words: "Every woman gives her life for what she believes. Sometimes people believe in little, or nothing. One life is all we have, and we live it as we believe in living it, and then it's gone. But to surrender what you are, and live without belief—that's more terrible than dying—more terrible than dying young" (*Joan of Lorraine: A Play in Two Acts* [Washington, D.C.: Anderson House, 1947], 127).

My prayer is that we will be true.

> *True to the faith that our parents have cherished,*
> *True to the truth for which martyrs have perished,*
> *To God's command,*
> *Soul, heart, and hand,*
> *Faithful and true we will ever stand.*
> (*Hymns*, no. 254)

Mark D. Ogletree lives in McKinney, Texas, with his wife, Janie, and their seven children: Brittany, Brandon, Bethany, McKenzie, Madison, Cassidy, and Callie. He is the director of the Plano Texas Institute of Religion, and is a family counselor with LDS Family Services. He holds a bachelor's degree from Brigham Young University, a master's degree from Northern Arizona University, and a doctorate from Utah State University. He enjoys racquetball, soft-ball, and being a dad.

14

LIKE UNTO THE SONS OF MOSIAH

Steve Adams

The sons of Mosiah—Ammon, Aaron, Omner, and Himni—have been some of my greatest heroes since the first time I read about their incredible adventures and missionary experiences. A poster of Ammon defending the flocks of king Lamoni hung on my wall from my Primary days. I used to pretend to be one of the four sons of king Mosiah and would relive their adventures of bringing thousands of Lamanites back into the kingdom of God. I remember looking at that picture and dreaming of the days when I would have the privilege of donning the "Black Name Tag" and serving a full-time mission. I never thought that day would come and now, in what seems the blink of an eye, I have been home from my mission for fourteen years, the same amount of time Ammon and his brothers served. As I look back, it seems like such a brief moment in time; but what an incredible influence it had on my life!

Our promise to help all of our brothers and sisters enjoy the blessings of the gospel was eloquently expressed by Elder John A. Widtsoe: "In our preexistent state, in the day of the great council, we made a certain agreement with the Almighty. The Lord proposed a plan, conceived by him. We accepted it. Since the plan is intended for all men, we became parties to the salvation of every person under that plan. We agreed, right then and there, to be not only saviors for ourselves but measurably, saviors for the whole human family. We went into a partnership with the Lord. The working out of the plan became then not merely the Father's work, and the Savior's work, but also our work. The least of us, the humblest, is in partnership with the Almighty in achieving the purpose of the eternal plan of salvation"

("The Worth of Souls," in *Utah Genealogical and Historical Magazine*, Oct. 1934, 189).

We all promised our Heavenly Father to do our best to help all of our brothers and sisters return safely home to Father and receive all that he has to offer.

WHO SHOULD SERVE

If you are a young woman and do not plan to go on a mission, I hope you will still read this chapter and not tune out, feeling that this subject does not apply to you. The principles ascribed to mission preparation will bless everyone's life, whether they choose to serve or not. The Prophet Joseph Smith said, "After all that has been said, the greatest and most important duty is to preach the Gospel" (*History of The Church of Jesus Christ of Latter-day Saints*, 7 vols. 2d ed. rev., ed. B. H. Roberts [Salt Lake City: The Church of Jesus Christ of Latter-day Saints, 1932–51], 2:478). It is everyone's duty and privilege to share this glorious gospel with the entire world. Whether you have been called to serve or not, you can be a missionary every day of your life.

I believe it is *as important* for young women to practice the principles of missionary preparation as it is for young men, even if the young woman chooses not to serve a mission. The principles associated with mission preparation, if lived, will do nothing but make young women better people, better wives, better mothers, and better servants in the Lord's kingdom.

President Gordon B. Hinckley clarified for young women that the choice to serve a mission is theirs. He stated: "There seems to be growing in the Church an idea that all young women as well as all young men should go on missions. We need some young women. They perform a remarkable work. They can get in homes where the elders cannot. . . . I wish to say that the First Presidency and the Council of the Twelve are united in saying to our young sisters that they are not under obligation to go on missions. I hope I can say what I have to say in a way that will not be offensive to anyone. Young women should not feel that they have a duty comparable to that of young men. Some of them will very much wish to go. If so, they should counsel with their bishop as well as their parents. If the idea persists, the bishop will know what to do" ("Some Thoughts on Temples, Retention of Converts, and Missionary Service," *Ensign*, Nov. 1997, 52).

A full-time mission can be one of the most wonderful and rewarding adventures in life. My mission did more to prepare me for service in the

Lord's kingdom for the rest of my life than perhaps anything else. It helped me build my foundation (Matthew 7:24–28) on a solid rock (Helaman 5:12) of faith. It was definitely the best two years of my life up until that point, and prepared me to more fully understand, live, and apply the principles of this glorious gospel so that every year that passes now becomes the best year of my life.

President Ezra Taft Benson gave exceptional counsel on the importance of preparing to serve a mission and included a formula for preparing young men to perform miracles in the Lord's service:

"Yes, prepare well for a mission all your life, not just six months or a year before you go.

"We love all of our missionaries who are serving the Lord full time in the mission field. But there is a difference in missionaries. Some are better prepared to serve the Lord the first month in the mission field than some who are returning home after twenty-four months.

"We want young men entering the mission field who can enter the mission field 'on the run,' who have the faith born of personal righteousness and clean living so that they can have a great and productive mission.

"We want missionaries who have the kind of faith that Wilford Woodruff and Heber C. Kimball had, each bringing hundreds and thousands of souls into the waters of baptism.

"Give me a young man who has kept himself morally clean and has faithfully attended his Church meetings. Give me a young man who has magnified his priesthood and has earned the Duty to God Award and is an Eagle Scout. Give me a young man who is a seminary graduate and has a burning testimony of the Book of Mormon. Give me such a young man, and I will give you a young man who can perform miracles for the Lord in the mission field and throughout his life" ("To the 'Youth of the Noble Birthright,'" *Ensign*, May 1986, 45).

TYPES OF MISSION PREPARATION

I currently serve as the stake mission president and work with numerous missionaries. I have seen the difference between missionaries who are prepared and those who are not. Preparation precedes power. I love to look to the Savior as our example to provide the pattern for mission preparation. The only New Testament verse that describes Jesus' life between the ages of thirteen and thirty, when he was preparing for his mission, is Luke 2:52, which states, "And Jesus increased in wisdom and stature, and in favour with God and man." This scripture illustrates four areas in which the Savior prepared for his divine mission; all future missionaries should strive to improve in these areas.

Stature, or Physical Preparation. One of the most important aspects of missionary work is just that—work! Every future missionary needs to learn how to work. Even though your mission will be the best two years of your life up to that point, it certainly won't be the easiest two years. There is much of hard work and discipline involved. Many different mission presidents have echoed this comment from President Benson as they have discussed with me their best missionaries:

"One of the greatest secrets of missionary work is work! If a missionary works, he will get the Spirit; if he gets the Spirit, he will teach by the Spirit; and if he teaches by the Spirit, he will touch the hearts of the people and he will be happy. There will be no homesickness, no worrying about families, for all time and talents and interests are centered on the work of the ministry. Work, work, work—there is no satisfactory substitute, especially in missionary work" (*The Teachings of Ezra Taft Benson* [Salt Lake City: Bookcraft, 1988], 200).

Missionary work is physically taxing. It may require that you walk or ride bikes for miles in freezing and/or blazing temperatures. You need to be in good physical condition to excel during your service. You will be stretched, and you will push yourself to bounds you didn't think possible. A mission grinds you down to the very elements of which you are made, and then proceeds to rebuild you bigger, better, and stronger than ever before.

Follow the counsel described in Doctrine and Covenants 88:124, which states, "Cease to be idle; cease to be unclean; cease to find fault one with another; cease to sleep longer than is needful; retire to thy bed early, that ye may not be weary; arise early, that your bodies and your minds may be invigorated."

Establishing the habit of rising early is a key element to success on a mission. It is during the morning hours that you will spend time in scripture study, which will help qualify you for revelation to guide your day. There is spiritual strength that comes when one masters the enticements of the flesh.

Begin a program to save money so that you can pay for your own mission, or at least a significant portion of it. Those missionaries who have invested in their own missions tend to value their time in the field a little more. The principle of sacrifice is real, and those who are willing to sacrifice financially in preparation for their missions will reap the blessings associated therein. The cost of a full-time mission is around ten thousand dollars for twenty-four months of service. That's a lot of money to acquire in a short amount of time. If, however, you acquire it week by week over the first nineteen years of your life, it is only $10.12 a week. That doesn't seem nearly as intimidating. You will be grateful you prepared.

Favour with Man, or Social Preparation. One of the most important skills a missionary can develop is the ability to get along with people. You can practice those skills now by learning to get along with parents, siblings, family, friends, teachers, Church leaders, coaches, advisors, counselors, or administrators. These are skills that can be learned. Even if you struggle with them now, through prayer, patience, and practice you can learn to make them a pleasant part of your personality. (Just remember those P's.)

You will be assigned a companion with whom you will live, cook, clean, work, serve, teach, and be with twenty-four hours a day, seven days a week. Some companions will be your best friends, and you will return home from your missions, room together in college, and be friends for eternity. Others will not be quite so easy to get along with and may even try your patience and charity to the penultimate degree. Both types of companions will teach you a great deal. Whether it comes from the companion you want to emulate or the one who has the attributes you never want to become part of your character, there is always a lesson to be learned. Some lessons are learned with joy, others with sorrow (Jacob 4:3). Just make sure you are the one that brings joy and happiness to the life of others rather than becoming the teacher of patience, endurance, and long-suffering.

Social skills are very important for an ambassador of the Lord. Do you know how to carry on a conversation with adults? Are you comfortable going into the home of someone you don't know particularly well and carrying on an intelligible conversation? Home teaching and the collection of fast offerings will go a long way into the development of those skills. Do you have adequate table manners? Do you sit down and eat a meal without making everyone else in the room lose their appetite or lunch? Do you know how to resolve conflict? Do you maturely handle disagreements and differences (because there will be some) or do you throw tantrums that make two-year-olds jealous? All of these skills will be needed for successful companionships and will be applied in your future marriage companionship as well.

Wisdom, or Intelligence. As I have reviewed President Gordon B. Hinckley's counsel to the youth of today, I have been amazed at how often he mentions the importance of education. One of the six "B's" from his special fireside with the youth last November was "be smart." He impressed upon our minds the need for education, especially in our competitive era of vast technology:

"All around you is competition. You need all the education you can get. Sacrifice a car; sacrifice anything that is needed to be sacrificed to qualify yourselves to do the work of the world. That world will in large measure pay you what it thinks you are worth, and your worth will increase as you gain education and proficiency in your chosen field.

" . . . You have a mandate from the Lord to educate your minds and your hearts and your hands" ("A Prophet's Counsel and Prayer for Youth," *New Era*, Jan. 2001, 8).

Another important tactic of preparation is the discipline and training of the mind through memorization. Elder Richard G. Scott, one of our current apostles, said: "I suggest that you memorize scriptures that touch your heart and fill your soul with understanding. When scriptures are used as the Lord has caused them to be recorded, they have intrinsic power that is not communicated when paraphrased. Sometimes when there is a significant need in my life, I review mentally scriptures that have given me strength. There is great solace, direction, and power that flow from the scriptures, especially the words of the Lord" ("He Lives," *Ensign*, Nov. 1999, 87–88).

Do you practice memorizing verses of scripture or great literature? President Hinckley's father used to reward him monetarily for memorizing specific scriptures, writings, and poetry. Have you memorized the seminary scripture mastery verses? I guarantee you will use those on your mission and throughout the rest of your life. I used to invite former students of mine to speak to my seminary classes upon returning from their missions. Without question the most frequent comment went something like, "I wish I had learned my scripture mastery scriptures better and listened a little more closely in class." Don't waste this precious preparation time! You will have much to learn before, during, and after your mission, but the more you learn now, the better! It is just like the principle taught in Doctrine and Covenants 130:18–19 (Have you noticed all the scripture mastery verses used in this book?); you will have so much the advantage on your mission.

Favour with God, or Spirituality. The most important area of mission preparation is spiritual preparation—that relationship between Deity and us. Can you imagine the Savior ever forgetting to check in with his Father at least every morning and night? Do you think he ever missed a day of scripture study? Do you think he ever skipped his Sabbath-day meetings because he had more important things to do or just didn't feel like going that day? Do you think he took time to serve others even when it wasn't real convenient? We often want to excuse our unrighteous behavior, but the Savior taught us, "Therefore, what manner of men ought ye to be? Verily I say unto you, even as I am" (3 Nephi 27:27). Even though we do fall short in all areas, we should always be striving our best to follow his example. Becoming like him is a process we must never give up on.

As I reflected upon what made the sons of Mosiah such great and powerful missionaries, I first erroneously thought it was because they had seen the angel with Alma the Younger and witnessed that incredible heavenly manifestation. But as I read the scriptures more closely I realized the real reason for the success they experienced on their fourteen-year mission to the Lamanites:

"Yea, and they had waxed strong in the knowledge of the truth; for they were men of a sound understanding and they had searched the scriptures diligently, that they might know the word of God. But this is not all; they had given themselves to much prayer, and fasting; therefore they had the spirit of prophecy, and the spirit of revelation, and when they taught, they taught with power and authority of God" (Alma 17:2–3).

They "searched the scriptures diligently." What a powerful impact the scriptures can have on our lives, *if* we will let them! If our goal is to know the Savior and become like the Savior, and he is the author of the scriptures, can we expect to intimately know the author without reading his books? President Hinckley recently stated:

"Faith in the Lord, Jesus Christ—I hope there is no one here today who isn't constantly cultivating that faith through reading the scriptures—the New Testament, the Book of Mormon, the Doctrine and Covenants—and building the faith which he or she carries in his heart, concerning the Son of God, our Redeemer and our Lord" (*Church News*, 25 Apr. 1998, 2).

In like manner, President Benson said: "It is not just that the Book of Mormon teaches us truth, though it indeed does that. It is not just that the Book of Mormon bears testimony of Christ, though it indeed does that, too. But there is something more. There is a power in the book which will begin to flow into your lives the moment you begin a serious study of the book. You will find greater power to resist temptation. You will find the power to avoid deception. You will find the power to stay on the strait and narrow path" ("The Book of Mormon—Keystone of Our Religion," *Ensign*, Nov. 1986, 7).

The second principle mentioned in Mormon's description of the sons of Mosiah is prayer. Do we pray daily? If not, who are we listening to (2 Nephi 32:8–9)? Do we pray morning and night (Alma 37:36–37)? Do we pour out our souls to him and constantly have a prayer in our hearts (3 Nephi 20:1)? President Hinckley has admonished us in this regard:

"Believe in prayer and the power of prayer. Pray to the Lord with the expectation of answers. I suppose there is not a man or woman in this entire congregation today who doesn't pray. I hope that is so. The trouble with most of our prayers is that we give them as if we were picking up the telephone and ordering groceries—we place our order and hang up. We need to meditate, contemplate, think of what we are praying about and for and then speak to the Lord as one man speaketh to another. 'Come now, and let us reason together, saith the Lord' (Isa. 1:18). That is the invitation. Believe in the power of prayer—it is real, it is wonderful, it is tremendous" (*Teachings of Gordon B. Hinckley* [Salt Lake City: Deseret Book, 1997], 469).

Fasting is another principle mentioned in Alma 17 that brings spiritual power into our lives. President Kimball spoke of the blessings of fasting with these remarks: "This principle of promise, when lived in the spirit thereof, greatly blesses both giver and receiver. Upon practicing the law of the fast, one finds a personal well-spring of power to overcome self-indulgence and selfishness" ("Becoming the Pure in Heart," *Ensign*, May 1978, 80).

On another occasion, he said, "If we give a generous fast offering, we shall increase our own prosperity both spiritually and temporally" ("Welfare Services: The Gospel in Action," *Ensign*, Nov. 1977, 79).

I know that fasting has played an important role in blessing my life and the lives of others. It acts as an energy source. It provides focus, strength, discipline, and power to our common daily efforts. I love to read from Isaiah 58 concerning the true law of the fast, with its attendant blessings. It is amazing to read all the things promised to those who apply this doctrine in their lives. I challenge you to read it and underline all the promises found therein. It makes skipping two meals a whole lot easier and more desirable when I see it from an eternal perspective.

The final counsel I would share in regards to spirituality is to be clean and pure (Psalm 24:3–4). There is a power in purity that blesses the life of the obedient soul. Elder Kimball taught it this way: "Another error into which some transgressors fall, because of the availability of God's forgiveness, is the illusion that they are somehow stronger for having committed sin and then lived through the period of repentance. This simply is not true.

That man who resists temptation and lives without sin is far better off than the man who has fallen, no matter how repentant the latter may be. The reformed transgressor, it is true, may be more understanding of one who falls into the same sin, and to that extent perhaps more helpful in the latter's regeneration. But his sin and repentance have certainly not made him stronger than the consistently righteous person" (*The Miracle of Forgiveness* [Salt Lake City: Bookcraft, 1969], 357).

Follow the counsel of God's prophets, and you will be blessed and remain pure. Trusting the Lord and his servants will always bless your life. Our Father in Heaven wants only your happiness, and he has clearly marked that path through the standards he has set. "Wickedness never was happiness" (Alma 41:10), and the ultimate happiness comes from obedience to our Heavenly Father (Mosiah 2:41). You can't do wrong and feel right.

The Lord knew we would make mistakes along our mortal journey and provided a way for us to become clean. We are not perfect, but we can become clean. Through the incredible gift of our Savior Jesus Christ and his atonement, we can be washed clean from the filth of this world. He is willing to share his perfection with us (Moroni 10:32–33). By following the proper steps of repentance, feeling "godly sorrow" (2 Corinthians 7:10), and manifesting a broken heart and a contrite spirit (D&C 20:37), we can know that we are once again clean. If you are not sure you have taken the proper steps, counsel with your bishop. He is the Lord's chosen servant to help you become clean and declare your worthiness before God in those sacred interviews.

By worthily partaking of the sacrament we are cleansed; that is why it is so necessary to attend church weekly. I know that I make enough mistakes during the week that I am always in need of a good cleansing. The sacrament, when partaken of worthily, provides the needed spiritual "soap and water" to make us clean again. Don't let Satan prey on your feelings of guilt and unworthiness. His only goal is to make you as miserable as he is (2 Nephi 2:27). Satan wants you to hide and suffer, but the Savior wants you to come unto him (Matthew 11:28–30) and be healed and cleansed (Isaiah 1:18; D&C 58:42–43). Again, there is no better feeling than to know that you are clean!

In summary, one of the most important preparations we will ever make is to prepare to be missionaries. The principles and skills developed will follow us throughout our lifetime and be a constant blessing in our lives. The Savior's life exemplifies specific areas that we can develop to become more like him—physically, intellectually, socially, and spiritually. By following his example, we can prepare to be the types of missionaries with whom the Lord can perform miracles. We can teach with the same power, authority, revelation, and prophesy that the sons of Mosiah had on their missions. We can bless thousands of lives and have the same feelings of love and compassion for our converts that Ammon expressed in Alma chapter 26. We can be like unto the sons of Mosiah.

Steve Adams served in the Washington Spokane Spanish Speaking Mission. Upon his return, he worked a counselor at Especially for Youth for four years. He received a bachelor's degree in psychology from the University of Utah, a master's degree in youth leadership from Brigham Young University, and a Ph.D. in sociology from BYU. Steve is the institute director at Wichita State University and serves on the high council and as stake mission president in his stake. He met his wife at EFY, when they were both counselors. They are now the parents of three children. He loves all sports and outdoor activities and, above all, enjoys spending time with his family.

15

THE GREAT PLAN OF HAPPINESS

Steven T. Linford

OK, I'll admit it. I was a fashion king in junior high and high school. In seventh grade I had a cool-looking green-, orange-, and brown-striped shirt. I loved this shirt so much that I wore it three days in a row (and may have worn it four days had I not overheard some girls talking about me and my shirt). Furthermore, I had the finest-looking, rust-colored corduroy suit complete with vest and bell bottoms that I wore to church each Sunday. Combining my suit with my triple-wide tie and platform-type shoes made me something to behold! A true fashion king.

I'm not sure when the "smiley face" came out, but when it did, it was very popular. These faces could be found on hats, pants, socks, and ties. I remember T-shirts of various colors and styles sporting the big yellow face. I loved the smiley face because it served as a reminder of peace and happiness. I wonder if one of the reasons it was so popular is because deep down inside everyone wants to be happy.

Take it from a former fashion king, I know where true happiness is found. It is not found in striped shirts, or in rust-colored corduroy suits, or even in "smiley face" apparel. True happiness is found only in living, with excellence, our Heavenly Father's plan—the great plan of happiness. As we righteously strive to live and follow our Heavenly Father's plan, we can and should expect to experience great happiness.

The Prophet Joseph Smith taught: "Happiness is the object and design of our existence; and will be the end thereof, if we pursue the path that leads to it; and this path is virtue, uprightness, faithfulness, holiness, and keeping all the commandments of God" (*Teachings of the Prophet Joseph Smith*, sel. Joseph Fielding Smith [Salt Lake City: Deseret Book, 1976], 255–56).

Perhaps you have heard the saying, "Happiness is not a destination it is a journey." Well, according to Joseph Smith, it is also a destination. In other words, as we stay on the path of virtue, uprightness, faithfulness, holiness, and obedience in our mortal journey, we will experience great happiness. Imagine the joy we will experience as we stay on this path and reach our final destination—eternal life in the presence of our Heavenly Father and Jesus Christ, forever as families.

I left to serve my mission to Milan, Italy, on June 3, 19?? (I know if I wrote the exact year you would just think something like, *Wow, I was only three months old when he went on his mission* or, even better, something like, *Wow, I wasn't even born when he left.* So I won't tell you the year.) One of the first discussions I learned in the Missionary Training Center was about the plan of salvation. This discussion began with three questions: Da dove sono venuto? Perche sono qui sulla terra? Dove andro quando questa vita sara finita? Now, repeat these questions as fast as you can three times. In English these questions are: Where did I come from? Why am I here on the earth? and Where will I go when this life is finished?

Let's take a closer look at these three questions. First, Where did I come from? In the premortal life, we were spiritually begotten by Heavenly Father and are literally his spirit sons and daughters. We have all heard the saying, "Remember who you are!" Recently I heard someone change this to, "Remember whose you are!" You are a child of God, and he loves and cares about you. Our Heavenly Father desires that we remain close to him so he can bless us, guide us, and help us. His work and glory is to have us return home to live with him someday.

There are many other things we know about our premortal life from the scriptures (see Alma 12; Moses 4; Abraham 3). For example, there was a Grand Council held wherein Heavenly Father presented his plan. Heavenly Father chose Jesus to be our Savior. Lucifer desired to be the Savior; but he wanted to destroy our agency and sought to obtain our Father's glory. This caused a war in heaven in which Lucifer rebelled and was cast out with his followers. You supported Heavenly Father's plan and were among the most righteous of our Heavenly Father's sons and daughters (see *The Teachings of Ezra Taft Benson* [Salt Lake City: Bookcraft, 1988], 554–55).

Now, on to the second question, Why am I here on the earth? One of the main reasons we came to earth is to be tested—to demonstrate our faithfulness even during times of adversity. A young man I taught last year exemplifies one who is striving to faithfully pass this test. We will call him Ben Smith.

Let me describe Ben to you. He is an intense young man—bright, enthusiastic, good-looking (according to girls), confident, and definitely cool. I asked Ben to be my seminary class president. I grew to love him in just a short period of time. He is quick-witted, loves to laugh, and, like Nephi of old, delights in studying the gospel in depth.

Last spring, our seminary conducted a service project for a small struggling school in Africa. We raised money and school supplies that were later shipped over to this school. Ben worked hard each day trying to motivate us to donate more supplies and money. One day, a day I'll never forget, he brought in a glass container full of quarters. He said we needed to improve, that we needed to be more unselfish. Then, without warning, he pulled out a hammer and hit the glass. The jar shattered. Ben reached in and pulled out a fist full of quarters and, while raising his fist in the air, told us we needed to do better. Needless to say, the class was very generous that day.

On the last day of school, Ben came to the seminary, found me, and said, "I'm taking you to lunch today, and I'm going to pay."

I said, "Ben, you don't have to pay. I should pay for you."

Ben responded with increased determination, "No, Brother Linford, this one's on me, I'm going to pay."

Realizing I was not going to win this battle, I replied, "OK, let's go." We walked out to his old, large, long, and rusty car. This car was huge. If it were a boat it would be the Queen Mary. Well, the door handle didn't work on my side of the car, so Ben had to open it from inside. As I got into his car, he looked at me and said, "Brother Linford, you won't believe this, but I paid thirty bucks for this car."

I smiled and said, "I believe it," I mean I said, "Wow, what a great deal!"

We went to the restaurant, were seated, and began looking at the menu. Ben looked at me and said, "You need to have the Cajun chicken. It is the best."

"OK," I responded, "Cajun chicken sounds great."

As the waiter approached the table, Ben said, "Hey, this is my seminary teacher. Take good care of him."

As we were waiting for our meal, Ben looked at me and said, "Brother Linford, have I ever told you about my background?"

I told him he hadn't.

He continued, "You know I don't live at home any more, right?"

I responded that I did.

Ben continued, "Brother Linford, when I was young my parents divorced. To this day my mother and father hate each other, refuse to talk to each other, and can't stand to be in the same room. My father stopped going to church. In fact, none of my brothers or sisters go. My father turned to alcohol and has rarely had a job. My family has lived in poverty and has been on welfare most of my life. We lived in a run-down home under terrible conditions. One night my father became angry and told me to leave. I have been living with other families ever since."

As I listened to this tragic story, I finally replied, "Ben, how have you been able to deal with such difficult circumstances? You seem to be doing so well."

Without hesitation, Ben responded, "It's the gospel." He went on, "When I was in ninth grade I was making a lot of poor choices; I was doing a lot of things that were wrong. But, I felt terrible inside. I decided to live the gospel. That is the only way I've been able to make it—living the gospel and staying close to Heavenly Father and Jesus." Ben then shifted to talking about the excitement he felt in anticipation of receiving the Melchizedek Priesthood, attending the temple, and serving a mission. As he spoke I thought of my gratitude for the gospel and the strength it gives us in dealing with trials and adversity.

Besides being tested, other purposes of this life include obtaining a body, making and keeping covenants, proving our faithfulness in keeping the commandments, using our agency wisely, and resisting temptations and overcoming sin (see Abraham 3:25; D&C 98:11–12; D&C 136:31). We need to try our best to pass the test of mortality, relying completely on the Lord and his atoning sacrifice.

Life is so short and, yet, so much is riding on what we do here. President Boyd K. Packer taught, "Mortal life is temporary and, measured against eternity, infinitesimally brief. If a microscopic droplet of water should represent the length of mortal life, by comparison all the oceans on earth put together would not even begin to represent everlasting life" ("The Moving of the Water," *Ensign*, May 1991, 9).

Think about it. A droplet of water placed on a glass slide under a microscope represents the time we spend here on earth, which, when compared to all the oceans of the earth, doesn't even come close to representing eternity. And yet, so much of what we enjoy in eternity is determined by what we do here in mortality. Alma 34:32–33 reads, "For behold, this life is the time for men to prepare to meet God; yea, behold the day of this life is the day for men to perform their labors.

"And now, as I said unto you before, as ye have had so many witnesses, therefore, I beseech of you that ye do not procrastinate the day of your repentance until the end; for after this day of life, which is given us to prepare for eternity, behold, if we do not improve our time while in this life, then cometh the night of darkness wherein there can be no labor performed." It is so important that we don't waste valuable time in doing things that distance us from God. But we must focus on preparing to meet him.

The third question—Where will I go when this life is finished?—was a concern of Alma's son Corianton in the Book of Mormon (Alma 39–42). Corianton had sinned and was deeply concerned about his eternal welfare; therefore, Alma taught him about repentance, death, judgment, and resurrection. Part of the challenge of the test of mortality is not knowing when it will end—we never know when we will pass from this life.

I met a young woman, Katie, a few years ago at a square-dancing activity in our ward. Katie was a sweet young woman. She had a warm, contagious smile and was so cheerful and happy. I noticed she would often come to church alone or with her younger sister. She was always so friendly and genuinely nice to everyone (even to me).

A few months after the square-dancing activity, I was invited to be a "priesthood man" at girls' camp. (Now, I need to issue a warning at this stage of the story. Never, ever, I mean, never, ever, trust a young woman at girl's camp. These girls might look innocent, they might give the impression they can be trusted, but they can't. Learn from my experience, they are wolves in sheep's clothing. Now, with that precaution in place, I will continue the story.) On this particular day, as I arrived at girls' camp, I was greeted by at least ten innocent-looking girls. It was obvious they were having a great time at camp. They excitedly escorted me into their camp and offered me a plate of Oreo cookies. Well, I love cookies. There is something about putting them in my mouth, chewing them, and swallowing them that I really enjoy. I took one of the cookies and bit right into it. As soon as I bit into the cookie, the cunning girls started laughing hysterically. I moved the cookie around in my mouth to get a good taste of the delicious cream flavor. But much to my astonishment, I quickly determined that the cream filling had been mischievously removed and replaced with—no, not toothpaste—shaving cream. It tasted like menthol, or maybe cologne-scented, either way it was hideous! I quickly expectorated (polite word for spit) the substance from my mouth and began looking for any beverage that would wash this horrendous taste away. And these girls, the girls I once trusted, the girls I once loved, these telestial girls, couldn't stop laughing. Again, learn from me, never, ever, I mean, never, ever, trust girls at girls' camp.

After a while I forgave these girls and actually began enjoying time with them. Following a fireside and a session of sharing scary stories, I climbed into my little tent, crawled into my sleeping bag, and fell asleep. The following morning I got up and found myself ambushed by the young women. It was me against them in a pinecone fight. I want you to know that I battled them like a fierce warrior and held my own for approximately five seconds until they completely annihilated me. Shortly after the war we ate something that resembled breakfast and I then departed for home. As I pulled out of camp, I waved to Katie, who was standing by the campfire. I did not know that I would never see her alive again.

That weekend, as the result of a tragic accident, Katie died. I learned of the accident early Sunday morning when my bishop and his first counselor came to my home. They told me the news and invited me to come to a meeting with the youth later that day. I went to the meeting, and we talked with the youth about the plan of salvation. Later, the bishop called and said Katie's family had asked if I would speak at her funeral. I accepted and then drove to Katie's house to offer my condolences and to begin my preparation for the talk. Once I arrived, I expressed my love and concern to her family and asked if Katie had kept a journal. Her mother said she had faithfully kept one. I asked if I could borrow it and use it in preparation for my remarks. Katie's mother excused herself and shortly returned with her journal. I thanked them and left. Once I returned home, I opened the journal to the last entry. This entry was written a few days before the accident and reads:

"My Testimony: (I hate to say it out loud)

"I know this church is true w/ all my heart and soul (how can anyone not)! I want to be perfect so badly—I don't want to not be able to see my Heavenly Father (ever) I can't stand that thought—he is my best friend—he knows every thing about me. I know that Jesus is my (our) Savior. And I love him so much. I want to be with them so bad right now so I can just skip over the hard trials, but I know it's for my own good!"

Then, in the vintage teenage style that I love, were written the last three words in her journal: "*I love Troy.*" She had a crush on a boy named Troy.

There's no doubt in my mind that Katie had been prompted to leave her testimony to her family and friends. And, certainly, because of the righteous way she had lived her life, she would live with Heavenly Father and Jesus again. I shared her last journal entry with the congregation at the funeral. Her written words brought peace to troubled souls as did the knowledge of the plan of salvation.

In Doctrine and Covenants 42:46 we read that when the righteous die, it is sweet unto them. They are freed from the pains of this world. The separation is painful, but we can find peace in knowing that it is temporary. We will one day rejoin our departed loved ones.

My best friend in junior high school was Brian Anderson. In seventh grade I ran for seventh-grade vice president, and Brian was my campaign manager (we don't need to discuss the outcome of that race). Then, Brian ran for ninth-grade president, and I was his campaign manager (again the outcome of that race is irrelevant). In eighth- and ninth-grade basketball, the coach liked me better than Brian and so I sat next to the coach during most of the games while Brian played. In ninth-grade football, the coach liked Brian a little better than me, so Brian got to stand next to the coach more than I did during the games. Needless to say, we were great friends. Soon, after our ninth-grade year I received the bad news: my best friend, Brian Anderson, was moving with his family to Colorado. Now, speaking from experience, it is no fun to lose your best friend just before high school. We did everything we could think of to stop the move. We even tried hiding their "For Sale" sign by putting it in their neighbor's garage, but even that didn't work. Brian Anderson moved just weeks before our sophomore year in high school started. As the years passed I lost touch with him. After high school I attended college, worked, and prepared for my mission. I left for the Missionary Training Center on June 3, 19?? (you really didn't think I was going to write the year did you?).

It didn't take long to become friends with the missionaries who had also been called to serve in Italy. From the very first day we began an intense, but wonderful, study of the gospel, the language, and the Italian culture. I loved the MTC and had been there a month when the new missionaries arrived. We were all excited to meet the new "greenie" missionaries. On the day they arrived I was studying at my desk in my room. From my desk I looked down the long hall of our dorm and saw the new missionaries coming down the hall carrying their luggage and looking for their rooms. As I watched them, my eye caught one of them. I looked harder at a familiar looking missionary. As I was staring at him, I could see that he was staring back at me. Our eyes met. I pushed my chair back from my desk. He stopped walking. I stood up. He dropped his luggage. I started running towards him. He started running towards me. It was like a scene from an old romance movie where a couple runs towards each other in a beautiful meadow. I held out my arms. He held out his. We embraced. I said, "Brian, is that you?" The missionary responded, "No"—I mean, the missionary responded, "Yes! Steve is that you?" I said, "Yes!" It was Brian Anderson, my best friend from junior high. He said, "Where are you going on your mission?" I replied, "I'm going to Italy, Milan. Where are you going?" Brian answered, "I'm going to Italy, Milan!" Then we exclaimed simultaneously, "No way!" Brian looked at me and said, "How was high school?" Summarizing I said, "It was cool. How was high school for you?" He said, "Good." That was it, we had just summed up the last four years of our life by using short, simple sentences. Note: guys are good at this; girls, however, must take hours, days, weeks, even months and years to catch up on lost time.

Although there was a separation, almost four years in this case, we were still best friends. Time had not erased or diminished our friendship. Similarly, that is what happens when someone close to us dies. There is a painful separation, we mourn and miss the person. But the glorious day will come when we will be reunited again. We will catch up on lost time and we will feel the same closeness—perhaps greater—we felt during mortality.

In 2 Nephi 2:25 it reads, "Adam fell that men might be; and men are, that they might have *joy*" (emphasis added). If we want to be truly happy in this life, and in the life to come, then we must faithfully live the gospel and righteously follow the great plan of happiness.

Steven T. Linford is married to Melanie Coombs Linford and is the father of C.J., Kilee, and Kolby. The mascots of the schools he has attended or taught at include the Eagles, Vikings, Utes, Aggies, Cougars, Lions, and Dons. Brother Linford's favorite thing to do is to spend time with his family. He loves to lift weights, climb mountains, run 10k's, swim, and play any sport with a ball. He is the principal at the Spanish Fork Senior Seminary and teaches part time in the Department of Religious Education at Brigham Young University. Steve has served as bishop and currently serves on the stake high council.

16

HELPING PARENTS SUCCEED

Michael Weir Allred

I enjoyed being a teenager. But now I enjoy being a parent. One of my sons, a preschooler, had been asked by his teacher to give her some information about me, his dad. She wrote down his answers as he responded to the questions.

"What is your dad's favorite color?"

"Black," he said. And so the teacher wrote it down and moved to the next question.

"What's his favorite food?"

"Little tiny seed things." (His word for sunflower seeds.)

"OK. How old is he?"

"Twenty."

"Where does he work?"

"Seminary."

"How tall is he?"

"Seven feet."

"What's his favorite drink?"

"Milk."

"What makes him happy?"

"Coming home."

Wow! He hit the bull's-eye. Out of all the things I get to do, coming home is my favorite. And when I get home, he often runs up to me yelling, "Daddy!"

I love being a daddy.

I would like to share with you something that is dear to me, one of my favorite subjects. I would like to teach you how we can help our parents succeed.

Study these four practical tips for getting along better with your parents, then try following them and see what happens.

1—LIFE IS TOUGH, AND THEN YOU DIE

When life is tough for you, it is still tough on your parents. One of the misconceptions many of us seem to have is that when we become old, life becomes easy: there are no more trials and no more temptation. This is certainly not true. As parents, we still have weaknesses that we need to work on and overcome. And many times when things are bad in the home for you, they are bad for your parents. Just like you have bad days at school, they have bad days at work and at home. Life can be tough for everyone—young and old.

I read somewhere that there are four categories of feelings and concerns that every teenager experiences (see Alex J. Packer, *Bringing Up Parents: The Teenager's Handbook* [Minneapolis, Minn.: Free Spirit Pub., 1992], 17–21).

> *Number 1: Breaking away*—Teenagers want to break away from their parents and become independent.
> *Number 2: A sense of belonging*—Teenagers want to belong to something, to be part of a group.
> *Number 3: Physical bodies*—Teens start to notice their physical bodies and how they are developing, or not developing.
> *Number 4: A sense of becoming*—Teenagers discover that it's about time to decide what they are going to be. They start to get a little scared. They feel like they want to get out of school, but don't want to start working for the rest of their lives. (Does this sound familiar?)

The author also mentioned four categories into which fall the concerns of people in their forties (people like your parents).

> *Number 1: Breaking away*—Their children are beginning to break away from them, and it hurts.
> *Number 2: A sense of belonging*—Parents are, amazingly, still concerned about fitting in. "Do I fit in with the other Relief Society sisters?"
> *Number 3: Physical bodies*—Parents begin to feel the effects of aging. Sometimes we don't even know if we can make it a day without taking an antacid.

Number 4: A sense of becoming—Parents start to ask themselves, "Have I become what I once set out to become?"

Now, what's interesting about this is that these parent and teenage crises usually happen at the same time. (It must be part of a divine plan.) In other words, while you are going through teenage crises, guess what, your parents are going through midlife crises.

Breaking away. Have you ever been embarrassed to be with your parents? You know, parents can seem embarrassing at times. Now that I am older and I look back—to my tight, high-waisted bell-bottom jeans, platform shoes, and huge lapels on slick polyester shirts, with long hair to fit the fashion of the day—I realize that even though my dad loved me unconditionally, he might have been just a little embarrassed by me. In other words, while I might have been at times a little bit embarrassed by him, he was probably at times a little embarrassed by me.

Belonging. Have you ever gone on a trip with your parents and had them make you go to church, even though you knew nobody there? I remember as a kid thinking, "I don't know anybody." But guess what, now that I'm an adult, I still don't know anybody. But I still go. Our kids don't know anybody, and if they say they don't know anybody, I say, "Yeah, me too."

Physical bodies. My father had a lot of health problems when I was in my teenage years. But I had my own problems. It was my senior year of wrestling, first match of the year; we were wrestling a great team. My opponent took my arm and pulled it back farther than it can go. My shoulder popped out. To this day, I can't lift it up without it making a popping sound. My physical body had lost the match.

During this same period of time, my father had a massive heart attack and was unable to work again. So while I was worried about the teenage crises affecting my physical body, he was worried about the effects of a midlife crisis on his physical body. And his crisis wasn't going too well.

Sense of becoming. How does the question "What am I going to become?" compare to "Did I become what I wanted to become?"

Let me share an example from the scriptures about what happened when a father and son's crises met. You probably already know this story, but I want to teach you a different principle concerning Abraham and Isaac.

"And it came to pass after these things, that God did tempt Abraham, and said unto him, Abraham: and he said, Behold, here I am. And he said, Take now thy son, thine only son Isaac, whom thou lovest, and get thee into the land of Moriah; and offer him there for a burnt offering upon one of the mountains which I will tell thee of" (Genesis 22:1–2).

Out of all the people who abhor human sacrifice, perhaps it is Abraham who was most sickened by it. I'm sure he had not forgotten similar circumstances in his young life when he had been on the altar, ready to be sacrificed to false gods by wicked priests. Abraham's life had been spared because Jehovah himself had appeared to rescue him. Now, after many years of prayer, he and his wife finally have a son, whom Abraham is asked to take and offer up as a human sacrifice.

"And Abraham rose up early in the morning" (v. 3). I wonder why he rose up early? I wonder if he couldn't sleep?

"And Abraham took the wood of the burnt offering, and laid it upon Isaac his son; and he took the fire in his hand, and a knife; and they went both of them together.

"And Isaac spoke unto Abraham his father, and said, My father: and he said, Here am I, my son. And he said, Behold the fire and the wood: but where is the lamb for a burnt offering?

"And Abraham said, My son, God will provide himself a lamb for a burnt offering: so they went both of them together.

"And they came to the place which God had told him of; and Abraham built an altar there, and laid the wood in order, and bound Isaac his son" (vv. 6–9).

I believe Isaac was old enough to push his dad down and run away. Abraham was, after all, an old man by now. Certainly Isaac was man enough that he could have gotten away, but he was also spiritual enough that he obeyed his father.

Can you see that when Isaac's dad was having a hard time, someone else was too? It was not a good day for Isaac. It was not a good day for Abraham. Life was tough on both of them.

Being a parent is not necessarily easy because your choices now affect your children, not just yourself. Elder Howard W. Hunter said, "Even though parents strive to choose wisely, an unwise choice will sometimes be made. . . . We should remember that errors of judgment are generally less serious than errors of intent" ("Parents' Concern for Children," *Ensign*, Nov. 1983, 64).

What should you do if your parents make a poor choice with good intent? You should honor them and obey them. Then when you become a parent, you can be more wise—having learned from another's mistake—and make a different choice. But errors of judgment are less serious than errors of intent. Honor your parents.

2—ONE GOOD TURN DESERVES ANOTHER

I had a student who one day said, "My parents are going to Utah for the weekend. And I don't want to go. I just want to stay home all by myself and they won't let me."

"Have you talked to your parents?" I asked.

"No. I just know that they won't let me," my young student replied.

"Talk to them," I said, "tell them how you feel."

So, he came back to school the next day and said, "Guess what? They are going to let me stay home, by myself."

"That is so cool," I said, "good job. Make sure you do everything they said."

When the weekend was over I heard about the party. The police had been called. Do you think the next time Mom and Dad are going out of town that they will let him stay home by himself? No. Because one good turn deserves another. Had that young man listened to his parents and shown himself to be honorable and dependable, then the next time he may have been offered a little bit more freedom, and the next year a little bit more, until one day he was in total control of his own life. But control doesn't come instantly. And it doesn't come when we are making poor choices.

Consider the life of the Savior.

"And when he was twelve years old, they went up to Jerusalem after the custom of the feast.

"And when they had fulfilled the days, as they returned, the child Jesus tarried behind in Jerusalem; and Joseph and his mother knew not of it.

"But they, supposing him to have been in the company, went a day's journey; and they sought him among their kinsfolk and acquaintance.

"And when they found him not, they turned back again to Jerusalem, seeking him.

"And it came to pass, that after three days they found him in the temple, sitting in the midst of the doctors, both hearing them, and asking them questions.

"And all that heard him were astonished at his understanding and answers.

"And when they saw him, they were amazed: and his mother said unto him, Son, why hast thou thus dealt with us?" (Luke 2:42–48).

Now, if Jesus is perfect, and even his mother said, "Why did you do that?" isn't it logical that we, being imperfect, would once in a while cause our parents to say, "Why hast thou thus dealt with us?"

Our parents will logically be a bit nervous about us once in a while. Look at what happened next: "And he [the Creator of heaven and earth, the Son of God, the Redeemer of all worlds] went down with them, and came to Nazareth, and was subject unto them" (v. 51). Even though he was their Creator and Redeemer, he was a teenager—or at least he was at the beginning of his teenage years—and he was subject unto them. This is the will of the Lord. For a second witness of this principle, look at Colossians 3:20. It reads, "Children, obey your parents in all things: for this is well pleasing unto the Lord."

It's possible that you are more spiritual than they are. You might know so much more, but you are still the child and under the command of God; you must honor them and obey them. And if you think that that's tough, wait until you are the one to be honored and obeyed and hopefully never make a mistake.

Elder Dallin H. Oaks said, "Young people, if you honor your parents, you will love them, respect them, confide in them, be considerate of them, express appreciation for them, and demonstrate all of these things by following their counsel in righteousness and by obeying the commandments of God" ("Honour Thy Father and Thy Mother," *Ensign*, May 1991, 15).

Because it is vital to honor them, here are a few tools of the trade.

Have you ever had a situation like this in your home: Mom says, "Steve, take out the garbage!"

You say, "OK, Mom, soon as it's a commercial." Four hours later, you are in trouble for not taking out the garbage. Have you ever been accused of being disobedient, when you had really only been forgetful?

Tool #1: Do it as soon as possible.

Whenever your parents ask you to do something, do it as soon as possible. You are going to do it anyway, so you might as well do it as soon as possible and not take the chance that you'll forget about it.

How about this one? Mom says, "Steve, take out the garbage."

You say, "OK, Mom." And you take out the garbage. Later on that night someone else does something wrong, and Mom or Dad gets upset and says,

"Nobody does anything around here." But you do—you took out the garbage.

Tool #2: Learn to return and report.

Say, "Mom, I took out the garbage." You see, parents sometimes forget too. Remember, parents are imperfect people just like you. We sometimes need to remind them of all the good that we do. It doesn't always work. In fact, sometimes the return and report leads to, "OK, now I want you to . . ." But you never know when their knowledge that you did something good will pay off.

A lot of us have a difficult time with the next one.

Mom says, "Steve, take out the garbage. Oh, and by the way, while you're out there, feed the horses, and then come in and empty the dishwasher."

You start thinking, "OK, I'm taking out the garbage and watering the horses and phew, shoot, I think I did it all." Right? And then you get in trouble because you didn't get one or two of the things done she had asked.

Tool #3: Prioritize.

While being asked to do a task, you hear, "Steve, take out the garbage and while you are out there, feed the horses and then . . ." At this point, ask your mom, "Which one's most urgent?" Then go out and do the task she said to do first. Then return and report and ask, "What would you like me to do next?" One of the reasons teens do not like to do it this way is because they think their parent will just keep telling them to do more and more. But the odds are, because you are reporting and reminding them of each task you do, that they will eventually say, "Well, you've done enough. Don't worry about it."

Here is another one. Your family has been on vacation three hundred miles from home. You're on the trip back, but still have one hundred miles to go when your father says, "Now, Steve, remember when we get home to take out the garbage."

You know you are going to fall asleep in the car, have three dreams, listen to your walkman, and be so tired by the time you get home that you just want to go straight to bed. How are you going to remember to take out the garbage?

Tool #4: Ask for reminders.

"Dad, when we get home will you please remind me to take out the garbage?"

Now if you forget, whose fault is it? You've invited a reminder. This way your parents will not have to remind you over and over again.

This next skill is my favorite. Have you heard something like this before?

"Lisa, do the dishes."

"It's not my turn."

"Do them anyway!"

"That's not fair!"

"Life's not fair."

These complaints don't work. They don't work because parents know how to answer all of them. So what do we do? How do we handle this situation?

Tool #5: Agree to do everything your parents ask.

Watch how well this works.

Mom says, "Lisa, do the dishes."

To which you calmly reply, "Mom, I'd be happy to help out Steve tonight."

Now what did you say in reality? "Yes, I'll do it, but it's not my turn, it's Steve's turn." You agreed, and in an agreeable way you mentioned whose turn it is.

Of course, there is a chance she might say, "Thank you for not talking back to me and for still doing the dishes." On the other hand, she might say, "That's right. Steve, get in here and do these dishes!" Be patient with yourselves and with your parents. They might be working on these skills too.

Tool #6: Apologize.

This tool is very important. Write this down on a big piece of paper, glue it to your mirror, and practice. Practice. Practice. Learn to apologize. Practice in front of the mirror. "Mom, I am way sorry." "Mom, please forgive me." "Dad, sorry."

Now, you have to give sincere apologies. They shouldn't be phony, sarcastic, or untrue.

What if you already have a damaged relationship? Spencer W. Kimball said, "Nothing we could give them [our parents] would be more prized than righteous living" (*The Teachings of Spencer W. Kimball*, ed. Edward L. Kimball [Salt Lake City: Bookcraft, 1982], 348). This applies even if your parents are not active in the Church. Just try harder to be better. Once in a while let them see you bear your testimony, or read your scriptures, or say your prayers.

3—PERFECT PRACTICE MAKES PERFECT

Learn to be better than normal. If you are always saying, "I'm not doing anything wrong," ask yourself, "Am I doing anything good?" If you aren't doing any good, then you're doing something wrong.

"The natural man is an enemy to God, and has been from the fall of Adam, and will be, forever and ever, unless he yields to the enticings of the Holy Spirit, and putteth off the natural man and becometh a saint through the atonement of Christ the Lord, and becometh as a child, submissive, meek, humble, patient, full of love, willing to submit to all things which the Lord seeth fit to inflict upon him, even as a child doth submit to his father" (Mosiah 3:19).

And always remember the promise we have in Philippians 4:13, which reads, "I can do all things through Christ which strengtheneth me." We can practice. We can become better. We can develop our skills.

4—NOBODY LIKES A TATTLETALE. OR DO THEY?

Do you remember the very first thing Nephi tells us in the Book of Mormon? "I, Nephi, having been born of goodly parents" (1 Nephi 1:1). A lot of people now know how Nephi felt about his mother. How do you think that made Sariah feel?

First acknowledge that your parents love you. Then express your love for them to them and to others. Isn't that what Nephi did? Sometimes you might have a difficult time expressing your love for them. And sometimes grown-ups still have a difficult time. If we don't learn to conquer our fears of saying "I love you" in our youth, we will still be trying to conquer them as parents.

Remember that you want to "tell on them" the most to Heavenly Father. Let him know how they are doing. Be grateful. Learn to say, "Thank you." President Spencer W. Kimball said, "No gift purchased from a store can begin to match in value to parents some simple, sincere words of appreciation" (*Teachings of Spencer W. Kimball*, 348).

I want you to know that of all of the things that we need to be successful in, it is most important that we are successful in our homes. We can be awesome missionaries, but if we can't get along in our homes, then we aren't living the gospel and we're not making it. We can have an awesome football team and be in the state play-offs, but if we can't be better in our homes, we are missing the boat. The Church can keep growing; but the home is the basic organization of the Church and it is we who need to strengthen the home so that others in it can grow.

Michael Weir Allred lives in West Haven, Utah. He served a mission to Japan, graduated from Weber State University, received a master's degree in counseling from the University of Phoenix, and is now principal of the seminary in Morgan, Utah. He spent seven years in the National Guard and Reserves as a counterintelligence agent. He has served in two bishoprics and is currently serving as the stake mission president. He and his wife, Kathy, have four sons: Tyson, Josh, Cody, and Kade.

17

GREATER JOY

Scott Anderson

Author and lecturer Russell Conwell once shared a profound story about a man and his quest for a fortune in diamonds. He wrote: "There once lived not far from the River Indus an ancient Persian by the name of Ali Hafed. . . . Ali Hafed owned a very large farm, . . . he had orchards, grain-fields, and gardens; . . . he had money at interest, and was a wealthy and contented man. He was contented because he was wealthy, and wealthy because he was contented. One day there visited that old Persian farmer one of these ancient Buddhist priests, one of the wise men of the East. He sat down by the fire and told the old farmer how this world of ours was made. He said that this world was once a mere bank of fog, and that the Almighty thrust His finger into this bank of fog, and began slowly to move His finger around, increasing the speed until at last He whirled this bank of fog into a solid ball of fire. Then it went rolling through the universe, burning its way through other banks of fog, and condensed the moisture without, until it fell in floods of rain upon its hot surface, and cooled the outward crust. Then the internal fires bursting outward through the crust threw up the mountains and hills, the valleys, the plains and prairies of this wonderful world of ours. If this internal molten mass came bursting out and cooled very quickly it became granite; less quickly copper, less quickly silver, less quickly gold, and, after gold, diamonds were made.

"Said the old priest, 'A diamond is a congealed drop of sunlight.' Now that is literally scientifically true, that a diamond is an actual deposit of carbon from the sun. The old priest told Ali Hafed that if he had one diamond the size of his thumb he could purchase the county, and if he had a mine of diamonds he could place his children upon thrones through the influence of their great wealth.

"Ali Hafed heard all about diamonds, how much they were worth, and went to his bed that night a poor man. He had not lost anything, but he was poor because he was discontented, and discontented because he feared he was poor. He said, 'I want a mine of diamonds,' and he lay awake all night.

"Early in the morning he sought out the priest. I know by experience that a priest is very cross when awakened early in the morning, and when he shook that old priest out of his dreams, Ali Hafed said to him:

"'Will you tell me where I can find diamonds?'

"'Diamonds! What do you want with diamonds?' 'Why, I wish to be immensely rich.' 'Well, then, go along and find them. That is all you have to do; go and find them, and then you have them.' 'But I don't know where to go.' 'Well, if you will find a river that runs through white sands, between high mountains, in those white sands you will always find diamonds.' 'I don't believe there is any such river.' 'Oh yes, there are plenty of them. All you have to do is to go and find them, and then you have them.' Said Ali Hafed, 'I will go.'

"So he sold his farm, collected his money, left his family in charge of a neighbor, and away he went in search of diamonds. He began his search, very properly to my mind, at the Mountains of the Moon. Afterward he came around into Palestine, then wandered on into Europe, and at last when his money was all spent and he was in rags, wretchedness, and poverty, he stood on the shore of that bay at Barcelona, in Spain, when a great tidal wave came rolling in between the pillars of Hercules, and the poor, afflicted, suffering, dying man could not resist the awful temptation to cast himself into that incoming tide, and he sank beneath its foaming crest, never to rise in this life again. . . .

" . . . The man who purchased Ali Hafed's farm one day led his camel into the garden to drink, and as that camel put its nose into the shallow water of that garden brook, Ali Hafed's successor noticed a curious flash of light from the white sands of the stream. He pulled out a black stone having an eye of light reflecting all the hues of the rainbow. He took the pebble into the house and put it on the mantel which covers the central fires, and forgot all about it.

"A few days later this same old priest came in to visit Ali Hafed's successor, and the moment he opened that drawing-room door he saw that flash of light on the mantel, and he rushed up to it, and shouted: 'Here is a diamond! Has Ali Hafed returned?' 'Oh no, Ali Hafed has not returned, and that is not a diamond. That is nothing but a stone we found right out here in our own garden.' 'But,' said the priest, 'I tell you I know a diamond when I see it. I know positively that is a diamond.'

"Then together they rushed out into that old garden and stirred up the white sands with their fingers, and lo! there came up other more beautiful and valuable gems than the first. Thus, . . . was discovered the diamond-mine of Golconda, the most magnificent diamond-mine in all the history of mankind, excelling the Kimberly itself. The Kohinoor, and the Orloff of the crown jewels of England and Russia, the largest on earth, came from that mine."

The old guide who first related this story to Russell Conwell told him that "had Ali Hafed remained at home and dug in his own cellar, or underneath his own wheat-fields, or in his own garden, instead of wretchedness, starvation, and death by suicide in a strange land, he would have had 'acres of diamonds.' For every acre of that old farm, yes, every shovelful, afterward revealed gems which since have decorated the crowns of monarchs" (*Acres of Diamonds* [Westwood, N.J.: Revell, 1960],).

Like Ali Hafed, many of us have the light of the gospel all around us but do not know how to mine its truths and make them real—we don't know how to respond to the gospel. Learning how to mine these truths can bring us incredible joy. The Book of Mormon story about Lehi and his family offers several classic examples of what happens when we respond to the gospel by mining its truths or by disregarding or looking elsewhere for its truths.

Let's first look at how the people of Jerusalem responded to the gospel. After Lehi received his vision, he set out to warn the people of Jerusalem that they must repent or be destroyed. How did Jerusalem respond to him? They rejected his words. Look for a moment at a similar example from our own time. Imagine that you sat at home tonight and watched television, how many of the Ten Commandments would you see broken in a two-hour period of time? Probably all of them. Paraded before us is a constant stream of individuals taking the name of God in vain, participating in adultery, showing disrespect for parents, bearing false witness, and so on. Like the people of Lehi's time, we're not doing so well. Keeping the commandments just doesn't seem to matter to the world. Many in the world are saying, "It won't do, forget it, reject the gospel." It is a response we see portrayed all around us.

Let's next look at the "Laman and Lemuel approach." How did they respond to the gospel of Jesus Christ (including direction from their father)? Was there a distinct difference between their reaction and that of Nephi? Were they disobedient? Let's review. Dad asks them to leave Jerusalem. Do they go? Yes. Dad asks them to go back and get the plates. Do they go? Yes. Who's the first one to go in and try to get the plates? Laman. Does he go in the second time even though he almost died the first time? Yes. (Wow, how about that! I sometimes read that part and think Laman shows more obedience than I do.) When they finally get the plates, does Laman travel in the wilderness with the plates? Yes. Does he go back and get the girls? Yes. Does he murmur this time? No. The word *murmur* is not used on this trip back. Later on, does he help build the ship? Yes, after a little electrifying experience, he finally does. Does he get in the ship and sail across the ocean? Yes. Would it be an act of faith to sail in a ship you had built? Yes. Finally Dad asks one last thing of him, stay faithful. Does Laman do it? No. Are you shocked? Did you get to 2 Nephi 5 and say, "I'm shocked. Laman fell away." Not one of you did that. You said, "I knew it. Saw it coming the whole time."

What was the difference between Laman and Nephi? If it was not their outward obedience, was it something more? It seems that Laman practiced a "have to" approach to the gospel. He was like many of those in the Old Testament who murmured and kept the commandments only because, well, if they broke them, they would be killed.

In 1 Nephi 2:12 is a great insight to Laman's (and Lemuel's) behavior. Nephi writes, "Laman and Lemuel, being the eldest, did murmur against their father. And they did murmur because they knew not the dealings of that God who had created them." *They knew not the dealings of God.* They were not able to see the Lord's hand in their own lives or in the lives of Lehi or Nephi. They never really believed that this could be God's work, or that he was directing them personally. They obeyed out of fear, not belief.

Now let's look at Nephi. How did he respond to the gospel? "I, Nephi, being exceedingly young, nevertheless being large in stature, and also having great desires to know of the mysteries of God, wherefore, I did cry unto the Lord; and behold he did visit me, and did soften my heart that I did believe all the words which had been spoken by my father; wherefore, I did not rebel against him like unto my brothers" (1 Nephi 2:16). Nephi knew the dealings of God. He knew that the Lord would answer his prayers. He knew that the Lord had guided his father. Subsequently, the Lord changed

Nephi's heart. And when his heart was changed, he saw everything differently. So, how could we summarize Nephi's attitude toward the gospel—could we call it a "love to" attitude?

As I have experienced the challenges of life, I have noticed that each of these approaches to the gospel seems to affect my life. I worry because some of the commandments in my life are ones I'm not keeping as well as I should. They seem to fit in the "won't do" or "don't do" category. I also know that, for me, some of the commandments still fall in the "have to" category. I have, however, found out for myself in many ways what the "love to" approach to the gospel can mean. I know there is no joy in the "won't do" attitude—none at all. I know that there is a small amount of joy in the "have to" method of living the gospel. But, if we really want to learn to "mine the diamonds" of the gospel and find real joy, we must follow Nephi's example and adopt the "love to" view of the gospel of Jesus Christ.

So, how do we do this? One process whereby we can mine the diamonds of the gospel is found in Third Nephi chapter 12; it is also recorded in Matthew chapter 5. These verses are known as the Beatitudes. If you look at your Bible Dictionary, on page 620, you will find that the Beatitudes are an interrelated set of principles or character traits. They are progressive. Following these steps with any gospel principle will help you internalize the concept, just like Nephi did, and learn to love it. Simply stated, the steps are as follows: become poor in spirit, mourn, become meek, hunger and thirst for righteousness, be merciful, be pure in heart, act as a peacemaker, and endure persecution.

Take a principle of the gospel that you are living without finding much joy, a principle for which you are going through the motions but have not yet caught the spirit. Let's use scripture reading as an example and establish that you read every day but are not getting a great deal out of it. The first step you should take is to recognize that you really don't have the right spirit about scripture study (you are poor in spirit). As you realize this, you will likely begin to feel sincerely sorry about it (you will mourn). You will then become teachable, humble, and ready to learn (you will be meek). Your desire for learning will grow within you and soon become a strong, internal motivation that leads to study, pondering, prayerful consideration and effort (you will hunger and thirst). You will need to develop patience for yourself (and others) as you struggle to grow and progress (you will be merciful). As you put forth effort in this humble, contrite, and patient way, the Spirit will confirm the truth of the scriptures to your mind and heart and you will find a love for reading the scriptures (you will become pure in heart). You will feel a peace and joy that you will not be able to hold to yourself; you will want to share it (you will become a peacemaker). Then, you will have the wonderful challenge of learning to overcome past habits and continuing to apply your new love for the scriptures in your daily life (enabling you to overcome internal persecution).

By the time I was about seventeen, I had practiced the Beatitude cycle some in my own scripture study. I was beginning to develop a "love to" attitude when it came to scripture study. At this same time, my parents were going through a separation, and my dad was living alone in a little bachelor apartment. In the midst of this struggle I was hurting inside and felt lonely and empty. I remember thinking that I could sure use a father's blessing. As I contemplated that thought, I pictured myself going to my dad's little bachelor apartment and asking him to give me a blessing. I knew that he was depressed and despondent and things were not easy. And I thought, *I can't do that. I'll just go to my bishop.* At that moment, Nephi became real for me. I quietly heard the Spirit whisper to my heart, saying, "Don't you remember the broken bow? Don't you remember when Nephi came into camp and Lehi started to struggle a little? Don't you remember that he went away and carved a bow and then went right to his father and said, 'Dad, I need revelation in my life. And I need it from you.'" I suddenly knew I needed to go to my dad. I knew the Spirit had used the Book of Mormon as a tool to give me personal direction in my life. I remember going to my dad's apartment, knocking on the door, telling him I needed a blessing, and having him say, "Oh, I don't know if I feel like I could give you one right now."

And I said, "I didn't say I needed one right now."

And he said, "Great, are you willing to wait?"

I told him I'd wait, and he promised to get ready. He called me sometime later and said, "Do you still want that blessing?" We fasted together, and he gave me a blessing I will never forget. When I see Nephi (the Book of Mormon says I will have that chance), I just want to say, "You brought me back to my dad. You changed my life." I love this book. I love this book.

I believe that the Beatitude process can be used on each of the commandments to help increase our joy. When we internalize one, we can immediately start over on another commandment. We learn line upon line, precept on precept. How long are we going to do this? The rest of your life and long after. Why? Oh, this is growth, this is exciting.

Let me share with you an example. I was standing in my seminary classroom. Three weeks into the semester the back door opened, and in came ten young men wearing football jerseys. They stepped into my classroom and were soon standing around me. They were all much taller than I was, and I suddenly thought an eclipse of the sun might have taken place. It was getting dark. I looked up at them and said hi. They asked if I was the teacher.

I said, "Uh huh."

They said, "You give good grades?"

I said, "To you guys I probably would."

They didn't even smile. They said, "Good. We're checking into your class."

And I said, "Great. It's good to have you here."

One of them said, "Oh yeah. We'll see."

I'll never forget that statement. "We'll see."

They walked to the back of the room and occupied the whole back row, muscled arms folded across their chests. They looked at me like "I don't need the gospel. I got pecs." I thought to myself, *Oh, how can I reach them? How can I have them feel the reason for being here?*

One day I walked up to them and asked, "Why are you here?"

"I won't get my allowance if I don't come." "I won't get to use the car."

I thought, *Yep, I know right where you're coming from.* The old "have to" approach. Welcome, Laman and Lemuel.

Three weeks later, however, I had a bit of inspiration one day. I said, "Kelly, come here." And he came and stood next to me, all 235 pounds of him. I said, "Kelly, I'm going to teach you about athletics today. Sit down on the floor." And so he did, and I was glad. Now I could look at him eye to eye. I called up another kid in the class, and he came and sat down across from Kelly. They grabbed on this big wooden stick and put their feet together.

I counted down, "one, two, three," and they were off. The whole back row cheered loudly. The two young men pulled as hard as they could. Finally, the biggest one pulled the other one up off the ground. The boy who lost walked humbly back to his seat. The one who won was up in front. I said, "Kelly, I want you to try this with two people. I'll make them girls, OK?"

He said, "Girls? I thought you said people." Whoa! Kelly was in big trouble! We called up two young ladies. (Young ladies only act weak, they are really tough. I know, I have five sisters.) They came up and sat down across from Kelly. They had four feet, he had two feet, but he had fat feet so it worked just fine. They put their feet against his and grabbed onto the wooden stick; he reached up with one hand and waved at his buddies, "This will just take me a minute." Those girls were so angry they could have lifted him with their adrenaline alone. All of the sudden I said go. They pulled as hard as they could. He grabbed with both hands and tried, but within ten seconds they had beaten him. He walked back somewhat humbled toward his seat. In that little moment, as he was walking back toward his seat, I said, "How would you like to know about a man who could handle two men his own size doing that sport?"

He said, "No way." I said, "Oh yeah. Not only that, he'd been locked up in jail for four and a half months. He couldn't even stand up straight in the place he was living. He had been living on frozen, moldy straw all winter long, with no sanitation in the room, and eating one meal a day. How many do you eat?"

"Eight."

"What kind of shape would you be in if you ate only one meal a day?" I asked.

"Terrible," he said.

I continued, "Two days out of that place, and he's walking through a Missouri town and somebody sees him and says, 'Aren't you Joe Smith?' He says, 'Yes.' 'I understand you're pretty good at stick pulling.' 'That's what they say.' 'How about a contest?' 'Fine.' The entire town turns out to cheer for the state champ, Joseph's foe in this contest. Joseph sits in the middle of the street. When they say go, Joseph goes 'ha' once and throws the man over his head. Until you try this sport you won't understand what I just said. And then he stands up and says, 'It'd take two Missourians to hold me down. I challenge any two Missourians in town.' They get their two biggest men, and still cannot budge Joseph Smith. They pull until their arms cramp and they have to give up."

At that moment, this young man, who was still standing in the aisle staring at me, said, "Whoa." The whole back row said, "This is a muscle story. This is a good story." And they were listening. So I continued to tell them about Joseph Smith. I told them about Richmond Jail, where Joseph was chained to the wall and all his muscles wouldn't do any good. I told them how the guards came in boasting about murdering babies, attacking women, and torturing the Mormons. The guards boasted about it in such detail that Joseph and the other prisoners couldn't stand it any longer. At midnight, Joseph suddenly jumped to his feet and said, "Silence, ye fiends of the infernal pit. In the name of Jesus Christ I rebuke you, and command you to be still; I will not live another minute and hear such language. Cease such talk, or you or I die THIS INSTANT!" (in *Autobiography of Parley P. Pratt* [Salt Lake City: Deseret Book, 1985], 180). And then the guards dropped to their knees and slid back away into the corner out of fear that if they spoke they would die.

This gave me opportunity to ask that back row some challenging questions: "Is there something more to manhood than muscle? Is there something called priesthood manhood that matters much more than the machos?" Suddenly, for just a minute, the Spirit spoke to some of those young men, some great young men. A week later they walked into my office one morning and said, "We're in trouble."

I said, "It's 7:30 in the morning, how do you get in trouble so early?"

"We got up early," they said. "We went over to Corey's house and read scriptures."

"Wow," I responded, "You really did that?" They really had. "So why are you in trouble?" I asked.

"Well, you know what happens when you read scriptures. You get hungry," they replied.

I started to catch on. "All ten of you got hungry in the same house?"

"We did. We ate their whole two-year supply."

I just laughed. I watched one of those young men stand up shortly after that and grab his scriptures and say, "I love this book." They had completed the Beatitude cycle—every step. They had come in without the Spirit and recognized at some point that they didn't have it. They felt sorry about it. They decided they needed to do something to become teachable. They took their books and started to get up early and read every morning. When they started to read, the words started coming alive for them. And suddenly one of them was standing up saying, "I love this book." They went and grabbed their friends halfway through the year and checked them into seminary. They said, "Come on over. We talk about athletes and secret agents. It's great." They became peacemakers and shared it with others. They found the diamonds. They mined the diamonds in their own hearts. They found out that the Book of Mormon is incredible. They found that prayer really works, and that when you pray it really works, and he really listens.

Oh, incredible youth! The gospel of Jesus Christ is so exciting when we get it in our hearts, when it comes alive for us. We can willingly share it, and we can willingly be peacemakers. President Gordon B. Hinckley said,

"We have some of our own who cry out in pain and suffering and loneliness and fear. Ours is a great and solemn duty to reach out and help them, to lift them, to feed them if they are hungry, to nurture their spirits if they thirst for truth and righteousness.

"There are so many young people who wander aimlessly and walk at the tragic trail of drugs, gangs, immorality, and the whole brood of ills that accompany these things. . . . There are those who were once warm in the faith, but whose faith has grown cold. Many of them wish to come back but do not know quite how to do it. They need friendly hands to reach out to them. With little effort many of them can be brought back to feast again at the table of the Lord" ("'Reach with a Rescuing Hand,'" *Ensign*, Nov. 1996, 86).

Oh, young people. This life is an incredible quest. Once you get it in your heart and start finding out how great it is, you will just want to reach out and bless people.

I testify to you young people that the principles of the gospel of Jesus Christ are like diamonds, and that we can mine them and use them to make us more polished and beautiful. The Lord will help us through this wonderful process. All along the way, if we've got something to overcome, he will help us. He will help us see things differently and share it with others, and feel more joy than you have even imagined. I love the gospel. I know the Lord lives. I know he wants to change our very hearts and pray somehow that this mining experience can bring you some of the joy that I have felt.

Scott Anderson and his wife, Angell, live in Bluffdale, Utah, where they spend time working on home improvement projects, waiting for their children to come to family meetings, and ordering pizza as a reward for cleaning the house. His hobbies include teaching, writing, music, outdoor activities, sports, and building memories with his family. Brother Anderson has a Ph.D. in marriage and family therapy from Brigham Young University and is currently on the faculty at the Orem Institute of Religion adjacent to Utah Valley State College. His wife says that Scott is a "gratitude guru" and a "life enthusiast" who loves to serve.

18

"O MAN, REMEMBER, AND PERISH NOT"

Allen Litchfield

The lyrics of an old Beach Boys song—"two girls for every boy"—describe well the ratio of boys to girls at many Especially for Youth sessions. On occasion, I have taken advantage of the situation by reversing the ratio in an object lesson designed to show teenagers how hard it can be to remember certain things. I find a nice, popular slow dance tune and cue it up on the music system in the classroom on campus. Then I ask ten boys and one girl to volunteer to come to the front of the room and help with a demonstration. At that point I talk to the audience—the majority of whom are usually girls—about how fun it would be to attend an EFY session where there are ten boys for every girl!

Of course the girls eat this up and cheer loudly. The boys become quiet and fearful. Then I suggest we demonstrate how that would actually work, particularly at the dances, and call up the lone female volunteer. I put a walking microphone on the girl and, after dimming the lights a bit, encourage her to dance to the music with all ten boys, one at a time, for about fifteen seconds each. I ask each boy to tell the girl his name and where he is from as he begins his dance sequence. After that, he is free to try his best cheesy introduction line. That part of the demonstration is usually very funny and goes something like this:

BOY: "Are you interested in gardening?"

GIRL: "I guess so."

BOY: "Well, what do you say we plant our two lips (tulips) together?"

For some reason, the boys that race to the front of the class to volunteer

149

always know these type of introduction lines. In any event, I ask the boys to hide their EFY name tags and remain on stage after the tenth boy has had his short dance. The deliriously happy girl is then brought to the podium and asked one by one the names of the boys she has danced with. She nearly always does poorly with the names. In some cases the girl doesn't get even one name right. After all, she is on stage and trying to look cool in front of hundreds of kids, and I never say specifically that the purpose of the dancing demonstration is to remember the names; the boys are with her for a very brief time and they are usually saying funny things. These distractions make it very difficult to remember the ten names. After the girl has been sufficiently embarrassed, we discuss for a minute or two why some things are hard to remember.

To make that point more vivid I give the entire audience a memory test. I verbally present a series of numbers to the group and ask that each person repeat the numbers without writing them down. Nearly everyone can repeat the six-digit number and most people can recall the seven-digit number. The eight-digit number is a bit harder, and most people struggle to remember the nine-digit number after hearing it aloud only once. Finally I read a ten-digit number out loud and ask if anyone can say it back. Sometimes one kid with a super memory repeats back the ten numbers correctly. Then I ask the young number wizard to repeat back the earlier six-digit number. He never can. Although he may do very well with numbers, holding on to that earlier set of six numbers is just too much. The point is that it is hard to remember everything.

At one session I tried to make my point even clearer. I told the group that if anyone could come up and name each of the presidents of the United States in order without a single error, he or she would get a prize of twenty dollars. I lost the twenty, because a young girl came up and rattled off every president without a single slip. It was an expensive object lesson for me, but it demonstrated nicely that people can remember things when they have made the considerable effort required. Over the next few months I memorized the list of presidents myself, just to prove to myself that I could do it, and interestingly there have been many occasions in which this information has proved valuable. Remembering can really come in handy.

For example, years ago I directed an EFY session at Brigham Young University during the week of July 1—Canada's Dominion Day, which is similar to the Fourth of July in America. Brad Wilcox was teaching that week. Everyone was impressed that Brad could come up to the front of the morning devotional group and lead the participants in a rousing rendition of "O Canada." He knew every word, including those to the second verse, which even some Canadians don't know. Brother Wilcox had made the effort on one of his trips to our northern neighbors to memorize and remember the words to their national anthem. President Gordon B. Hinckley regularly demonstrates how passages and poems he memorized as a youth are still with him seventy-five or eighty years later (see, for example, "'A Humble and a Contrite Heart,'" *Ensign*, Nov. 2000, 88). I believe we too must make that kind of effort to the point that the material or matters we are studying actually become a permanent part of us. This is especially vital when it comes to the things the Lord has asked us to remember.

At the very end of king Benjamin's address in the Book of Mormon, he warns us, "O man, remember, and perish not" (Mosiah 4:30). So many things perish when important things are forgotten. A joke, for example, "perishes" if you forget the punch line. I have a cartoon of Calvin and Hobbes that makes this point. In the first frame Calvin comes up to his tiger and asks, "Want to hear a joke?" Hobbes says, "Sure." Calvin launches into the joke like this: "OK. This guy goes in to a bar. No wait, he doesn't do that yet or maybe it's a grocery store. OK. It doesn't matter. Let's say it's a bar. He's somewhere in the vicinity of a bar, right?" The joke loses its direction entirely as he continues, "So anyway, there's this dog and he says something odd, I don't remember what, but this other guy says, um . . . well, I forget. But it was funny." In the final frame the tiger looks kind of baffled and says, "I'll try to imagine." To which Calvin says, "Yeah, you'll really laugh." Jokes with forgotten elements really die.

Your dinner may "perish" if you forget to watch it on the stove. Your pet may perish if you forget to feed her. Your houseplant may perish if you forget to water it. Your school grades may perish if you forget to study and hand in assignments. Your car may perish if you forget to provide it with regular maintenance, such as oil changes and brake checks. Love connections may perish if partners forget to nourish their relationship. Testimonies may perish if their owners forget to nurture their faith. Many important things need to be remembered to survive.

That is why the Lord has told us repeatedly to remember some important things that will save our spiritual lives, our eternal perspective, our celestial commitment, and our relationship with him. For an example, look up Helaman 5 in your Book of Mormon. In the right-hand column of page 377 alone, how many times do you find the word "remember"? You will find that it is printed more times than there are pages in this chapter. Words that stem from *memory* or *remember* occur well over two hundred times in the Book of Mormon. You might want to highlight or shade in your own scriptures these reminders to remember. Some strategic passages in the Book of Mormon are just saturated with calls to remember. Then think about this: perhaps the Lord so often prompts us to remember because failing to remember these critical parts of the gospel plan may cause us to perish spiritually, dashing the Lord's hopes that we will return to him.

This little story about my baby daughter, Amber—who is now sixteen and attends EFY herself—helps to make that point. When she was six or seven years old, Amber didn't think she was a great artist. She had an assignment in school that involved drawing something on a poster. She had learned that if you make an overhead transparency of the thing you want to draw and then project that image with an overhead projector onto the poster, that anyone can draw really well because it is a simple matter of tracing. She asked me one evening to bring home the projector the next day so she could do her poster. I said I would, but got busy during the hectic day and forgot. That evening she reminded me again, but the next day I forgot as well. This may sound like I am a neglectful father, but actually I think that I am typical of people who have busy lives and fail to remember everything that has to be done. The next morning I found the following note, printed by my little Amber, lying on my briefcase by the front door:

> remember
> Dad get the pergector
> remember
> for Amber
> remember.

I still have that little note, partly because it reminds me of my precious Amber when she was small but also because it reminds me of the loving reminders of my God who gently encourages me to keep some important things in my mind and in my heart. The Book of Mormon is filled with similar reminders. King Benjamin, in his famous speech from the tower, pled with us to "remember, remember that these things are true; for the Lord God hath spoken it" (Mosiah 2:41). Passages like that are like little notes sent down from the Lord to prompt us to remember things that will save us.

One thing that the Lord keeps asking us to remember is his commandments. Nephi counseled his brothers to "remember to keep his commandments always in all things" (1 Nephi 15:25). Alma instructed his son Helaman: "O, remember, my son, and learn wisdom in thy youth; yea, learn in thy youth to keep the commandments of God" (Alma 37:35). With striking parallelism, Alma's grandson Helaman passed on the warning to his sons: "Behold, my sons, I desire that ye should remember to keep the commandments of God" (Helaman 5:6).

There are often things we can use to help us remember to obey the commandments. For example, some who lived during Moses' time put blue fringes on the borders of their clothing to help them remember. "And it shall be unto you for a fringe, that ye may look upon it, and remember all the commandments of the Lord, and do them; . . . That ye may remember, and do all my commandments, and be holy unto your God" (Numbers 15:39–40). Many young Latter-day Saints wear CTR rings to help them remember the importance of making wise decisions. Endowed persons wear temple garments under their clothing to help them remember the covenants and ordinances they made in the temple. When you take the sacrament, observe holy days such as Christmas and Easter with the proper focus, fast with the purpose of connecting with God, study the scriptures regularly, and even take in a session of EFY, you are doing things that will help you remember to keep the commandments.

The scriptures also regularly ask us to remember our gifts. Near the end of Moroni's final testimony, he says: "And I would exhort you, my beloved brethren, that ye remember that every good gift cometh of Christ. And I would exhort you, my beloved brethren, that ye remember that he is the same yesterday, today, and forever, and that all these gifts of which I have spoken, which are spiritual, never will be done away, even as long as the world shall stand, only according to the unbelief of the children of men" (Moroni 10:18–19). Only our unbelief will prevent those gifts from blossoming in our lives. The Lord through the Prophet Joseph said: "And again, verily I say unto you, I would that ye should always remember, and always retain in your minds what those gifts are, that are given unto the church" (D&C 46:10). The modern scripture then outlines the wonderful gifts of the Spirit that are still available to those who remember them and seek them out. We must not forget these glorious gifts that can and should make such a difference in our lives. We must not be like the servant in the parable who buried his talent instead of developing it.

There are other things the scriptures ask us to remember; but perhaps they ask nothing as important as remembering Christ and what he has done for us. Jesus himself placed the Nephites under covenant to "always remember" him and to keep the commandments which he had given them (3 Nephi 18:7). We initially make that covenant in the waters of baptism and then renew it every Sabbath as we partake of the sacrament. In the sacrament prayers we promise to remember his body and blood—his sacrifice on our behalf—and to remember him. The Lord in return promises us that we will have his Spirit to be with us. The Holy Ghost, which often imparts of the Lord's Spirit, will "teach you all things, and bring all things to your remembrance" (John 14:26).

We don't need to worry about God forgetting us. He has promised repeatedly that he will remember us. One of the main purposes of the Book of Mormon, as expressed in the title page, is to show that God remembers his children and the covenants he has made with them. One of the most beautiful promises he gives is that he will never forget us. "But Zion said, The Lord hath forsaken me, and my Lord hath forgotten me. Can a woman forget her sucking child, that she should not have compassion on the son of her womb? yea, they may forget, yet will I not forget thee" (Isaiah 49:14–15; see also 1 Nephi 21:14–15). Isaiah admits that in a very rare case a nursing mother might forget her little child, but assures us that our God will never forget us. The Lord even goes on to say that he has "graven [us] upon the palms of [his] hands" (v. 16), a reference to the reminders in his hands of his great sacrifice on the cross.

I don't have any trouble accepting the fact that my God remembers me, because I have been remembered by a valiant Sunday School teacher of my youth, Mary Murray. Sister Murray, a single sister from Australia, taught my class in Lethbridge, Alberta, Canada, when I was about ten years old. While she was my teacher she sent me birthday cards and Christmas cards right on time with a loving note inside. That act of kindness and thoughtfulness seemed nice, but not especially unusual. When I turned twelve, I moved away to another city. Cards from Mary Murray followed me to Calgary until I turned eighteen and went away to school to another city. I got cards there too. But then I went away on my mission to far-off Fiji. I received two birthday cards and two Christmas cards while serving in the South Pacific.

She always knew where I was and what I was doing, sort of like a stalker but not as scary, because she always sent warm wishes and good advice. I returned home and went back to the university. The cards continued. I got married and we started a family. The cards kept coming. We moved around a great deal. Her sweet cards found us, always right on time. Remember that most of these years, I wasn't very good about writing back. But she never commented on that and her gentle cards did not depend on my reciprocity. She invariably knew about new children and changes in our situation. Around this time she retired and moved back to Australia. But the cards never stopped. The picture on one of her cute Christmas cards from Australia was of koala bears, kangaroos, and a platypus surrounding the manger. Many of the birthday cards contained pictures of those down-under creatures, as well as crocodiles, bringing the message of love.

I always assumed that I must have been her favorite and that she only kept in touch with me for all those years. But upon checking with Debbie, Brad, Brian, Craig, Kent, Bruce, and other members of that class from 1960, I found that the cards had been sent to all of us. A few years ago I didn't get a birthday card on May 16. That surprised and worried me because Mary hadn't missed me for about thirty-seven years. I learned shortly after that that this wonderful teacher had passed away. If this kindly Australian sister could remember my classmates and me for almost four decades, I suppose the Supreme Being can do at least as well. I testify that the Lord remembers each and every one of us. He knows where we are and how we are doing. In a number of interesting ways he sends down regular reminders of his love and care. When I am in tune with the Spirit I notice and recognize those tender transmissions. I am sure that he has sent many messages addressed to me that I missed because I was too busy, distracted, or unworthy.

The real problem is not that God might forget us. I am satisfied that he will never forget. The challenge is that we keep forgetting him. I'd like to place before you a short analogy from the classic movie *The Lion King* (Jim Capobianco, *The Lion King,* dir. Roger Allers and Rob Minkoff, 88 min., Walt Disney Pictures, 1994, videocassette). In the film, the young lion Simba runs away and links up with Pumbaa and Timon. For a while, the three of them live a life of "Hakuna Matata"—no cares, worries, responsibility, or growth. Simba never does anything wicked, but he *has* forgotten who he is—a lion king. Instead of living up to his potential or the purpose of his creation, he survives by living on bugs and grubs and playing around. Rafiki, the monkey, who is sort of like a good bishop, parent, seminary teacher, youth leader, or EFY counselor, tries to wake up Simba so that he can experience the vision. Finally Simba does receive the vision of his father, who reminds him who he is. Mufasa tells Simba that he is the son of a king, with the potential of becoming a king himself someday. If only he can remember who he is, he will return to the circle of life. He might have to fight some hyenas and face some other challenges, but it will be worth it, because he will then be able to fulfill his destiny and become like his father.

I pray that you will remember who you are and why you are here. I know that we generally can't remember how things were beyond the veil. But I pray that we will remember those times when the Lord has reached through the veil with his love, his truth, his message of hope, his blessed peace, his healing embrace, his maps pointing the way, his notes outlining the plan, and his promise that he is with us.

Allen Litchfield and his wife, Gladys, are the parents of six children. Brother Litchfield has taught seminary and institute classes and has taught in the Department of Religious Education at Brigham Young University. He is currently serving in a stake presidency of a BYU stake for single students, the stake taking up the smallest geographic area in the Church—the Deseret Towers. He has taught the gospel to the youth of the Church in thirty-one states and looks forward to teaching in those last nineteen.

19

THE FIRST PRINCIPLE
OF THE GOSPEL

Curtis Jacobs

Several years ago while teaching seminary in Tempe, Arizona, a young lady came to me after school with a major question. It wasn't one of the typical questions a seminary teacher is often asked. She didn't ask about guys or school or family; she asked about something deeper. She was a wonderful example of what it meant to be a "CTR" kind of Latter-day Saint. She always attended church, helped out at activities, and was known as a good member of the Church. Her question surprised me. She said, "Brother Jacobs, I know that I have a testimony, but how do I know if I have faith?" I thought for a moment about what to say. I could have simply said, "Well, if you have a testimony, you had to have faith to get one." But I knew that wasn't what she was looking for.

How would you answer her question?

How do you know if you have faith?

If you look at the definition of faith given in the scriptures, you will see that virtually everyone has faith in something. Look up Hebrews 11:1, for example: "Now faith is the substance [notice footnote b, GR: assurance] of things hoped for, the evidence [footnote d, GR: proof] of things not seen."

Now, look up Alma 32:21 (a scripture mastery verse!): "Now as I said concerning faith—faith is not to have a perfect knowledge of things; therefore if ye have faith ye hope for things which are not seen, which are true."

Based on these two definitions, we can determine (1) that faith is the *hope* of something you have not seen but is true, and (2) faith is *evidence* that something you haven't seen *is* true.

Now, let me illustrate how everyone has faith in some way. If you have a job, it is likely that you *hope* for something in return for your hard work. A paycheck, perhaps. If you were just hired, however, it is likely that you have never seen your paycheck. Not yet, anyway. But is there any *evidence* that you will be paid? Any *assurance* that you will be paid? Of course there is. You can talk to other employees who have been paid. They may even be able to show you their paychecks—solid proof!

In this example of faith, your paycheck is the "hope for things which are not seen." There is evidence that you will see your paycheck because others who have worked there receive theirs. You have "faith" in your employer. You trust that he will pay you, if you do your part.

Here is another example. Think about what it is you "hope" for by going to school. Would I be too far out to suggest that you hope to graduate someday? Don't you hope to get that piece of paper called a diploma? Have you even seen it? Not yet, right? Well, how in the world do you know you can actually graduate then? Well, you could talk to others who have done so. They could even show you their diplomas. Again, you "hope for things which are not seen," your diploma, and you seek evidence that you can graduate, because others have! You have faith in your school administrators (they usually are pretty good people; besides they want you to get out . . . I mean graduate from school).

I could mention other places that you show faith, but I think you get the message. Frankly, you probably wouldn't even get out of bed in the morning if you didn't have faith in something. We all have some type of "hope." It may not be a religious hope; nonetheless, it is a simple hope for something not seen but true.

The preceding examples all involve having faith. The first principle of the gospel, however, is not just having faith; it is having "faith in the Lord Jesus Christ." You may have faith in your employer, or your school district, or the sun in the morning, but none of those things get you into the celestial kingdom. Each of us needs faith in Christ.

So, when it comes to faith in Christ, what is it we hope for? Moroni gives us a great answer to that question: "And what is it that ye shall hope for? Behold I say unto you that ye shall have hope through the atonement of Christ and the power of his resurrection, to be raised unto life eternal, and this because of your faith in him according to the promise" (Moroni 7:41). We hope that through Jesus' atonement we can receive the greatest of all the gifts of God, eternal life. Do we really hope that we can make it? Do we really desire to be saved in the celestial kingdom?

What evidence is there that you can receive this exaltation? Well, for one thing the scriptures clearly teach that each of us can receive it! In fact, the scriptures are a great source of faith themselves. Samuel the Lamanite taught that the scriptures can bring us to have faith in the Lord (Helaman 15:7). The scriptures teach us what our Heavenly Father and his Son Jesus Christ are like. By really understanding them, I have learned that I can trust them. I can have faith in them.

So how does a person get started? Let's take a look at the Book of Mormon and Alma chapter 32. Alma is trying to get these people to believe. He says, "But behold, if ye will awake [are you still awake?] and arouse your faculties, even to an experiment upon my words, and exercise a particle of faith, yea, even if ye can no more than desire to believe, let this desire work in you" (v. 27). Your first step is to desire to believe. Some people, sadly, couldn't care less about spiritual things; they have no desire to learn, to gain a testimony, or do anything about religious matters. This type of people have no desire to know. But if you and I can at least have a desire, then we have begun exercising a particle of faith.

What comes next? Well, go back to hoping for your paycheck. What would happen if you never went to your job and you never put in the hours? Would you be paid? No way. True faith requires more than desire, it requires that we act on our desire. The Prophet Joseph Smith taught: "Faith is the assurance which men have of the existence of things which they have not seen, and *the principle of action* in all intelligent beings" (*Lectures on Faith* [Salt Lake City: Deseret Book, 1985], 1; emphasis added). In the mission field I had a great companion, Michael Dean Fluckiger, who taught me this little statement:

> Faith is an action.
> Without action there exists only belief.
> Belief becomes faith when acted upon.

So, if I "desire to believe," what action must follow to have faith? Missionaries all over the world teach people the discussions. Missionaries hope that the people they are teaching will have a desire to find out for themselves if what they have been taught is true. Do you know what the missionaries ask their investigators to do at the end of each discussion?

Read, ponder, and pray! "Now, we will compare the word [the scriptures] unto a seed. Now, if ye give place, that a seed may be planted in your heart, behold, if it be a true seed, . . . it will begin to swell within your breasts; and when you feel these swelling motions, ye will begin to say within yourselves—It must needs be that this is a good seed, or that the word is good" (Alma 32:28). First you have a desire, then you act upon that desire by "giving place"—by reading, pondering, and praying that you will "feel" the Spirit testify!

Do you remember Moroni's promise? "I would exhort you that when ye shall read these things . . . and ponder it in your hearts . . . if ye shall ask with a sincere heart, with real intent, having faith in Christ, he will manifest the truth of it unto you, by the power of the Holy Ghost" (Moroni 10:3–4). I can bear you my own personal testimony that I have felt those feelings. One day I was simply reading part of a book entitled *Teachings of the Prophet Joseph Smith*. While reading, I had this marvelous feeling come over me, and the thought came into my head, *You are reading the words of a prophet of God*. I've never forgotten that.

Several years ago I read an article in the *Ensign* about a young man who decided to tell his bishop that he wasn't going to serve a mission. It wasn't that he didn't like the Church, he just didn't like all the rules. He had long hair. His attendance at church had begun to slip. Then one day he received a new home teaching assignment. His companion was to be Bill Brothers. He had thought about how to get out of it. But just then Bill approached him; he'd known Bill since Primary. He couldn't tell him no. Bill said, "Why don't we show the guys in our ward how home teaching should really be done?" The young man decided to show these members he could do it.

They were assigned to the Smith family, who were reading the Book of Mormon as a family. Their children were young, so Brother Smith asked if the home teachers would tell the basic stories to his family each month. The first month, this young man didn't really prepare and felt badly about it. He decided he would be ready the next month. As he began to read, he soon began to ask himself, *What if this is really true?* He read of Nephi, Lehi, Jacob, and others. He read of Alma's prayers about his wayward son. He thought about his own parents. He read about the destruction of the wicked at the time of Christ's coming to America. He read Moroni's warning about Judgment Day and how the Lord would hold us responsible for the words contained in the Book of Mormon. He felt like those were words written directly to him.

He prayed about the Book of Mormon. He later wrote, "I knew the Book of Mormon was true! The seed of faith had been planted!" (see Derek Preece, "What If This Is Really True?" *Ensign*, Sept. 1990, 21). He drove over and told the bishop he was going to serve a mission.

Can you see what happened here? At first the young man wasn't reading the Book of Mormon in search of a witness of its truth; he didn't have a desire to know. But something happened. He wanted to prepare a better lesson for the family he home taught. He *desired.* Then he read, pondered, and prayed. He exercised a particle of faith. Anyone who has ever had an experience like this—whether by reading the scriptures, listening to a general conference talk, and so on—has exercised at least a particle of faith!

Another way we can exercise our faith is in living the principles of the gospel. Christ taught, "If any man will do his will, he shall know of the doctrine, whether it be of God, or whether I speak of myself" (John 7:17). Take the principle of the Word of Wisdom, for example. What blessings do you hope for by being obedient to the Word of Wisdom? Read Doctrine and Covenants 89:18–21. Is there any evidence that obeying the Word of Wisdom can bring these blessings? Of course—medical science has proven this again and again during our lifetime. So exercise your faith by living the principle! That is how you will know it is of God! The same can be said of prayer, fasting, tithing, and any other gospel principle.

Now, remember, we do not exercise faith in Christ so that we can have an easy life; we do so with the hope of receiving eternal life. Sometimes hard things happen to good people. Moroni said, "ye receive no witness until after the trial of your faith" (Ether 12:6). Think of the many prophets who suffered death and punishment because of their faith. The Book of Mormon teaches us that "the Lord seeth fit to chasten his people; yea, he trieth their patience and their faith" (Mosiah 23:21). Perhaps you have been made fun of because you are willing to live the gospel. Maybe you have seen tragedy in your life, or the life of a friend. It is at these times that our faith is tried! It is at times like these that our faith will help us endure.

When I was in the mission home, I met a wonderful young man. He was a convert. His family had been devout in their beliefs. He had heard about the Mormons and begun to investigate. He read the Book of Mormon, pondered and prayed, and received a witness. He decided to serve a mission. His family was completely against it. When he went on his mission, his letters from home were full of anti-Mormon literature. Yet, he endured. He frankly was one of the best missionaries in my mission. He is now married to a beautiful lady he met at BYU! They have a wonderful family. He is unashamed of the gospel. He shares it constantly! No one in his family has yet joined the Church. But because of his faith, he can stand firm.

During general conference in October 1997, President Gordon B. Hinckley asked of the Lord: "I say again, as did the Apostles to Jesus, 'Lord, increase our faith.' Grant us faith to look beyond the problems of the moment to the miracles of the future. Give us faith to pay our tithes and offerings and put our trust in Thee, the Almighty, to open the windows of heaven as Thou hast promised. Give us faith to do what is right and let the consequence follow" ("Lord, Increase Our Faith," *Ensign*, Nov. 1987, 53).

Young friends, you are a generation with faith. It takes faith to observe the Sabbath day when others around you are making it a play day instead of a holy day. It takes faith to pay tithing. It takes faith to fast, to have family prayers, and to observe the Word of Wisdom. It takes faith to do home teaching, to serve a full-time mission. It takes faith to say no to the many temptations that are all around you. It takes faith to refuse certain movies, videos, or music when the whole world seems to say these things are acceptable. It takes faith to keep the law of chastity. It takes faith to be found keeping the commandments of God. Yes, you are a generation of faith.

To the young lady who asked, "How do I know if I have faith?" I answer that her very life shows that she does. She has a hope and trust in Christ, in his gospel, and in his promises. May each of us grow in faith until the promise of eternal life is ours. I have faith we can do it.

Curtis L. Jacobs has worked for the Church Educational System since 1979 and with the Especially for Youth program since 1984. Brother Jacobs has taught seminary and institute in Arizona and Utah, where he has spent the last few years at the Institute of Religion at Utah State University. He and his wife, Jolene, are the parents of four very active children. Curtis is a racquetball fanatic and loves Les Misérables.

20

"FOR I AM NOT ASHAMED OF THE GOSPEL OF CHRIST"

Bruce W. Hansen

Going to seminary after school was a challenge for some of the high school students. They had been in school all day and now they were to walk across the street to the recently built chapel for fifty minutes of seminary. As I waited for them, a group of enthusiastic girls came into the classroom early to tell me what Billy had done. Periodically, a group of their non-LDS peers would make fun of these freshmen on their way to seminary. (See 1 Nephi 8:27 for a Book of Mormon analogy!) On this day, however, Billy had decided to respond by standing in the middle of the street and quoting a scripture mastery verse that we had recently memorized, "For I am not ashamed of the gospel of Christ: for it is the power of God unto salvation to every one that believeth" (Romans 1:16). It was a remarkable action and increased the girls' enthusiasm for the gospel. It also added to the admiration I already had for that young man.

On another occasion, seminary students were sponsoring "Bring a Friend to Seminary" day. At first I was disappointed by the low number of non-LDS youth in attendance at my 12:30 class. Then, just before the devotional, a large number of students, with their teacher's permission, walked in from the United States history class across the street. We almost had a majority of non-LDS kids in the seminary class. I was even more impressed by the devotional that followed. A young lady shared her testimony in front of her peers; thereafter she called on several other students to tell their friends why they were Latter-day Saints. A wonderful spirit filled the classroom. I sat in the back in awe of the faith and courage of the youth in the Church!

President Gordon B. Hinckley said, "This work requires sacrifice, it requires effort, *it requires courage to speak out and faith to try*. This cause does not need critics; it does not need doubters. It needs men and women of solemn purpose. As Paul wrote to Timothy: 'God hath not given us the spirit of fear; but of power, and of love, and of a sound mind.

"'*Be not thou therefore ashamed of the testimony of our Lord*' (2 Tim. 1:7–8)" ("Be Not Afraid, Only Believe," *Ensign*, Feb. 1996, 5; emphasis added). How do you develop or sustain the faith and courage necessary to not be ashamed of the gospel of Jesus Christ? The following are four suggestions to assist in developing such enthusiasm.

1. Realize that Jesus Christ is the only name whereby we can be saved. If anyone ever asks you how important Jesus is in the Church, I recommend quoting these verses from the Book of Mormon:

"And we talk of Christ, we rejoice in Christ, we preach of Christ, we prophesy of Christ, and we write according to our prophecies, that our children may know to what source they may look for a remission of their sins. . . .

"And now behold, I say unto you that the right way is to believe in Christ, and deny him not; and Christ is the Holy One of Israel; wherefore ye must bow down before him, and worship him with all your might, mind, and strength, and your whole soul; and if ye do this ye shall in nowise be cast out" (2 Nephi 25:26, 29).

Jesus Christ is more than just our elder Brother. He is the Father of our spiritual rebirth (Mosiah 5:7–8; D&C 25:1). He is the Creator of "worlds without number" (Moses 1:33; D&C 76:24). Imagine that—worlds without number! When we look up in the heavens without the aid of a telescope, we can see approximately six thousand stars. With the use of technology and huge telescopes, however, we get a glimpse of the marvelous expanses that can help us appreciate the reality of so many worlds. For example, in the space that we view outlined by the Big Dipper, astronomers estimate that there are one million galaxies; and each of those galaxies has an average of approximately one hundred billion separate stars! (see Kenneth F. Weaver, "The Incredible Universe," *National Geographic*, May 1974, 589–625; Gerald N. Lund, "'Let This Mind Be in You,'" in *New Testament Symposium Speeches, 1988* [10–12 Aug. 1988], 2). Not only is Christ the Creator of these worlds, Elder Marion G. Romney reminded us that he is also their Redeemer:

"Jesus Christ, in the sense of being its Creator and Redeemer, is the Lord of the whole universe. Except for his mortal ministry accomplished on this earth, his service and relationship to *other worlds* and their inhabitants are the same as his service and relationship to this earth and its inhabitants. . . .

" . . . [Jesus] voluntarily submit[ted] himself to a torturous death, whereby winning victory over the grave and assuring *universal* resurrection. In short, Jesus Christ, through whom God created the universe, was chosen to put into operation *throughout the universe* Elohim's great plan 'to bring to pass the immortality and eternal life of man'" ("Jesus Christ, Lord of the Universe," *Improvement Era*, Nov. 1968, 46, 48; emphasis added).

When one ponders the reality of Jesus' greatness, it is easier to understand what Moses meant when he said, "Now, for this cause I know that man is nothing, which thing I never had supposed" (Moses 1:10). Ammon made a similar comment when he testified, "I know that I am nothing; as to my strength I am weak; therefore I will not boast of myself, but I will boast of my God" (Alma 26:12). It seems that we need to recognize and remember our "own nothingness" without the Lord before we can truly benefit from his greatness (Mosiah 4:11).

After king Benjamin finished quoting the words of an angel, he "cast his eyes round about on the multitude, and behold they had fallen to the earth, for the fear of the Lord had come upon them.

"And they had viewed themselves in their own carnal state, even less than the dust of the earth. And they all cried aloud with one voice, saying: O have mercy, and apply the atoning blood of Christ that we may receive forgiveness of our sins, and our hearts may be purified; for we believe in Jesus Christ, the Son of God, who created heaven and earth, and all things; who shall come down among the children of men" (Mosiah 4:1–2). Note the blessings that came into their lives after repenting and coming unto the great Jehovah with full purpose of heart: "the Spirit of the Lord came upon them, and they were filled with joy, having received a remission of their sins, and having peace of conscience" (Mosiah 4:3). Even Ammon, after testifying of his "nothingness," exclaimed, "I will boast of my God, for in his strength I can do all things; yea, behold, many mighty miracles we have wrought in this land, for which we will praise his name forever" (Alma 26:12).

The words of a favorite hymn bring these declarations together: "When I in awesome wonder *Consider all the worlds thy hands have made. . . .* Then sings my soul, my Savior God, to thee, How great thou art!" (*Hymns*, no. 86; emphasis added). No one who truly realizes our Redeemer's greatness could ever be embarrassed by his gospel.

2. Follow the living prophet. When I was serving as a Young Men president, we challenged the youth to read the entire Book of Mormon and do seven acts of service each month in preparation for a trip to Temple Square. A number of the young men and women had never been to Salt Lake City before. It was exciting for them to see the temple for the first time. A group of our young men, however, was upset at the sight of individuals passing out anti-Mormon literature at the entrance to Temple Square. I remember their challenge to me, "Go get 'em, Brother Hansen." I admit the opportunity for a quick "Bible bash" intrigued me for a moment, but I overcame the temptation and encouraged the young men to simply ignore them.

An hour or so later we were visiting the Church Office Building and enjoying a question-and-answer session with Elder Ronald Poleman. As we were leaving, a rumor quickly spread that President Ezra Taft Benson was going to take a moment to visit with us. It was no rumor! Into the main foyer walked President Benson. No one said a word. The prophet said to our youth, "Do you know who you are? Do you really know?" Again, no one said a word (not that they weren't paying attention!). Finally, Elder Poleman broke the spiritual silence by asking if we'd like to shake hands with the prophet. Despite his age, President Benson's firm grip left a lasting impression.

At long last, one young man had the courage to raise his hand and ask, "President Benson, could we shake your hand again?" "Sure," came the prophet's response, and we again got in line and shook hands with the Lord's spokesman.

After this experience it was time to return to our bus. As I walked behind the same young men who had been offended earlier by the passing out of derogatory literature, I was grateful for their new attitude. They expressed sympathy for those people that wasted their time distributing such falsehoods while a prophet of God was just up the street. No longer did these young men desire a "Bible bash." They had simply felt the love of God as shown through his living prophet.

Remember, all prophets represent Christ and speak his words (D&C 1:14, 38; Amos 3:7). When we follow the prophet "there is safety and peace." I love the booklet *For the Strength of Youth.* When I was a bishop, I'd sometimes tell the young people that this pamphlet could also be called,

How to Be Happy When You Are a Teenager. These are writings and teachings that "the First Presidency and Quorum of the Twelve have reviewed, accepted, and endorsed . . . , which is printed at their request and with their approval for the information, guidance, and blessings of the youth of the Church" (Salt Lake City: The Church of Jesus Christ of Latter-day Saints, 1990, 1).

A consistent message found in the scriptures is that God blesses those who follow his prophets, and curses those who reject them. I testify that one cannot follow the counsel of Gordon B. Hinckley *and also* feel ashamed of the gospel. As we abide by his counsel we'll know it is from God (John 7: 17).

3. Be clean. During the summer before my junior year in high school, my parents were faced with trying to decide whether to go on a two-week vacation without me. My summer job would not permit me to be gone that long. In the end, they decided to leave their "baby boy" home alone and go on a much-needed trip. I was so excited . . . for them, of course! The night before they left, Dad invited me into the back room of the house for a short visit. After telling me of his love and trust, Dad also said that there was one rule that I had to strictly follow, "Never be alone with a young lady in the house, never!" I promised that I wouldn't do anything wrong. . . . Dad said again, only this time more firmly, "Never be alone with a young lady in the house!"

At that time, my dad was also my bishop. He knew that I was a worthy Aaronic Priesthood holder. But he also understood the nature of temptation better than did his sixteen-year-old son. Bishop Hansen (Dad) then explained, "It's not you I don't trust, it is the situation." He went on to explain how influential Satan could be at such times and that nothing would hurt him (Dad) more than to have his son break such a serious commandment. Although I didn't fully appreciate the "no girls" restriction at the time, I will forever be grateful for loving, yet firm, counsel from my bishop/father.

The prophets have *always* admonished us to remember how imperative it is to keep the law of chastity. In a special satellite broadcast to the youth of the Church, President Hinckley said, "My dear young friends, in matters of sex you know what is right. . . . I plead with you to be careful, to stand safely back from the cliff of sin over which it is so easy to fall. Keep yourselves clean from the dark and disappointing evil of sexual transgression" ("A Prophet's Counsel and Prayer for Youth," *New Era*, Jan. 2001, 13).

Elder Henry B. Eyring told of a situation in which he was counseling a girl who had become disappointed about her patriarchal blessing. It seems that it warned her of a situation, wherein if she yielded, it would lead to great heartache and sorrow. The young lady said she wasn't even dating and was disappointed to be warned of a situation that currently seemed so remote from her personal life. Elder Eyring went on to explain:

"I remember better the interview I had with her less than a year later. She sobbed for a while, sitting in a chair on the other side of my desk in the bishop's office. And then she blurted out her tragedy and how it happened, exactly as she had told me the patriarch so long before had described. In her little season of doubt that a patriarch could see with inspiration, she had made choices that led to years of sorrow" ("And Thus We See," an evening with Elder Henry B. Eyring, Feb. 5, 1993, 1).

Wise counsel from your Church leaders and parents is given because they love you and want you to have your "confidence wax strong in the presence of God" (D&C 121:45). The First Presidency taught, "The physical relationship between a husband and a wife can be beautiful and sacred. It is ordained of God for the procreation of children and for the expression of love within a marriage. . . .

"Because sexual intimacy is so sacred, the Lord requires self-control and purity before marriage as well as full fidelity after marriage" (*For the Strength of Youth*, 14–15). You will never be ashamed of the gospel of Jesus Christ if you let virtue garnish your thoughts unceasingly (D&C 121:45) and obey the law of chastity!

4. Realize that the gospel turns lives around, "for it is the power of God unto salvation to every one that believeth" (Romans 1:16). I have always appreciated the blessings of the Church given to my immediate family. It wasn't until I went to prison (fortunately only as a visitor!) that I saw how the gospel could literally change the life of anyone who comes under its healing influence.

While I was serving as bishop, a less-active member of my ward made some serious mistakes and was put in prison. I called the prison to arrange for a time that I could come and visit. When I spoke with the bishop of the "prison ward" he asked if I'd like to speak in their Sunday worship services. I said yes, but had some reservations about speaking to such a *captive* audience.

As the time for my visit came closer, I was quite nervous. What do you say to members (and nonmembers alike) who may not be allowed to *leave their ward boundaries* for up to twenty years? After much prayerful consideration, I was prompted to look into the November 1995 *Ensign*. Therein, I came across President Boyd K. Packer's talk entitled, "The Brilliant Morning of Forgiveness" (18–21). I believe it was just what the Lord wanted these inmates to hear.

As I drove to the prison, I wondered how I would be received. *Do I call the prisoners by name, or address them as "brother 24601"? What kind of spirit will accompany a meeting held behind bars?* I was hardly prepared for the spiritual feast I was about to take part in. The bishop greeted me and asked me to accompany him to where the prisoners would enter. After a thorough security check, each inmate entered the makeshift chapel. Their bishop's warm handshake and smile greeted them. Then they gave their nervous guest speaker a sincere greeting and reverently sat down for the beginning of the meeting.

In prison, the inmates do not have the privilege of partaking of the sacrament. Therefore, the service was made up of a few announcements, a couple of hymns (including a medley of Primary songs played by one of the prisoners), and the speaker. I felt every eye on me as I walked to the podium and began reading from President Packer's talk:

"Letters come from those who have made tragic mistakes. They ask,

"'Can I *ever* be forgiven?'

"The answer is *yes!* The gospel teaches us that relief from torment and guilt can be earned through repentance. Save for those few who defect to perdition after having known a fulness, there is no habit, no addiction, no rebellion, no transgression, no offense exempted from the promise of complete forgiveness" (Packer, "The Brilliant Morning of Forgiveness, 19).

By the time I had finished reading and commenting on President Packer's talk, I felt the Spirit of the Lord like I had seldom felt in my entire life. This message from an apostle of the Lord had given them encouragement and hope. In a small way, it was like witnessing the Nephites falling down at the feet of Jesus after he had allowed them to feel and bear witness of the marks in his hands and in his feet (3 Nephi 11:17). By the spirit felt in the meeting and the large number of requests for a copy of President Packer's talk, it was apparent that the hope offered by the Atonement had touched their hearts.

Before departing from this sacred experience, the bishop showed me around the prison. I asked him about the effect the gospel has on the life of a convicted criminal. He told me about several non-LDS prisoners who had requested baptism after their release from prison. I wondered about the long-term impression the gospel makes on the lives of all those who are released after getting reactivated into the Church. After considering this question, the kind bishop responded that of the approximately 130 prisoners released since he'd been called as bishop more than six years earlier, he was aware of only *three* ever being arrested again. The national average for those getting arrested after being released from prison is over 60 percent! (see www.ojp. usdoj.gov/bjs/crimoff.htm for similar findings). Suddenly, the scripture in 3 Nephi 5:4 about preaching the gospel unto those cast into prison took on a whole new meaning. Nothing in this world can relieve the burden of sin and discouragement like the gospel of Jesus Christ (Alma 33:23; Matthew 11:28–30). A gospel that can literally turn around the life of *anyone* who will come unto Christ with full purpose of heart is nothing to be ashamed of (2 Nephi 31:13).

I testify that this gospel "is the power of God unto salvation to every one that believeth" (Romans 1:16). As we put Christ first in our lives, follow the living prophet, keep ourselves clean and pure, and allow the gospel to change our lives and those around us, we will *not be ashamed.* As President Hinckley recently said: "We want you to have fun. We want you to enjoy life. We do not want you to be prudes. We want you to be robust and cheerful, to sing and dance, to laugh and be happy.

"But in so doing, be humble and be prayerful, and the smiles of heaven will fall upon you" ("A Prophet's Counsel and Prayer for Youth," 14). Surely, such smiles are for those who are "not ashamed of the gospel of Christ."

Bruce W. Hansen is an instructor at the Las Vegas Institute of Religion. He has been teaching for the Church Educational System for eighteen years and has been a speaker for EFY since 1989. Bruce holds a master's degree in counseling and educational psychology. He served a mission in Frankfurt, Germany, while his future wife was serving in Paris, France. Brother Hansen has a been a bishop and is currently a member of the stake high council. He enjoys playing Ping-Pong at the institute and basketball anywhere. He and his wife, Leanne, have five children.

21

THE TIMES OF THE SIGNS

Victor W. Harris

We definitely live and breathe in an interesting time and in an interesting culture, don't we? For example, the other day I retrieved this off the Internet (see Cliff Martin, "Jargon," www.ldsfriends.com):

> *My son's a CTR . . . I go to PEC.*
> *I work for CES . . . I study the TG.*
> *I read the B of M . . . I probe the D&C.*
> *I search the KJV . . . I ponder the JST.*
> *Today in BYC . . . we planned for EFY.*
> *I stayed a little after . . . and had a PPI.*
> *The YM and YW . . . are putting on a play.*
> *It's one that I remember . . . we did in MIA.*
> *Before our oldest son . . . went in the MTC,*
> *He helped the BSA . . . complete their SME.*
> *Soon our oldest daughter . . . is headed for the Y.*
> *Soon our oldest clothing . . . is going to DI.*
> *Now, if you've understood . . . this alphabetic mess,*
> *The chances are quite good . . . that you are LDS.*

I am grateful to be a Latter-day Saint, in spite of this alphabetic mess. As you know, throughout the ages, prophets of God have looked forward with great steadfastness and anticipation to our day. Their lives and testimonies stand as a profound witness of Jesus' first visit to our earth. Their words and warnings evidence the divine truth that he who is "Wonderful, Counsellor, The mighty God, The everlasting Father," will return again and usher in a millennial age as the Prince of Peace (Isaiah 9:6). We live in this day—the day when the fulfillment of all of the prophecies will come to pass as a part of the restoration of all things (see Ephesians 1:10).

As we seek to understand the prophecies concerning the Second Coming, it is natural to experience a desire to also understand how we can more fully prepare to embrace and to endure them. As the coming of our Lord approaches, it is the scriptural words of our ancient and modern prophets that can most fully prepare us to "abide the day" (D&C 35:21).

In June of 1995, President Gordon B. Hinckley said, "I love our scrip-tures. I love these wonderful volumes, which set forth the word of the Lord—given personally or through prophets—for the guidance of our Father's sons and daughters. . . .

"I have read these volumes again and again. As I have pondered their words there has come, by the power of the Holy Ghost, a witness of their truth and divinity" ("Feasting on the Scriptures," *New Era*, June 1995, 6, 8).

What follows is my attempt to let some of the words of our ancient and modern prophets tell the story of the Second Coming and teach us how we as Latter-day Saints can prepare for this glorious day.

So what can we do to prepare? Do you recall the story of the three little pigs and their three different levels of preparation? Two of the pigs cried, "Who's afraid of the big, bad wolf?" until the big bad wolf arrived on the scene. As he attempted to deceive them with his cunning words and to enter their shoddily prepared houses, they then cried, "Not by the hair of our chinny, chin, chins," to which the wolf responded, "Then I'll huff and I'll puff and I'll blow your house in."

Their homes were no match for the destruction that followed. One little pig, however, heeded the counsel and warnings of those who were wise—he built his home out of brick, a material that makes for a strong foundation.

Concerning our spiritual houses, Nephi counseled: "Remember, remem-ber that it is upon the rock of our Redeemer, who is Christ, the Son of God, that ye must build your foundation; that when the devil shall send forth his mighty winds, yea, his shafts in the whirlwind, yea, when all his hail and his mighty storm shall beat upon you, it shall have no power over you to drag you down to the gulf of misery and endless wo, because of the rock upon which ye are built, which is a sure foundation, a foundation whereon if men build they cannot fall" (Helaman 5:12).

On 2 July 1839, the Prophet Joseph Smith said, "I testify . . . that the coming of the Son of Man is nigh, even at your doors" (*History of The Church of Jesus Christ of Latter-day Saints*, 7 vols. 2d ed. rev., ed. B. H.

Roberts [Salt Lake City: The Church of Jesus Christ of Latter-day Saints, 1932–51], 3:390). If the coming of our Lord was close in 1839, how much closer do you think it is at the dawn of this new millennium? It was Jesus himself who said, "But if ye are prepared ye shall not fear" (D&C 38:30). So again, what can we do to prepare so that we can avoid the fear that many will feel upon his return?

I testify that for those who are pure and who have taken the Holy Spirit as their guide, the Second Coming will not be a fearful experience (see D&C 45:57). For those who are unprepared, however, his coming will occur as a "thief in the night" (1 Thessalonians 5:2). "Of that day, and hour," Jesus said to his disciples, "no one knoweth; no, not the angels of God in heaven, but my Father only" (Joseph Smith—Matthew 1:40).

Concerning what we can do to prepare, Doctrine and Covenants 87:8 reads, "Wherefore, stand ye in holy places, and be not moved, until the day of the Lord come; for behold, it cometh quickly, saith the Lord." Have you ever wondered where these holy places can be found? I believe they can be found in temples and in churches; in seminaries and institutes of religious instruction; in emotionally healthy and happy homes; next to bedsides on bended knee; at uplifting activities; and in wholesome, building, and loving relationships. Ultimately, a holy place is anywhere the Spirit of the Lord can continue to dwell in our hearts. Therefore, Zion can be found anywhere a people who are "pure in heart" dwell (D&C 97:21).

A spiritual Zion built upon purity of heart must be established before the Lord and the City of Zion will return. Concerning this beautiful occasion, Jesus said, "Then shalt thou and all thy city meet them there, and we will receive them into our bosom, and they shall see us; and we will fall upon their necks, and they shall fall upon our necks, and we will kiss each other;

"And there shall be mine abode, and it shall be Zion, which shall come forth out of all the creations which I have made; and for the space of a thousand years the earth shall rest.

"And it came to pass that Enoch saw the day of the coming of the Son of Man, in the last days, to dwell on the earth in righteousness for the space of a thousand years;

"But before that day he saw great tribulations among the wicked; and he also saw the sea, that it was troubled, and men's hearts failing them, looking forth with fear for the judgments of the Almighty God, which should come upon the wicked.

"And the Lord showed Enoch all things, even unto the end of the world; and he saw the day of the righteous, the hour of their redemption, and received a fulness of joy" (Moses 7:63–67).

Did you notice in these words that the Lord's judgments will come only upon the wicked? The righteous will be redeemed and experience joy. What a beautiful promise! It is my testimony that nothing that the Lord sends as a part of the Second Coming will harm us if we have learned to *stand in holy places* and to *take the Holy Spirit as our guide*.

With this promise in mind, let's discuss some of the events that we can expect to occur prior to the Second Coming in an attempt to further dispel any fears we might have. To his disciples, Jesus said that in the last days "iniquity shall abound" and "the love of men shall wax cold" (JS—M 1:30). Each of us have witnessed that this is an everyday occurrence—iniquity and a general lack of love abound in television, in newspapers, at school, and in the workplace.

President Ezra Taft Benson stated that the root of such iniquity and lack of love is *pride*. In his April 1989 general conference talk, he stated, "This message has been weighing heavily on my soul for some time. I know the Lord wants this message delivered now" ("Beware of Pride," *Ensign*, May 1989, 4). I feel impressed to share with you some of his words concerning the many faces of pride that directly affect us *now* in our lives.

President Benson said, "Pride is essentially competitive in nature. . . .

"The proud make every man their adversary by pitting their intellects, opinions, works, wealth, talents, or any other worldly measuring device against others. . . .

"Pride is a sin that can readily be seen in others but is rarely admitted in ourselves. Most of us consider pride to be a sin of those on the top, such as the rich and the learned, looking down at the rest of us. (See 2 Ne. 9:42.) There is, however, a far more common ailment among us—and that is pride from the bottom looking up. It is manifest in so many ways, such as fault-finding, gossiping, backbiting, murmuring, living beyond our means, envying, coveting, withholding gratitude and praise that might lift another, and being unforgiving and jealous" (ibid., 4–5).

President Benson also identified one of the most common elements of pride among teenagers and adults: "Selfishness is one of the more common faces of pride. 'How everything affects me' is the center of all that matters—self-conceit, self-pity, worldly self-fulfillment, self-gratification, and self-seeking. . . .

"Another face of pride is contention. Arguments, fights, unrighteous dominion, generation gaps, divorces, spouse abuse, riots, and disturbances all fall into this category of pride" (ibid., 6).

President Benson then offered the antidote to pride, when he testified, "The antidote for pride is humility—meekness, submissiveness. (See Alma 7:23.) . . .

"God will have a humble people. Either we can choose to be humble or we can be compelled to be humble" (ibid., 6).

As President Benson concluded, he uttered some of my favorite words. I think they apply to all of us who are trying so hard to prepare for the Second Coming: "Let us *choose* to be *humble*. We can *do it*. I know *we can*" (ibid., 7, emphasis added). I love these words of hope. I testify that we can overcome pride and become humble as we prepare for the exciting events to come.

With these words and warnings in mind, I would like to conclude with some of the incredible signs of the times that are being fulfilled before our eyes or that yet await us:

GENERAL PROPHECIES AND SIGNS OF THE TIMES

- Each nation will hear the gospel in their own tongue (D&C 90:11).
- World knowledge will increase (Daniel 12:4).
- The gospel will go to the Gentiles first, then to the Jews (1 Nephi 13:42; Matthew 20:16).
- Christ will come suddenly to his temple (Malachi 3:1; D&C 36:8; 110).
- Men's hearts shall fail them (Luke 21:26).
- The mark of the beast will be upon the wicked (Revelation 13:16).
- Spiritual darkness will cover the minds of the people (D&C 112:23–24).
- Churches will forgive sins for money (Mormon 8:32).
- False Christs will show many signs and wonders (JS—M 1:22).
- Men will not believe the signs of the times (2 Peter 3:3–4).
- Fear shall come upon all people (D&C 63:33; 88:91).
- Precious things "in an hour [will be] made desolate" (Revelation 18:19).
- 144,000 High Priests will be called (D&C 133:18; 77:11).
- Wars and rumors of wars will be upon the face of the earth (D&C 63:33).
- Peace will be taken from the earth, and the devil will have great power (D&C 1:35).

- The whole earth will be in commotion (D&C 45:26; 88:89–91).
- Iniquity shall abound on the earth (JS—M 1:30).
- The spirit of Christ will be withheld from the wicked (D&C 63:32).
- Angels are waiting (and have been released) to reap destruction upon the tares or wicked (D&C 38:11–12).
- A great hailstorm will destroy the crops of the earth, each hailstone weighing a talent or approximately 75.6 pounds (D&C 29:16; Revelation 16:21; see Bible Dictionary, p. 789: "Talent").
- No flesh will be completely safe upon the waters (D&C 61:4–5, 14–15; 88:90).
- The moon will reflect a blood-red color, and sea waves will be huge (D&C 45:42; 88:87, 90).
- Flesh shall fall from bones and eyes from sockets (D&C 29:18–19).
- The spirit of Christ shall be poured out upon all flesh (Joel 2:28–32).
- There will be famines, pestilences, and earthquakes in divers places (JS—M 1:29).

PROPHECIES CONCERNING THE CHURCH OF JESUS CHRIST OF LATTER-DAY SAINTS

- The Church of Jesus Christ will be restored (Daniel 2:44–45; Revelation 14:6–7).
- The Book of Mormon will come forth (Ezekiel 37:15–20; Isaiah 29).
- The times of the Gentiles will commence (D&C 45:28–30).
- Much tribulation will affect the Saints (D&C 58:1–4; 63:33–34; 112:24–26).
- Zion (the Church) will be established in the mountains (Isaiah 2:2–3).
- Church membership in comparison with the world will be relatively small (1 Nephi 14:12; 2 Nephi 28:14).
- Elijah will come again and bestow the sealing keys to perform sacred ordinances for both the living and the dead (Malachi 4:5; D&C 110:13, 14).
- Speculation and extravagance will afflict the Saints (see Heber C. Kimball, *Deseret News*, 23 May 1931, 3).
- False Christs and prophets will deceive some of the elect (Revelation 13:13–14; JS—M 1:22).
- The gospel will go to all the world before the end comes (Matthew 24:14).
- Christ and the Church leaders will meet at Adam-ondi-Ahman (see Joseph Smith, *History of the Church*, 3:386–87; D&C 116).

- The center stake of Zion will be in Jackson County, Missouri (D&C 57:3).
- The elders will be called home from the world (see Kimball, *Deseret News*, 23 May 1931, 3).
- The righteous will not be deceived (JS—M 1:37).
- Those who consecrate and offer tithes will not be burned at his coming (D&C 64:23–25).
- One half of the Saints will not abide the day of his coming (Matthew 24:40–41; 25:1–13; D&C 112:24–25).
- Some of the Saints who remain will be "caught up" to meet the Great Jehovah (D&C 88:96).

PROPHECIES CONCERNING THE AMERICAS

- The Lamanites will "blossom as the rose" (D&C 49:24).
- The U.S. Constitution will be on the brink of disaster (Brigham Young, *Journal of Discourses*, vol. 2, 182).
- The Saints will gather to Zion and to her stakes (3 Nephi 21:28; D&C 115:6).
- Salt Lake City will become a wicked city of the world (see Kimball, *Deseret News*, 23 May 1931, 3).
- The New Jerusalem is Independence, Jackson County, Missouri (D&C 84:2–3).
- Zion will be the only place not subject to war (D&C 45:69).
- The ten tribes will be gathered spiritually through missionary work (3 Nephi 21:26).
- The ten tribes as a body will come from the north to the New Jerusalem (D&C 133:26–34; see also *Teachings of the Prophet Joseph Smith (TPJS)*, sel. Joseph Fielding Smith [Salt Lake City: Deseret Book, 1976], 17).

PROPHECIES CONCERNING ISRAEL

- The Jews will be persecuted and scattered until the "times of the Gentiles" are fulfilled (Luke 21:20–24; D&C 45:24–25).
- The scattered Hebrew nation will again be reunited (Isaiah 11:12; 52:9).
- Moses will restore the keys of Israel's gathering (D&C 110:11).
- Jerusalem (Israel) will be a fruitful land (Isaiah 61:4; Ezekiel 36:8).
- The temple will be rebuilt in Jerusalem (Revelation 11:1–2; *TPJS*, 286).

- Some of the scattered Jews will begin to believe in Christ (2 Nephi 30:7).
- Gog and his mighty nation will arise. Ezekiel uses the name *Gog*, which is the name of an evil prince from his day, to describe an evil prince in the last days who will lead his nation against Israel. The ensuing battle will begin in the valley of Megiddo which is about sixty miles north of Jerusalem. This battle will be called the battle of Armageddon (Ezekiel 38–39).
- Jerusalem's peace and wealth will be envied by Gog (Ezekiel 38:11–16).
- Gog and two hundred million of his followers will fight against Israel (Revelation 9:16).
- The battle of Armageddon will be the greatest war since the time of Adam (Daniel 12:1).
- Jerusalem will fall to Gog and his army with one half of the city being taken captive (Zechariah 14:2).
- Two prophets will defend Jerusalem for three and a half years (D&C 77:15; Revelation 11).
- These two prophets will be captured and killed, their bodies will lie in the streets for three and a half days, and then they will be raised up (Revelation 11).
- In the midst of this great battle, one of the many appearances the Savior will make at his coming will be to the Mount of Olives. The mount will cleave in two and thereby prepare a way for the remaining Jews in Jerusalem to escape (D&C 133:20; Revelation 14:1; Zechariah 14:3–4).
- These survivors will then approach the Savior, look upon him, and ask, "What are these wounds in thine hands and in thy feet?" Jesus will solemnly reply, "These wounds are the wounds with which I was wounded in the house of my friends. I am he who was lifted up. I am Jesus that was crucified. I am the Son of God." The scriptural record then records the response of the Jews, "And then shall they weep because of their iniquities; then shall they lament because they persecuted their king" (D&C 45:51–53).

PROPHECIES CONCERNING THE COMING OF OUR LORD

- Christ's second coming will be at the beginning of the seventh thousand-year period. After the seventh thousand-year period begins, will be a one-half-hour space—according to the Lord's time frame—and then he will come (D&C 77:6, 12; 88:95; Revelation 8:1).

- A great earthquake will cover the whole earth (Jeremiah 4:23–26; Revelation 6:12).
- All the continents and the land will be reunited (D&C 133:23–25).
- The land of Zion will join the land of Jerusalem (D&C 133:23–25).
- The earth shall reel, the sun shall be darkened, and the stars shall fall from heaven (D&C 88:87).
- The angels will begin the sounding of their trumpets, and all nations will hear it (D&C 88:92, 94).
- The three great cities of Boston, Albany, and New York will be destroyed (See Wilford Woodruff, "Construction of Logan Temple Foretold," in N. B. Lundwall, comp., *Temples of the Most High* [Salt Lake City: Bookcraft, 1968], 98).
- The Lord's voice will be heard throughout the earth (D&C 45:49).
- Christ will come in glory and power (Isaiah 40:5).
- When the rainbow is withdrawn, the coming of our Lord is nigh (*TPJS*, 340).
- Christ will appear the same way he left (Acts 1:9–11).
- The face of the Lord will be unveiled (D&C 88:95).
- Everyone on earth will witness the Second Coming (Isaiah 40:4–5).
- Christ will appear in a red robe (D&C 133:48).
- The great and abominable church will be destroyed (D&C 29:21; 1 Nephi 22:23).
- The righteous will rejoice (D&C 133:44–62).
- The earth will burn, and only the terrestrial things will survive (Isaiah 24:6; D&C 29:9; 64:23–25; 101:23–31; Malachi 4).
- The Saints who are alive on the earth shall be quickened and caught up to meet Christ (D&C 88:96).
- The Saints who are sleeping in their graves shall be resurrected and caught up to meet Christ (D&C 88:97).

After all of this, the purposes of our God, his Son, and his disciples will then be fulfilled. Until that glorious day when the coming of our Lord occurs, however, we must continue to wage the battle of the eternities—the battle begun long ago in our premortal life.

Concerning this ongoing battle, President Gordon B. Hinckley has said: "There are two powers on the earth . . . —the power of God and the power of the devil. . . . When God has had a people on the earth, it matters not in what age, Lucifer, the son of the morning, and the millions of fallen spirits that were cast out of heaven, have warred against God, against Christ, against the work of God, and against the people of God. The war goes on. It is waged in our own lives—day in and day out—in our homes, in our work, in our school associations. It is waged over questions of love and respect, of loyalty and fidelity, of obedience and integrity. The victims who fall are as precious as those who have fallen in the past. It is an ongoing battle" ("The War We Are Winning," *Ensign*, Nov. 1986, 43–44).

These are powerful words from a powerful servant of God. May I bear you my witness that I know that our Lord will come again a second time. Further, I testify that just as the Lord watched over and protected those who became pure in heart from Adam to Noah, so will he also protect those who repent, become pure, and stand in holy places today.

Adam, Enoch, Noah, and many other ancient prophets came to prepare and warn the people before the flood. Joseph Smith, Ezra Taft Benson, Gordon B. Hinckley, and many other modern-day prophets, apostles, and Saints have come to prepare and warn us before the fire.

We truly are living in the "Times of the Signs." May we choose to be prepared so we will not have to fear, is my prayer.

Victor Harris has been teaching since 1985. He is a frequent speaker at Especially for Youth, fireside programs, and BYU Education Week. He is also an entertainer, having toured with BYU's Young Ambassadors and USO. He graduated from Brigham Young University with a bachelor's degree in psychology and holds a master's degree from Utah State University in family and human development, specializing in adolescence and marriage and family relations. He enjoys tennis, basketball, traveling, and spending time with his family. Victor and his wife, Heidi, have three children—Mckay, Avenlea, and Jaeden—and live in Logan, Utah.

22

IT IS WRITTEN!

Michael Kidd

Years ago, while standing in the grocery store checkout line, a headline from a tabloid newspaper caught my attention. The 10 May 1994 *Weekly World News* reported, rather humorously, "Bible Prayers to Flush Out Body Fat." The teasers for the story were: "Eat all you want and still lose 10, 20, 30 pounds or more! Holy Scriptures show you how to lose weight fast!" Because I was a new seminary teacher at the time, I just had to buy the tabloid. I figured I would be able to use it in a scripture reading lesson some-time. Who would have thought that one of the blessings of reading the scriptures would be a blessing of weight loss!?

That same year, the principal of my seminary shared with me another "blessing" of scripture study. It was a quote he found from Heber C. Kimball, an early Church apostle. Apparently, Elder Kimball was addressing a gath-ering of Saints about the labors of missionary work. Here's what he said:

"I have often told you that all my lazy hairs were gone; and I have often told the young Elders, to encourage them, that the first mission I took, after I was ordained one of the Twelve, was through New England and into Nova Scotia. . . . Soon after I started I found that I was rather unlearned, though I knew that before, but I knew it better after I started.

"I began to study the Scriptures, . . . and I had so little knowledge that the exercise of study began to swell my head and open my pores insomuch that the hairs dropped out; and if you will let your minds expand as mine did you will have no hair on your heads" (in *Journal of Discourses*, 26 vols. [London: Latter-day Saints' Book Depot, 1854–86], 4:107).

How inspiring is *that* blessing of scripture study? I like to remind my seminary students of this thought when they mock me for my baldness.

181

So, it seems, you and I have a few interesting blessings to choose from when it comes to reading and studying the scriptures: we can either lose weight or lose hair. But let me share a secret with you. When it comes to reading and studying the scriptures, you and I really have nothing to lose; we have everything to gain. So, in this chapter, I hope to share a thought or two about the power of scripture study to motivate us a little more to "feast upon the words of Christ" (2 Nephi 32:3) as found in his holy scriptures.

Dear friends, the Lord is counting on you to know what he has said in the scriptures. In fact, he expects it. He once declared, "And now I give unto you a commandment . . . to give diligent heed to the words of eternal life. For you shall live by every word that proceedeth forth from the mouth of God" (D&C 84:43–44). He knows you will be spiritually protected from the adversary when you do. As such, the Lord is also depending on you to search, study, and ponder his words. When you do, you follow in his footsteps and you will be prepared to meet the challenges of your lives—especially the tempting ones.

Allow me to illustrate by sharing an experience that has become a parable for me.

Growing up in California, my chance to visit ski resorts, canyons, and fish-loaded rivers was limited by a distance too far to travel. A little more than seven years ago, my wife and I made Utah County our permanent home, which put us relatively close to great skiing, beautiful canyons, and the blue ribbon fishing water called the Provo River.

I have enjoyed driving through Provo Canyon, and I marvel at the gracefulness of the fly fishermen who line up along the Provo River to test the waters. Amazed and entranced, I have often pulled off the road to watch the graceful, flowing movements of each fly fisher's cast. After watching those fly fishermen (and loving the outdoors), I decided that I wanted to be part of the sport.

My chance came rather unexpectedly. My brother-in-law was living in Logan at the time. He had just taken up fly-fishing as a sport and was eager to teach me. So, in his parking lot he showed me the mechanics of casting a dry fly.

A few weeks later, after watching an outdoors program, he called me to see if I would be interested in fishing the Provo River on Thanksgiving Day. He told me that the outdoor program recommended the use of artificial spinners—not dry flies—since the brown trout were spawning and much more aggressive. He then explained that if the spinners didn't work, we could try our luck at fly-fishing.

To prepare for my first Provo River fishing trip, I went to a local sporting goods store. I figured that if anyone could impart precious Provo River fishing secrets, the guys at the sporting goods store could. I told the first employee I saw about my fishing trip and asked for his help in picking out the perfect artificial spinners. He walked me over to an enormous display of Panther Martin lures—the costliest lures in the store. He told me that there were many spinners manufactured by different companies, but, in his experience, Panther Martin lures yielded the most success.

Success on the river, not a depleted pocketbook, mattered more to me, so I asked the salesman to show me which of the Panther Martin lures I should buy. He pointed out two: a dark one with yellow spots, and a shiny, metallic one. I grabbed them quickly and asked when to use either lure. The salesman explained that the dark one was best for sunny, bright, clear days. The reflection and movement would draw the attention of even the most intelligent fish. On the other hand, if the day were overcast, cloudy, and gloomy, he said, I would do best using the shiny, metallic one. It, too, he said, had given many a fisherman tremendous success. With that, I purchased the lures and headed for home, confident that I would guide an unsuspecting brown trout into my fishing net.

Finally Thanksgiving Day arrived. And, a few hours later, so did my brother-in-law. We wasted no time traveling into the canyon, seeking the perfect fishing hole—the one where the biggest trophy brown trout hid. After donning our chest waders and wading boots, we tied on the spinners. Because it was a beautiful, warm, sunny day, I attached the dark lure with yellow spots. Five minutes later, we stood in the river, casting and reeling.

I cast upstream, figuring that the spinner would look best flowing with—not against—the river's current. That assumption proved correct, and within a half hour I watched an eleven-inch brown trout chase my spinner. The chasing continued for nearly five minutes.

Each time I would cast upstream and reel in my lure, I would watch the same trout pursue the spinner and then turn back upstream. I guessed that my spinner presentation wasn't realistic enough so I tried casting further upstream. Then, instead of reeling in my line quickly, I decided to match the speed of the river's current. By the second cast, my luck started to change.

As I cast upstream and reeled in my line at the speed of the river's current, that same trout chased my lure and, just before I lifted it out of the water to recast, my brown, aquatic friend took the lure! Surprisingly, though, the fish didn't fight to free itself. I figure that after five minutes of chasing my lure, the fish had insufficient strength to attempt to break free. I caught my fish, held it up for my brother-in-law to see, and then carefully released it back into the river's cool, clear water.

I have reflected often on that experience and, like a parable, have found several applications for life. Consider a few of them.

Like the fanciest of fishing lures, Satan has the perfect one for each of us. For those sunny days in our lives when things are comfortable, the devil will use lures (perhaps black, with attractive yellow spots) designed to "pacify, and lull [us] away into carnal security, that [we] will say: All is well . . . and thus the devil cheateth [our] souls" (2 Nephi 28:21). But because not every day of our lives is sunny, the devil often takes from his tackle box other shiny, metallic lures designed to prolong depression or discouragement, invite contention, or "stir [us] up to anger against that which is good" (2 Nephi 28:20). Either way, the devil's design is to cast at us whatever lure will be most appealing for the day—be it sunny, stormy, or overcast. He is neither afraid to try dozens of different lures nor tie his own custom-made-for-us flies until we bite.

Satan is also an extremely accomplished fisherman. He is superb at matching the river's current and unbelievably patient. He will cast and reel as long as necessary, convinced that if we give in to inner passions and appetites we'll eventually bite his deadly hooks. He knows that, once we do give in, landing us into his horrifying net of misery will be easy. We will be too helpless, worn out, and tired to break free; our spirits may be willing, but our flesh will be too weak.

Perhaps worst of all, Satan is not a catch-and-release fisherman. Since the day we cast our "vote" in the Council in Heaven, the devil has labored unceasingly to make mankind miserable like himself. No one is exempt from that ghastly, search-and-destroy effort. The apostle Peter testified, "Your adversary the devil, as a roaring lion, walketh about, seeking whom he may devour" (1 Peter 5:8). Elder Spencer W. Kimball echoed that thought when he said, "Satan is very much a personal, individual spirit being, but without a mortal body. His desires to seal each of us his are no less ardent in wickedness than our Father's are in righteousness to attract us to his own eternal kingdom" (*The Miracle of Forgiveness* [Salt Lake City: Bookcraft, 1969], 21).

With such a discouraging portrait of this dangerous fisherman, one may be led to ask if there is any hope for safety. Is there any way a young woman or a young priesthood holder can recognize Satan's homemade fishing lures, flies, and barbed hooks and thus avoid them? Isn't there someone or something, like the employee at the sporting goods store, who can warn us about Satan's lures and flies? Nephi seems to think so. He declared, "My soul delighteth in the scriptures" (2 Nephi 4:15). Interesting, isn't it? Nephi found safety in the scriptures because he pondered the things he both saw and heard as he read them (2 Nephi 4:15–16). They gave him precious information. And surely he found the strength to protect himself from Satan's tempting lures. I challenge you to see if reading your scriptures will fill you with the same hope and extend the same knowledge and protection.

President Ezra Taft Benson also recognized the power of the scriptures. He taught that the Book of Mormon "exposes the enemies of Christ. It confounds false doctrines and lays down contention. (See 2 Nephi 3:12.) It fortifies the humble followers of Christ against the evil designs, strategies, and doctrines of the devil in our day" (*A Witness and a Warning* [Salt Lake City: Deseret Book, 1988], 3).

Knowing of the spiritual protection that comes from scripture reading, can there be any wonder that Nephi would write, "My God hath been my support . . . and he hath preserved me upon the waters of the great deep" (2 Nephi 4:20)?

Friends, we cannot afford NOT to read the scriptures! We must not be ignorant of Satan's destructive fishing efforts by reading the scriptures one day and then letting considerable time pass before we read them again. There is too much at stake. Paul warned young Timothy: "In the last days perilous times shall come" (2 Timothy 3:1). Then, continuing, he enumerated those things that would characterize the last days. He said: "Men shall be lovers of their own selves, covetous, boasters, proud, blasphemers, disobedient to parents, unthankful, unholy, Without natural affection, trucebreakers, false accusers, incontinent, fierce, despisers of those that are good, Traitors, heady, highminded, lovers of pleasures more than lovers of God; Having a form of godliness, but denying the power thereof" (2 Timothy 3:2–5).

Can any of you not sense the adversary's relentless fishing efforts to create such conditions? Paul did. So, in an effort to teach Timothy how to avoid the lures that would lead him into such reprehensible behavior, Paul counseled, "But continue thou in the things which thou hast learned and hast been assured of, knowing of whom thou hast learned them; And that from a child thou hast known the holy scriptures, which are able to make thee wise unto salvation" (2 Timothy 3:14–15). The scriptures, then, become the daily protection that can ward off the multicolored fishing lures, flies, and hooks the devil uses most; they can give us a glimpse of the kinds of fishing tackle he chooses.

The Savior understood the power of the scriptures, too. Because he is our Master and our Exemplar, we are to do as he did in every instance— nothing more, nothing less. Observe how he overcame the adversary's ruth-less attack by using the scriptures.

Matthew tells us that following Christ's baptism, he went into the wilderness to be with God (Matthew 4:1; see footnote b), fasting forty days and forty nights. Perhaps as a matter of understatement, Matthew then says that the Savior was "an hungred" (Matthew 4:2). Who wouldn't be? Taken literally, we could observe that if the Savior's fast were to open on New Year's Day, 1 January, he would close it in the middle of February—9 February! Or, take a look at your calendar. Circle today's date and then count ahead forty days. Are you impressed? Amazed? Well, after so many days of fasting, a piece of bread would taste like cake! So, following what must have been a precious, sacred, holy experience (perfect conditions for a sunny-day lure?), "the tempter came to him, [and] he said, If thou be the Son of God, command that these stones be made bread" (Matthew 4:3).

The Savior's response is intriguing, if not instructional and indicative of the power of the scriptures in combating the devil. Jesus "answered and said, It is *written*, Man shall not live by bread alone, but by every word that proceedeth out of the mouth of God" (Matthew 4:4; emphasis added). To combat the devil's temptation the Savior quoted a scripture that is "written" in the book of Deuteronomy.

Clearly, that retort frustrated the devil, for, in the next verse, "Jesus was taken up into the holy city . . . on the pinnacle of the temple" (Matthew 4:5, footnote a). Then, "the devil came unto him" (Matthew 4:6, footnote a) with a new temptation: "If thou be the Son of God, cast thyself down" (Matthew 4:6). Again, defending himself, "Jesus said unto him, [quoting yet another scripture!] It is *written* again, Thou shalt not tempt the Lord thy God" (Matthew 4:7; emphasis added).

Later, Jesus was tempted a third time, being shown "all the kingdoms of the world, and the glory of them" (Matthew 4:8). The devil promised the Savior, "All these things will I give thee, if thou wilt fall down and worship me" (Matthew 4:9). For the third time, Jesus responded with—and note it well!—"it is *written*, Thou shalt worship the Lord thy God, and him only shalt thou serve" (Matthew 4:10; emphasis added)—another scripture.

Each of the three major temptations cast at the Savior failed. Why? I believe it is because Jesus Christ knew his scriptures, he knew the plan, and he knew the will of the Father. He knew the power of the word of God. He memorized passages of scripture and he pondered their deep and hidden meanings (see Bruce R. McConkie, *The Mortal Messiah: From Bethlehem to Calvary*, 4 vols. [Salt Lake City: Deseret Book, 1979–81], 1:368). And, most powerful and instructional of all, the Savior called upon God's words in the scriptures to evade the dangerous lures of the adversary.

So, the important question is, Do we value God's word the way the Savior did? Are we willing to invest at least ten to fifteen minutes each day in scripture reading? If your time appears to be stretched too thin, maybe you can at least commit to reading a few verses in the scriptures each day. Anybody can do that. Elder Joseph B. Wirthlin suggested, "Every one of you can read something in the scriptures each day. You should spend some time pondering and studying the scriptures. It is better to read and ponder even one verse than none at all. I challenge each young man [and woman] to read something in the scriptures every day for the rest of your lives. Few things you do will bring you greater dividends" ("Growing into the Priesthood," *Ensign*, Nov. 1999, 40). Can we afford not to read the scriptures each day, knowing the very real nature of the adversary's efforts to destroy the children of God? If you really think about it, a few minutes of scripture reading each day is such a little amount of time compared to so much protection.

My friends, what I have presented is but one illustration of the power of the scriptures. What you have seen is what they can do for each of us if we will commit this very instant to search, ponder, and pray about them. The scriptures are true treasures of spiritual knowledge and guidance. The scriptures "speaketh harshly against sin, according to the plainness of the truth" (2 Nephi 33:5) and yet "persuadeth [us] to do good; . . . speak[ing] of Jesus, and persuad[ing us] to believe in him, and to endure to the end, which is life eternal" (2 Nephi 33:4). The scriptures protect and bless those who read them. They reveal the adversary's motives and strategies and "will tell you all things what ye should do" (2 Nephi 32:3) to combat his temptations.

I hope that you sense much more of the eternal power of the scriptures. I hope you have developed a deeper commitment to read and live by God's holy, spoken word. Indeed, there really is nothing to lose, like weight or hair, when you read the scriptures. Rather, there is everything to gain—absolutely everything.

Michael A. Kidd was born and raised in Southern California. He served a Spanish-speaking mission to New York City. Following his mission he attended Brigham Young University, where he studied English and Spanish. While there, he also met and married his wife, Holly. He has loved his seven years of teaching seminary in Pleasant Grove, Utah. In his spare time, Michael enjoys sports, music, watching movies with his wife, playing with his little boy and girl, reading, and fly-fishing. He and his family currently live in Eagle Mountain, Utah.

23

YOUTH OF THE NOBLE BIRTHRIGHT

Ron Bartholomew

On many occasions, President Gordon B. Hinckley has said: "You are youth of the noble birthright. . . .

"You are great young people. I have said again and again, we have the finest generation of young people ever in the history of this Church. . . . You are intrinsically better. You are wonderful young people!" (*Teachings of Gordon B. Hinckley* [Salt Lake City: Deseret Book, 1997], 711, 714). He also said, "You represent a great generation in the history of the world and in the history of this Church. In terms of the Church, I feel that you are part of the greatest generation we have ever had" ("True to the Faith," Salt Lake Valley-Wide Institute Fireside, January 21, 1996). You have heard it many times—chosen generation—youth of the noble birthright. Exactly what does that mean? Let's answer this question by explaining: (1) *when* you were chosen, (2) *why* you were chosen, (3) for *what purpose* you were chosen, and (4) *how* you can fulfill your part of Heavenly Father's plan for you while you are on this earth.

WHEN WERE YOU CHOSEN?

We are all Heavenly Father's spirit children, and we lived with him in the premortal life, before we were born. The apostle Paul taught that during our premortal lives, the Lord assigned each of us a specific time and place to come and live on this earth: The Lord "hath made of one blood all nations of men for to dwell on all the face of the earth, and hath determined the times before appointed, and the bounds of their habitation" (Acts 17:26). These two assignments—*where* we would live and *when* we would live—were part of the "foreordination," or the "ordination" we received before we were born. Elder Bruce R. McConkie further explained that in addition to a specific time and place, "the *race and nation* in which men are born in this world is a direct result of their pre-existent life. All the spirit hosts of heaven deemed worthy to receive mortal bodies were foreordained to pass through this earthly probation in the particular *race and nation* suited to their needs, circumstances, and talents" (*Mormon Doctrine*, 2d ed. [Salt Lake City: Bookcraft, 1966], 616; emphasis added).

WHY WERE YOU CHOSEN FOR THIS TIME AND STATION?

The gift of agency began in the premortal life. Because every spirit used its agency differently there, some became more faithful to Heavenly Father than others. President Joseph Fielding Smith explained: "God gave his children their free agency even in the spirit world, by which the individual spirits had the privilege, just as men have here, of choosing the good and rejecting the evil, or partaking of the evil to suffer the consequences of their sins. Because of this, some even there were more faithful than others in keeping the commandments of the Lord. . . .

" . . . The spirits of men were not equal. They may have had an equal start [see Alma 13:5–7], and we know they were all innocent in the beginning; but the right of free agency which was given to them enabled some to outstrip others, and thus, through the eons of immortal existence, to become more intelligent, more faithful, for they were free to act for themselves, to think for themselves, to receive the truth or rebel against it" (*Doctrines of Salvation*, comp. Bruce R. McConkie, 3 vols. [Salt Lake City: Bookcraft, 1954–56], 1:58–59). We know that Jesus became the most righteous of any spirit in the pre-earth life through his constant righteous use of agency there. We also know that every spirit chose to follow either Heavenly Father or Satan. You are here *now* because of your faithfulness *then*.

The Lord explained to Abraham that among those who followed Heavenly Father, some were so exceptionally faithful they were chosen to be his "spiritual leaders" here on earth. Abraham records: "Among all these there were many of the noble and great ones;

"And God saw these souls that they were good, and he stood in the midst of them, and he said: These I will make my rulers; for he stood among those that were spirits, and he saw that they were good; and he said unto me: Abraham, thou art one of them; thou wast chosen before thou wast born" (Abraham 3:22–23). In other words, because they were "noble," "great," and "good," some were chosen in the world of spirits to be "rulers," or spiritual leaders here on earth.

You are part of that chosen or select group of "noble and great" spirits. According to President Ezra Taft Benson, "For nearly six thousand years, God has held you in reserve to make your appearance in the final days before the Second Coming of the Lord. . . . While our generation will be comparable in wickedness to the days of Noah, when the Lord cleansed the earth by flood, there is a major difference this time. It is that God has saved for the final inning some of his strongest children, who will help bear off the Kingdom triumphantly. And that is where you come in, for you are the generation that must be prepared to meet your God.

"All through the ages the prophets have looked down through the corridors of time to our day. Billions of the deceased and those yet to be born have their eyes on us. Make no mistake about it—you are a marked generation" ("In His Steps," in *Speeches of the Year, 1979* [Provo: Brigham Young University Press, 1980], 59).

You are part of this "marked generation"!

In order for you to accomplish this special mission, you needed to be born into a situation where you would have access to the restored gospel of Jesus Christ. Moses taught that this was also part of your premortal foreordination. He said that among all of Heavenly Father's spirit children, the most faithful were chosen to come forth as members of the royal, chosen family lineage of Jacob (Israel): "When the most High . . . separated the sons of Adam, he set the bounds of the people according to the number of the children of Israel" (Deuteronomy 32:8). Elder Melvin J. Ballard wrote that being born into this family lineage is an additional reward for faithfulness in the premortal life: "There was a group of souls tested, tried, and proven before they were born into the world, and the Lord provided a lineage for them. That lineage is the house of Israel, the lineage of Abraham, Isaac and Jacob and their posterity. Through this lineage were to come the true and tried souls that had demonstrated their righteousness in the spirit world before they came here" (in *Melvin J. Ballard—Crusader for Righteousness* [Salt Lake City: Bookcraft, 1966], 218–19).

When you receive your patriarchal blessing (the word patriarchal means "father," so this is a father's blessing from your Heavenly Father), the Lord tells you from which of Jacob's (Israel) sons you have descended. This is of utmost importance, because Jacob was Isaac's son, and Isaac was the son of Abraham. Abraham was so faithful that the Lord promised him that all who ever received the gospel and the blessings of the priesthood would either be born into his family line through his son Isaac and his grandson Jacob or adopted into it (see Abraham 2:9–11; Genesis 17:19–21; 28:13–15).

Elder McConkie explained the great spiritual advantage it is to you to be born into this chosen family line: "To bring to pass the salvation of the greatest possible number of his spirit children the Lord, in general, sends the most righteous and worthy spirits to earth through the lineage of Abraham and Jacob. . . .

" . . . Those so grouped together during their mortal probation have more abundant opportunities to make and keep the covenants of salvation" (*Mormon Doctrine*, 216).

Because you were chosen in the pre-earth life to be born into the family of Abraham, you now have the opportunity to enjoy the blessings of the gospel, all the ordinances of the priesthood, and ultimately eternal life. Have you ever wondered why you were so fortunate to be born here and now, where you are able to accept and enjoy the blessings of the gospel? It is because of your faithfulness in the premortal life!

President Harold B. Lee testified of this when he said: "You are now born into a family to which you have come, into the nations through which you have come, as a reward for the kind of lives you lived before you came here. . . .

"All these rewards were seemingly promised, or foreordained, before the world was. Surely these matters must have been determined by the kind of lives we had lived in that premortal spirit world. Some may question these assumptions, but at the same time they will accept without any question the belief that each one of us will be judged when we leave this earth according to his or her deeds during our lives here in mortality. Isn't it just as reasonable to believe that what we have received here in this earth life was given to each of us according to the merits of our conduct before we came here?" ("Understanding Who We Are Brings Self-Respect," *Ensign*, Jan. 1974, 5).

FOR WHAT PURPOSE WERE YOU CHOSEN?

President Hinckley said this: "You are good. But it is not enough just to be good. You must be good for something. You must contribute good to the world. The world must be a better place for your presence. And the good that is in you must be spread to others. . . .

"But in this world so filled with problems, so constantly threatened by dark and evil challenges, you can and must rise above mediocrity, above indifference. You can become involved and speak with a strong voice for that which is right" ("Stand Up for Truth," in *Brigham Young University 1996–97 Speeches* [Provo: Brigham Young University Press, 1997], 22).

President Spencer W. Kimball taught that before we were born we made sacred covenants with our Heavenly Father that, if we were allowed to be part of the youth of the noble birthright, we would stand for that which is right and make a difference in the world in which we live. He explained: "We have made covenants. We made them before we accepted our position here on the earth. . . .

" . . . We committed ourselves to our Heavenly Father. . . . This was a solemn oath, a solemn promise" (*Be Ye Therefore Perfect* [Salt Lake Institute of Religion devotional, Jan. 10, 1975], 2).

With your great premortal legacy comes the greatest responsibility ever placed upon a group of people in the history of the world. Read the following excerpts from President Hinckley regarding your noble and great generation:

"[You're] not just here by chance. You are here under the design of God" (*Teachings of Gordon B. Hinckley*, 720).

"Truly, my dear young friends, you are a chosen generation. I hope you will never forget it. I hope you will never take it for granted" ("'A Chosen Generation,'" *Ensign*, May 1992, 70).

"Never forget that you were chosen and brought to earth as a child of God for something of importance in his grand design. He expects marvelous things of you!" ("News of the Church," *Ensign*, Feb. 1983, 76).

"We are on stage, you and I, at this glorious season. We have so much to do, so very, very much to *do to move forward the work of the Lord toward the marvelous destiny which He has outlined for it.* . . . None has a more compelling responsibility than do you. You are young. You have energy. You have convictions in your hearts. . . . I challenge you to stand for that which is right and true and good. . . . Regardless of your way of doing things in the past, I offer you a challenge to square your lives with the teachings of the gospel, . . . to live your life as an example of what the gospel of Jesus Christ will do in bringing happiness to an individual" ("True to the Faith," Salt Lake Valley-Wide Institute Fireside, January 21, 1996).

Another prophet of God, President Spencer W. Kimball, said this: "If the . . . members of the church would live the gospel principles all the errors of the world would evaporate. The world would come to us, and we would change the frustration of the world to the peace of the gospel" (in "President Kimball Enjoys His Work," *Church News*, 26 Feb. 1972, 13).

HOW CAN YOU KEEP THE PROMISES YOU MADE BEFORE YOU WERE BORN?

I have met young people all over the Church who have lived up to their premortal promises and are truly "youth of the noble birthright" in name and in deed. They are changing their world by standing up for that which is right and true and good, "at all times and in all things, and in all places" (Mosiah 18:9).

One such young man was Rick, an all-state running back on his high school football team. One day I was working in my office when he came in to see me.

"I need some help, Brother Bartholomew," he started.

"OK, what can I do for you?"

"Well . . . there is a swearing problem with many of the LDS guys on the team, especially the seniors. Some of the younger guys are starting to swear just to impress them."

I knew many of these young men, and I was a little surprised to hear that. "Oh . . ." I replied, "So . . ."

"I've decided to ask each one of them, starting with the team captains, to stop swearing at the practices and games and start setting a better example for the younger players. . . . But those guys are *tough*, Brother Bartholomew . . . I'm afraid of what might happen if I start preaching to them . . ."

They *were* an unusually tough group of young men. But Rick was a star athlete, and I knew he had the respect of the entire team. If anyone could get through to them, it was probably him.

"I think you'll be OK. Why don't you talk to a couple of them and see what happens?" I replied, trying to be encouraging.

Still unsure, but totally committed, Rick left my office.

Several weeks passed, and I had completely forgotten about our conversation in my office. Then one day in class when we were discussing the Aaronic Priesthood, I posed this question: "Does anyone know someone who is a good example of an Aaronic Priesthood holder?" To my surprise, several young men on the football team raised their hands all at once! As they all looked at each other and realized what had just happened, they were shocked. They were good guys, but they had never responded to any question I had ever asked with that kind of enthusiasm!

I pointed to one of them, who immediately blurted out, "Rick!"

"Why?" I asked.

In a serious tone, he recounted how Rick had approached him one day after practice and had asked him to start setting a better example for the other guys on the team by not swearing. He said Rick had done it in such a way as not to offend him, but that it had actually motivated him to clean up his language.

No sooner had the young man shared his experience than the other football players began to share similar experiences. Each of these young men realized that Rick had taken the time to talk to them individually about this difficult and personal issue.

I wish you could have seen the looks on their faces as these young men became aware that one of their friends had cared enough about them, the gospel, and the other LDS young men on the team to take a stand. Rick changed the world he lived in that year because he wasn't afraid to stand up for what was right and good and true.

Heather is another young person who wasn't afraid to take a stand in a difficult situation. Though she is a beautiful girl, she didn't date as much as she would have liked to during high school. After class one day she burst into my office: "*He* asked me out, Brother Bartholomew!"

"Who?" I asked.

"*He* did," came her reply. "It's one thing to get a date," she explained, "but I've been waiting for *this guy* to ask me out, and he did!"

When the day of their date finally arrived, I asked her: "Where is prince charming taking you tonight?"

"To the movie. I hope it is a good one."

"Well, he is a nice guy, isn't he?" I asked.

"He is a *great* guy," she responded, and with that she was off to class.

The next day I could hardly wait to ask her about her date. "So, how was it?"

"It was wonderful," she replied, "but it sure got off to a scary start! As we were walking across the parking lot toward the theater, I scanned the movie titles and ratings and realized there was only one good movie, and it was rated G!"

Heather had set a pretty high standard for herself. She had listened carefully to *everything* the prophets and apostles had said. She knew they had specifically asked us not to view R-rated movies, but she also knew they had also asked us not to view anything that is "vulgar, immoral, inappropriate, suggestive, or pornographic in any way" (*For the Strength of Youth* [Salt Lake City: The Church of Jesus Christ of Latter-day Saints, 1990], 12). She had told me that if the movie industry didn't think her little brothers and sisters should be seeing a particular movie because of violent or inappropriate content, it would probably be offensive to the Spirit as well. So, she had set a personal standard not to view any PG-13 movie or even some PG movies if they were questionable in any way. Her personal motto was this: "Keeping the companionship of the Holy Ghost is more important than a movie—*any* movie."

As they approached the ticket booth she heard the young man ask for two tickets to a very popular movie. Her heart sunk. What was she going to do? She had wanted to make a good impression on her first date with him, but she knew this particular movie was inappropriate by any gospel standard. Everyone at school who had seen it had raved about it, but she knew from their description of it that it contained several scenes that would be completely offensive to the Holy Ghost. As she stood there, a line from the Young Women theme popped into her mind: "I will stand as a witness of God at all times and in all things, and in all places, as I strive to live. . . ." Nervously, she leaned over and whispered to her date: "I'm sorry, but I don't watch those kind of movies."

Startled, his face went from shock to relief as he blurted out, "Really? Neither do I!" He apologetically explained how he had truly wanted to impress her, and had decided, against his own best judgment, to take her to this movie because of its popularity among their peers. They laughed out loud, bought two tickets to *Anastasia*, and enjoyed the rest of the evening together.

Heather is on a mission in Argentina at the time of this writing. As I have watched her over the years, I have noticed the profound effect she has on many people. She has truly stood as a witness of God "at all times in all things, and in all places."

"Standing as a witness" is doing what Jesus would do if he were here. It doesn't always mean that you'll have to defend the standards of the Church; sometimes it just calls for treating others the way the Savior would—even when it is inconvenient. I saw a remarkable example of this in a young woman named Kristen. She served as a student leader at the school where I taught seminary. She changed her world by treating others in a Christlike manner.

Because of her position, she spent her fair share of time "up in front" conducting assemblies, planning student activities, and being a leader. She was in a position where she could really have an influence on her peers. But sometimes the *real* opportunities to do this come in unexpected ways.

One day while she was eating lunch with her friends, a group of special-needs students came by and sat down beside them. These special young people were physically and socially awkward. One of them was learning disabled to the point that she had to live in a care center close enough to the high school that she could attend the resource classes during the day. Her name was Robyn. She was the only African-American student in the entire school. These new friends were warmly welcomed into the group, and eating lunch together became a daily occurrence.

As the school year progressed, Kristen began to develop a love for Robyn. She would visit her at the care center and would often take her to sporting events and other student activities. Although this was not always easy or convenient, she freely gave the love the Savior would have given to this special daughter of our Heavenly Father.

One day, while Kristen was conducting a student assembly, Robyn saw her and unexpectedly stood up and began pushing her way towards the front of the room. All eyes watched as she worked her way up the aisle. When she reached Kristen, she threw her arms around her, pinning the microphone between them. This allowed everyone in the audience to hear her tender, heartfelt words over the loud speaker: "Kristen, I love you! You are the only friend I have!"

Robyn's sincere expression of love penetrated deep into Kristen's heart. Unable to control her emotions (or finish conducting the assembly), she ran off the stage, went home, and spent the rest of the day crying. How could someone so sweet, so full of love, and so innocent think that only one person in the whole world loved her?

Shortly after graduation, Robyn lost her life in a tragic automobile accident. However, she died knowing that someone loved her. Young people, you have an opportunity to make a difference: seize the day! Kristen was able to make the world she lived in a better place because she treated people the way the Savior would—while she still had the chance.

Sometimes the Lord gives us a second chance to make a difference. If we fail to "stand as a witness" the first time, we shouldn't give up! I saw an example of this in a sweet young sister in Detroit, Michigan, named Mary. As one of the only members of the Church in her school, she knew she had a great responsibility to keep the commandments and show others the way to live. However, sometimes that is difficult when other "things" get in the way.

Mary had always been a great example to her friends at school and was willing to talk openly about the Church. Bobby, who was one of these friends, had actually developed an interest in the Church because of her. However, when he asked her to the end-of-the-year school dance, she decided to go even though it was several months before her sixteenth birthday. *After all*, she thought, *it is just a big group of friends*. When an article appeared in the *New Era* a short time later about the dating standards of the Church, she read it and realized she had made a mistake.

She invited Bobby over one day and read the entire article to him. Confused, he asked her if they were breaking up before they had really even gotten together. Mary explained her feelings about these standards to him, and he agreed to just hang out as friends until her sixteenth birthday. In the meantime, she invited him to attend Mutual, sacrament meeting, and even an occasional family home evening lesson.

When Mary turned sixteen she began to date other young men as well as Bobby. Jealous and angry, he broke off their relationship and began spreading untrue things about Mary and the Church. Mary's mother tried to comfort her, but finally decided to take matters into her own hands. She went to talk to Bobby herself, and explained that if he was really that interested in Mary, he should take the time to find out what she was all about. He did. At Mary's invitation, he began to take the missionary discussions.

Shortly after that, his father unexpectedly passed away. Because of what the missionaries had taught him, he knew where his father was, and how they could be together forever as a family again someday. He and his father had been very close, and this newfound knowledge of the gospel gave him the strength to endure the most difficult trial of his life to that point.

I met Bobby at their stake youth conference. As the chairman of the stake youth committee, he conducted the meetings. I was so impressed with him, and also with Mary. Several months later I called to see how he was doing. He had been a star on the football team his junior year, and was being actively recruited by several colleges. I asked him how his senior year was going, and which college he had decided to sign with. His response took me by surprise. He said: "I'm not playing football this year, Brother

Bartholomew. My mother was having a hard time making ends meet since my father's death, and so I decided to take on a part-time job to help out with the family finances. . . . Besides, I have to start saving for my mission, right?"

Look at the difference that was made in one man's life because a young woman was willing to take a stand. Even though she made a mistake along the way, she went back and made it right. Now a young man in her world found the Savior and his gospel, was able to make it through the loss of his father, and serve faithfully in the Church.

My young friends remember who you are. Remember that you made promises to our Father in Heaven who sent you here to this earth, "for such a time as this" (Esther 4:14). As the "youth of the noble birthright" you can and will make a difference as you "stand as witnesses of God at all times and in all things, and in all places" (Mosiah 18:9).

Ron Bartholomew is the principal of the LDS seminary adjacent to Timpanogos High School in Orem, Utah. He and his wife, Kristen, are the parents of seven children: Scott, Laura, Kyle, Emily, Nathan, Nickelle, and John. He served a mission to Pusan, Korea, and received a bachelor's degree in Korean language from Brigham Young University. He also received his master's degree from that same institution. He has served as stake Young Men president and has taught seminary for the past seventeen years. He loves walking with his wife, bicycling, woodworking, gardening, working on computers, and eating gummi bears.

Hey, i'm so glad you i got to meet you! Don't forget to keep in touch! I ♥ U! Malwaiz

Alyssa Haskell

Hey, so cool to know you at EFY + thanks for teaching me how to swing!
♥ ya,
Beth Hiatt

Wuz Up? You were awsome and turned out to be a real ladies man!
Jon, Paulie

Hey Richard It was nice meeting you. Your a good dancer. KIT. goldygirl86 Love ya, Crystal Temple

Richy
★ Hey! Cool pen!!
★ You are great! CTR & go on that mission! Live your testimony! Go Book of Mormon! The church is true!!!

Keep in touch...
Sasha I. Kirby

hey Jude
thanx for
being here. keep
it always! Don't
touch me!

Allen F.

rachel
thinks you're
cool! I hope that
letter is big enough